1000 Houseplant Hints

1000 Houseplant Hints

Contributors

DR JOE STUBBS

RON MENAGE

JOCK DAVIDSON

DAVID SQUIRE

CHANCELLOR
PRESS

CONTENTS:

HOW TO DISPLAY YOUR PLANTS

HOUSEPLANT CARE AND SELECTION CHART

AT-A-GLANCE GUIDE TO PLANT TYPES AND CONDITIONS

INDEX

First published in Great Britain in 1984 by
Octopus Books Limited
part of Reed International Books

This edition published in 1992 by
Chancellor Press
Michelin House, 81 Fulham Road, London SW3 6RB

© 1984 Reed International Books Limited

Printed and bound in Great Britain by The Bath Press

INTRODUCTION

Gardening in the home with houseplants is a hobby with a double blessing. The joy of tending to the everyday needs of houseplants – their watering, potting, feeding and propagation – is an occupational blessing. The effort of raising houseplants that fit in well with the furniture, carpets and decorations will produce a 'home' in which everyone feels peaceful and content, and is both absorbing and fulfilling. There is also a pleasing and continuing satisfaction in just sitting and admiring plants. And, unlike plants in the garden, both flowering and foliage plants in the home can be admired at close quarters throughout the year.

This pocket-sized illustrated book has been created by experts to assist both knowledgeable and novice houseplant enthusiasts to get the best from their plants. Expert houseplant growers are always looking for ways to extend their hobby, perhaps displaying plants in a more stimulating and exciting way or growing a plant that demands more dedicated care, while the novice houseplant enthusiast often just wants clear and concise practical information on which to build a hobby. Both of these will delight in the information packed between the covers of this stimulating book that will find a useful place in any home, whether lodged between cookery books in a plant-packed kitchen, beside a favourite and comfortable chair, or on a small bedside table for easy reading late at night.

The first part of the book guides the reader clearly through the often complex and confusing requirements of plants in the home: the temperatures and humidity essential for good growth; cleaning foliage plants; staking and supporting them; their propagation and potting into larger pots; the recognition and control of pests and diseases; and even growing plants without traditional composts, by hydroculture. There are also invaluable notes on leaving plants unattended during holidays, and settling new plants into the home so that their growth is not checked or retarded.

The A-Z section illustrates and describes more than 300 plants for the home, including those grown for their beautiful leaves as well as the ones famed for their seasonal flowers. Also, houseplant enthusiasts wishing to know more about specialist plants – whether seasonal bulbs, stately palms, delicate ferns, cacti, bromeliads or exotic-looking orchids – will appreciate the detailed information that brings certain success with these subjects.

And those enthusiasts who admire the oriental art of growing miniature trees and shrubs will find the information on bonsai invaluable; their care, positioning throughout the year and propagation are described in detail.

Using these plants in the home and the selection of suitable containers that enhance their appearance is another essential element of keeping houseplants. And positioning plants so that their foliage or flower colours complement rather than clash with each other and the decor is another vital element in the home. Both of these, as well as growing plants in hanging-baskets, in Wardian cases, terrariums and bottle gardens, are discussed and illustrated.

Grouping plants in large containers, setting them in floor-level containers and arranging them in troughs are also discussed, as well as those plants that can be used to hide bad features in the home, such as water and gas pipes, or to highlight good features, perhaps well-proportioned arches, ornate window surrounds or attractive Victorian fireplaces.

A special 16-page insert illustrates in full colour ways in which plants can be used in the home, in living and dining rooms, kitchens, bathrooms, in halls and on stairways. Each of these places poses problems for plants as well as the householder; some plants will survive low temperatures and gloomy surroundings, while others need warmth and plenty of light if they are to produce a spectacular array of flowers.

Choosing plants for specific places in the home can often present a problem for both novice houseplant enthusiasts and the more experienced. Therefore detailed information is given about foliage and flowering plants for table-centre decoration, large foliage plants to act as screens and focal points, foliage and flowering plants that climb or trail, or both, as well as those plants that bring colour through their flowers at specific times during the year.

At the back of the book is a useful quick-reference Care and Selection Chart detailing in chart-form the environmental requirements of more than 300 plants. And the comprehensive index of botanical and common names enables the reader to gain quick and easy access to any of the plants mentioned in the book.

Few books have such a pedigree of authority as this information-packed single volume. Houseplant experts have been brought together to create a book that can boast *all you need to know to successfully grow and display houseplants*. Too often gardening is not the inexpensive hobby it is frequently thought to be, but houseplants that can be admired daily and last for many years must be *real* value for money. A bouquet of flowers sold by a florist is expensive, but a small houseplant can be half the cost and last much longer.

The daily attention demanded by houseplants is ideal therapy for those people who live on their own or are alone most of the day. Dogs and cats are said to have a therapeutic influence in that they require regular attention, and plants are no less important in this respect. And although unlike dogs they do not need to be taken for 'walkies' they can be regularly moved around the house to vary the decor. Jogging may be good for the heart, but so, too, is the sight of a well grown houseplant bursting with cheerful colour when you arrive home tired from the office or a long shopping expedition.

Contributor
Dr Joe Stubbs

PLANT CARE

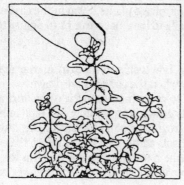

BASIC CONDITIONS

LIGHT

Light is essential for plant life since it provides the energy needed for growth. The light requirements of different plants, however, vary widely. Some types will only flourish in bright sunlight whilst others tolerate shadier conditions. The levels of light indoors also show dramatic differences, not only in the different areas of the house but also within individual rooms. So one of the secrets of successful indoor growing is to position the plants where the light level is most suited to their particular needs.

Day length is another factor which influences plant growth. Plant food production reaches its peak during the long days of summer and declines as the nights lengthen with the approach of winter. Consequently, most foliage plants pass into a resting phase during winter regardless of the amount of sunshine. At the same time their requirements for water and plant foods are also at a low ebb. So liquid feeding is not needed and watering should be kept to a minimum.

The best lit place in a house is close to a window which faces south and so receives direct sunlight for most of the day. This suits pelargoniums, many other flowering plants and cacti, but there is a risk of leaf scorch with indoor foliage plants. Even in the case of flowering plants it is preferable to have net curtains to diffuse the light.

Plants on window sills are, however, subject to a big overnight fall in temperature, particularly when the curtains are drawn. Consequently it is advisable to move them into the room during the night in cold weather. Plants growing on window sills tend to bend towards the light and their growth becomes lop-sided. The easy way to prevent this is to turn the pots a little every few days, so that the plant is encouraged to remain upright, but don't do this to flowering plants which are budding as it may cause the flower buds to drop off.

Away from the window Moving back a little way from a south-facing window the light is still bright, but plants standing in this position are only exposed to direct sunlight for part of the day. So too are plants on the sills of windows facing east or west. These conditions suit most flowering plants and are also suitable for some foliage types.

Shady locations A limited range of indoor plants can even be grown in shady parts of the house, provided that the level of light is such that reading is possible. Plants which normally require higher light intensities can also be grown here temporarily for a month or two. They will, however, need to be moved into better lit areas to recuperate.

Effect of colour Indoor lighting levels are markedly affected by the colour of the walls and ceiling. Light colours reflect the light and increase the general level of illumination in a room. Dark shades on the other hand absorb the light and so lower the light intensity.

Many other factors such as the size of the windows and the presence or absence of nearby large trees or buildings affect the levels of natural lighting in a room. So it is impossible to lay down exact rules as to what types of plants can be grown successfully. What you need to do is experiment with placing the plants in different positions and then keeping a close watch on their appearance. When the light intensity is too low there will be little growth and what does develop is likely to be drawn out and spindly. Young leaves tend to be smaller and paler than those grown in adequate light whilst old leaves are likely to turn yellow and fall prematurely.

Low lighting levels have a particularly severe effect on flowering plants. Flower bud production is greatly reduced and any buds which do develop generally give poor quality blooms.

Most houseplants do best in bright but diffused light. Prolonged exposure to direct sunlight on the other hand can cause leaf scorch on many foliar plants and some flowering species. The degree of damage varies widely. Whole leaves of particularly

sensitive varieties may shrivel and turn brown whereas in more
resistant types the damage is usually restricted to the leaf tips and
edges. With so many variables it is not possible to specify exactly
which plants can be grown successfully in various areas of your
home. Information on the light requirements of a wide range of
houseplants is, however, given in the Care and Selection Chart and
this should provide helpful guidance on the choice of plants.

WATER

Adequate supplies of water are essential for plant health, wilting of
the foliage being the first sign of water shortage. The obvious
reaction to this situation therefore is to water the plant.
Unfortunately, wilting can be brought about not only by dryness at
the root but also, somewhat surprisingly, by waterlogging of the
growing compost. Consequently the application of more water may
only exaggerate the problem. When the plant is seen to be wilting,
therefore, you must first check on the condition before attempting
remedial action.

TOO LITTLE WATER

Modern peat-based composts shrink as they dry out and also
become very lightweight. So first of all you should check to see if
there is any sign of the compost shrinking away from the side of the
pot. Gross water deficiency can also be detected by the lightness of
the pot. Both these observations indicate extreme dryness of the
compost which is not easily remedied by top watering. Much the
best way of dealing with this situation is to immerse the pot in water
to just below the level of the compost and leave it there till the
surface of the compost begins to darken as it dampens.

Less extreme dryness is best checked by pushing a finger into the
compost and checking to see whether or not your finger tip remains
dry. If it does then the pot needs watering.

Light watering Failing to water the pots is one obvious cause of
the drying out of the compost but a much more common factor is
the use of frequent but very light watering. This only wets the top
layer of the compost and does not penetrate deeper into the pot
where plant roots are growing.

TOO MUCH WATER

Too frequent, heavy watering can lead to the compöst becoming waterlogged and soggy. This can have a lethal effect on plants since it restricts the flow of vital oxygen to the plant roots. These stop growing and can no longer supply the aerial parts with sufficient water, causing them to wilt. Waterlogging also favours root-rotting diseases so, unless the situation is quickly remedied, the roots start to rot and the plant dies.

Extreme heaviness of the pot is a clear indication of waterlogging. This diagnosis can be confirmed by knocking the plant out of the pot and checking on the condition of the compost and the plant roots. The remedy is to re-pot in fresh compost, having first of all washed off the old material and removed any damaged or browned roots.

WHEN TO WATER

Watering should be done to a fixed schedule. Not only does each type of plant have its own requirements but these vary according to the relative sizes of the plant and the pot and also to its situation. The type of pot also affects the frequency of watering since clay pots lose water more rapidly than do plastic pots. As a general rule, however, all plants require less water in winter. The only effective way therefore of determining when to water is to make regular checks on the state of the compost. First look to see if the surface has dried out and then carry out the finger test to check the state of the upper layers of the compost – if your finger stays dry when pushed into the compost, the plant needs water.

WATER REGIMES FOR HOUSEPLANTS

Although each type of houseplant has its own special requirements for water they can for practical purposes be split into three main groups:

1. Dry in winter Cacti and succulents need to be kept short of water during the winter and, in fact, the compost can be left to dry out almost completely. In spring and summer, however, they should be treated as moist/dry plants.

2. Moist/dry Most foliage plants belong to this group. Throughout the spring and summer they should be given a generous watering each time the top layer of compost has dried out.

Less frequent and lighter watering is needed in winter. Some drying out of the compost is desirable since it ensures that there is adequate aeration of the roots.

3. Moist at all times Only a few plants flourish if the compost is kept continuously wet. These include marsh plants such as *Acorus* and *Cyperus* which benefit from having the base of the pot standing in water. Azaleas, which are usually potted in very free-draining compost, also fall into this group.

HOW TO WATER
The easiest and most convenient method is to use a watering can fitted with a long fine spout to apply the water to the top of the compost whilst avoiding wetting the foliage. Filling the pot to its rim gives adequate watering in summer. In winter, however, the water needs to be applied more sparingly in order to avoid getting the compost waterlogged.

Exceptions This method is unsuitable for watering *Saintpaulias* since the velvety leaves can be damaged by water drops and it is difficult to insert the watering can spout under the closely packed rosette of leaves. Tuberous plants such as gloxinias and cyclamen also need special treatment since their crowns may become diseased if they are wetted. The best way of watering these plants is to immerse the pots in water to just below the top of the compost, leaving them there till the surface of the compost darkens. The pots should then be allowed to drain before they are put back on show.

Vase plants (Bromeliads) also require special treatment since, in addition to normal watering of the compost, the 'vase' (formed by the central core of leaves) needs to be kept filled with water. It is also advisable to empty and refill the 'vase' every couple of months. If possible, use rainwater, as in some areas alkaline top water can leave an unsightly residue on the leaves.

WARMTH

Warmth is an important factor in the growth of plants, but their individual requirements vary widely. This is particularly true of houseplants because of their diverse natural habitats. Many foliage plants, for instance, are natives of the tropics whilst others are from more temperate regions. Flowering houseplants generally show less variation and most do best in cool to average temperatures. One exception to this general rule is that bromeliads may need to be kept at 24°C (75°F) if they are to produce flower buds. Even these exotic plants, however, will survive quite happily in more normal temperatures once they have come into flower.

A modern, centrally heated house where the day temperature does not normally rise above 21°-24°C (70°-75°F) and the night temperature is above 10°C (50°F) can provide an ideal location for all types of houseplants. In fact, too much heat is detrimental even to exotic tropical species. In their natural habitats the high temperatures are balanced by bright light. Lighting levels indoors are much lower, so if the temperature is too high the plants become drawn up and spindly. High temperatures also tend to shorten the flowering period.

Dry atmosphere Another limiting factor, particularly in centrally heated homes, is dryness of the atmosphere. In such conditions most plants transpire very freely, losing a lot of water from their foliage. The rate of this water loss increases as the temperature rises and can reach the point where it exceeds the supply from the roots. Consequently the leaves dry up and wilt and, in extreme cases, can turn brown at the edges and fall prematurely. This type of damage can be prevented by increasing the humidity of the air surrounding the plants and the various ways of achieving this are described on pages 17-19.

Humidity Although it must be accepted that too high temperatures can be damaging to some plants it should also be realised that it is possible to minimise any ill effects by increasing the humidity of the air which surrounds them and at the same time giving them as much light as possible – even a few bowls of water in a room can help.

Low temperatures There are no such remedies for the injurious effects of excessively low temperatures. Consequently, homes where the temperature falls below 15°C (60°F) are not suitable for tender species such as *Acalypha*, *Aglaonema*, *Anthurium*, *Caladium*, *Calathea*, *Cissus discolor*, *Dieffenbachia*, *Dizygotheca* and *Syngonium*. Most other types will survive a drop to 10°C (50°F) whilst a few hardy plants such as aspidistra, *Maranta*, *Rhoicissus* and tradescantia will tolerate temperatures as low as 4.4°C (40°F).

Most popular flowering plants flourish best in cool to average heat but will survive quite well in centrally heated homes provided that they are kept in a brightly lit position. More difficulty is experienced with those that prefer rather cool conditions. This class, which includes azalea, *Beloperone*, *Browallia*, chrysanthemum and cyclamen, have only a short life indoors unless they are kept in well lit and really cool positions.

On the basis of their heat requirements houseplants can be divided into three main classes as follows:

Tender Require a minimum temperature of 15°C (60°F) but will flourish in temperatures up to 24°C (75°F) provided that the humidity is high enough.
Half-hardy These do best in cool to average temperatures. They will survive a minimum temperature of 10°C (50°F) but do best in the range 13-21°C (55-70°F).
Hardy Tolerate a minimum temperature as low as 4.4°C (40°F) and yet flourish in normal room temperatures.

Temperature drop All plants tolerate a small overnight drop in temperature so this fall is not normally a problem. Major lowering of the temperature, such as can occur near windows in frosty weather can, however, be damaging, particularly if the plants are trapped between drawn curtains and the window. Consequently it is advisable to move plants from the window sill in the evening before drawing the curtains – draw the curtains early so as to retain as much warmth as possible. Remember too that both doors and windows can be a source of draughts which are harmful to plants. Cacti are the exception to this rule since very low night temperatures are a feature of their natural desert habitat, so they find it easy to adapt.

SPECIAL CONDITIONS

HUMIDITY

Although it is well known that central heating dries out the atmosphere of a room it is not always appreciated that plants generally prefer more humid conditions. Houseplants whose natural habitat is a steamy tropical jungle are most affected, but even plants from more temperate regions suffer to some extent. Indeed the only plants which thrive in this unnaturally dry air are desert plants such as cacti and succulents.

PLANT REACTIONS TO LOW HUMIDITY

In a dry atmosphere the rate of water loss by transpiration is greatly increased. Consequently the leaves tend to dry out and begin to wilt. This effect is most pronounced in plants with thin papery leaves. With these the first sign of damage is that the leaves become brown and shrivelled. More resistant plants react by temporary wilting of the foliage. Continuous exposure to dry air induces early leaf fall and can eventually cause complete defoliation. Flowering plants generally suffer badly if they are kept in low humidity. The flowers soon fade while the flower buds dry up and fall without opening. Plants with leathery leaves such as *Sansevieria* and succulents are least affected and survive quite happily under these conditions.

METHODS OF INCREASING HUMIDITY

One partial solution to this problem is to display sensitive plants in the kitchen or bathroom where the air is usually moister than in the rest of the house. Another approach is to use humidifiers to increase the general level of humidity in the house. This is rather a drastic step to take, so it is better to use one of the following methods of increasing the humidity in the immediate surroundings of the plants.

Double potting This involves sinking the plant pot in moist peat in a larger waterproof display pot. All you need do then is to keep this peat continually moistened in order to ensure that the air around your houseplant remains moist. An added bonus is that the moist peat provides a reserve water supply for the plant and also insulates the growing compost from an overnight drop in the temperature.

Gravel trays These are shallow plastic trays which are designed to hold a thin layer of moist gravel on which the pots of houseplants can be placed. Plants grouped on gravel trays thus benefit from the humidifying effect on the moist gravel. Watering of the plants is also simplified since any surplus water can be allowed to drain into the gravel.

Large containers An attractive alternative to the use of gravel trays is to group the plants in deeper decorative containers and pack moist peat around the individual pots. It is of course essential that the container is waterproof. These large containers can also be used for multiple plantings of houseplants in growing compost. There are, however, some disadvantages associated with multiple planting. Firstly, it is not possible to water according to the individual needs of the various plants. Secondly, since drainage holes are not provided, there is a risk of the compost becoming waterlogged and so affecting root growth.

Terrariums An even more effective way of ensuring constant high humidity around the plants is to grow them in a large bottle or fish tank. This method has the additional advantage that watering requirements are minimized. It is, however, only suitable for the display of rather small, slow-growing plants. More information on this technique is given on page 225.

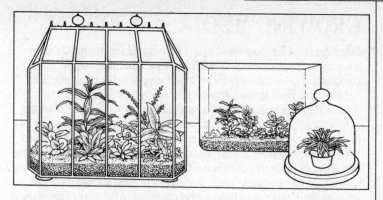

Misting This treatment is of particular value as a way of increasing the humidity of the air surrounding single plants, but is also suitable for use with groups of plants. All you do is lightly mist the foliage and surrounding air with tepid water using a small hand sprayer with the nozzle adjusted so as to give as fine a spray as possible. Misting is best done early in the day when the plants are not exposed to bright direct sunlight. Late evening applications should be avoided as these provide conditions which favour the development of grey mould.

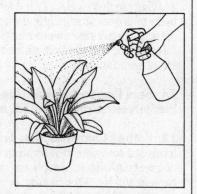

Most plants benefit from being misted, but with flowering plants such as *Achimenes*, begonia, calceolaria, cineraria, cyclamen and geranium it is important to restrict the misting to the surrounding air and to avoid wetting the foliage and flowers. Cacti and succulents are the only plants which must not be misted since they are liable to develop rot in moist air.

Where to mist Remember to watch out for your wallpaper and furnishings when misting. In a bathroom the plants can simply be placed in the bath for their daily syringe, but in other rooms it may involve removing them to a more suitable place. Local humidity will be increased if plants are misted together.

GROWING MEDIA

Even the most fertile garden soil is unsuitable for use in plant pots because in these artificial conditions it soon becomes tightly compacted. Consequently the vital air supply to the plant roots is reduced and their growth impeded. Furthermore, soil pests and disease flourish, posing serious risks to the plants. Special growing composts are therefore required which are specially designed for use in pots. Originally these were based on sterilised soil as in the John Innes growing composts. Nowadays, however, houseplants are more commonly grown in soil-less media which essentially means that the main ingredient is moss peat. Both types of growing compost are equally good, but nevertheless when re-potting becomes necessary it should be done with the type of compost used in the original planting.

SOIL COMPOSTS

These are available as the John Innes range of growing composts. They are made up of a mixture of sterilised loamy soil, peat and coarse sand with the addition of ground limestone or chalk together with a supply of fertilizer. This produces an open, fairly free-draining growing medium which is ideal for use in pots. This compost is less likely to dry out so rapidly and completely as a peat compost, and there is a better reservoir of plant food. There are various types of John Innes composts to meet the full range of growing requirements. These are as follows:

J.I. Seed Compost in which the added fertilizer is superphosphate. Used for seed sowing and for the rooting of cuttings.

J.I. Potting Composts Nos. 1, 2 and 3 which contain different levels of a complete NPK fertilizer (NPK stands for the major plant nutrients: nitrogen, phosphorus and potash), No. 1 having the lowest content and No. 3 the highest. No. 1 is generally recommended for use with seedlings whilst the higher numbers are suitable for use with established plants.

Ericaceous Composts which have no added chalk or limestone are designed for use as growing media for plants such as azalea and erica which dislike lime.

SOIL-LESS COMPOSTS

Various brands of peat, peat/sand and peat/vermiculite growing composts are available from garden shops and garden centres. Some are described as general purpose composts which can be used for seed sowing, rooting cuttings and potting on. Others are specialised seed or potting composts. Peat-based ericaceous growing composts are also available.

HOME-MADE COMPOSTS

Soil composts J.I. type composts can be made at home provided that your soil is a good quality loam. The soil, however, must first be sterilised by heating to just below 100°C (212°F) and this presents difficulties unless you own an electric soil sterilizer. One method is to put a thin layer of moist soil on a metal tray and heat in the oven for 15 minutes. Alternatively you can sterilize the soil by steaming. To do this you suspend a sack of dry soil over boiling water in a saucepan for 30 minutes. Allow the soil to cool and then mix it with peat and coarse sand in the following proportions by bulk:

	Seed compost	Potting compost
Loamy soil	2	7
Moss peat	1	3
Coarse sand	1	2

To complete the preparation of J.I. Seed Compost you then mix in 10g (¼ oz) of ground limestone or chalk and 40g (1½ oz) of superphosphate to 2 litres (8 gallons) of the mixture. When making J.I. P. 1 the superphosphate is replaced by 100g (4 oz) of J.I. base fertilizer which can be bought ready mixed. J.I. P. 2 and 3 contain double and treble the quantity of both chalk and fertilizer.

SOIL-LESS COMPOSTS

These are much easier to prepare since none of the ingredients needs to be sterilized. Furthermore it is possible to buy prepared packs of combined chalk and fertilizer. Consequently all you have to do is to mix these with either peat or a peat/coarse sand mixture. You can also make up composts to your own specification. Granular perlite, for instance, can be used in place of sand to give a more open mixture such as is needed by cacti. Fertilizer packs suitable for the preparation of ericaceous composts are also available.

HYDROCULTURE

This specialised growing technique is a relatively new development in the culture of houseplants. With this method the normal growing compost is replaced by spherical porous clay aggregates which are kept constantly wetted with a dilute solution of fertilizer. This ensures that the plant roots are not only well supplied with water and plant food but that they are also well aerated. Plants thrive in these conditions, the roots becoming thick and fleshy and quite different from those growing in soil or peat. The system is expensive to set up since it requires the use of special pots with a reservoir and special provision for the addition of liquid fertilizers. Its main advantage is that maintenance is minimized since the intervals between waterings are measured in weeks rather than days.

Not all plants are suitable for this method of cultivation. Another limitation is that the plants should be propagated in hydroculture if they are to thrive in this medium. Consequently hydroculture at present is mainly restricted to specialist contractors who lease out decorative plants to offices, hotels and public buildings.

CARE OF NEW PLANTS

It is a sad fact that all too many houseplants die within a few weeks of being brought into their new homes. Most of these casualties can be prevented if care is used in the selection of good plants from reliable suppliers and sensible precautions are taken to protect them from extremes of temperature when taking them home. The new plants also benefit from extra attention for the first week or two.

ADVICE ON BUYING HOUSEPLANTS

The first stage of their journey from the growers' greenhouse to the home usually involves transport to the retail outlet. Special delivery vans are needed for this to avoid the risk of delicate plants being exposed to damaging draughts and to extremes of temperature, all of which can cause irreversible damage. The plants can also suffer when they are on display if they are not properly looked after. Much the best guarantee against such troubles is to purchase the plants from reputable retailers who get them from reliable growers. Nevertheless it is still worthwhile checking the plants over yourself before buying.

PRE-PURCHASE CHECKS

Don't buy plants which show any of the following defects:

1. Roots growing in profusion out of the bottom of the pot, which indicates that the plant is pot-bound.
2. Compost has shrunk away from the pot showing that watering has been neglected.
3. Foliage wilting or yellowed. This may be simply due to lack of water, but it could also indicate that the root system is unhealthy.
4. Infestations of greenfly, whitefly, mealy bug or scale insects. Plants infected with rust, powdery mildew or grey mould diseases should also be rejected since these troubles spread all too readily to your other plants.

CARE AFTER PURCHASE

New houseplants are very much at risk when you are taking them home. Foliage and flowers may be bruised or broken off and the plants subjected to damaging draughts. In winter time there is the added danger of exposure to low temperatures. So it is important that the plant should be well wrapped either in paper or plastic film. Excessive heat can also affect them so do not leave them in the car boot in hot weather.

New plants also need time to settle in to their new quarters. During this time special care is needed over watering and they should be protected from draughts. Don't worry, however, if the odd leaf falls off since this is a common reaction to disturbance.

Remember that care over the selection of plants, their transport to your home and their early treatment pays big dividends in the longer term survival of your new houseplants.

PLANT POSITIONING

Where you choose to display your plants in the home can greatly affect their chances of survival. In any room the intensity of light is brightest close to the window and falls off rapidly as the distance increases. There are also temperature gradients depending on the distance from the radiators. Furthermore, even in a centrally heated house, there can be wide differences in temperature from room to room. Low levels of humidity are a constant problem in centrally heated houses. Consequently, special provision may have to be made to increase the humidity of the air in the immediate surroundings of the plants.

Success with houseplants therefore hinges on the selection of plants which are most suited to the conditions prevailing in the various display areas. Here the information on plant growth requirements given in Part 2 of this book should be invaluable.

The following notes on the general growing conditions in different rooms may also be helpful.

LIVING ROOM

This is the most popular display area for houseplants even though the conditions are by no means ideal for plant growth. Certainly the temperature is usually too high for flowering plants with the result that their flowering period is considerably shortened. Nevertheless there are plenty of houseplants which will grow satisfactorily in the living room, especially if they are positioned near to a window. Displaying the plants in groups also helps since this increases the humidity of the air around the plants.

DINING ROOM

Conditions here are generally similar to those in the living room.

BEDROOM

These are not widely used for the display of houseplants even though they usually provide an even, draught-free atmosphere. Unheated spare bedrooms, however, are ideal for plants such as geranium (pelargonium), which prefer cool conditions in winter. They are also useful for housing flowering plants such as Christmas and Easter cacti whilst they are budding. These plants can then be put on display elsewhere when they come into flower.

BATHROOM

This is normally somewhat cooler and certainly more humid than the living room and so is ideal for a wide range of houseplants. Furthermore, the frosted glass means that sensitive plants are not at risk from damage by direct sunlight. Bathrooms thus provide an excellent convalescent home for plants.

KITCHEN
Now that North Sea gas has replaced the old town gas, most houseplants flourish in the cooler and more humid conditions found in kitchens. So it is not surprising that this is a popular display area for houseplants.

HALLWAY
This is generally fairly cool and cold draughts can be a problem in winter. Light levels too are often rather low except close to a window. Unheated halls, however, provide good conditions for winter-flowering plants, provided that these are displayed in the light areas.

CONSERVATORY
This is usually the best-lit room in the house and so provides excellent growing conditions for most types of houseplants during the summer. Unless, however, the conservatory is heated, the range of plants which can be grown in it during the winter is restricted to those which can survive cold temperatures. High temperatures can be a problem in summer unless plenty of ventilation is given. The use of gravel trays or multiple plantings is also to be recommended so as to ensure that the atmosphere does not become too dry.

WATERING
This needs to be adjusted to the individual plant requirements. Some plants flourish only when the growing compost is kept constantly moist. Most, however, thrive best when the compost is allowed to dry out to some extent between waterings. Remember too that plants need less water when they are dormant than when they are active.

FEEDING
Modern peat-based composts have only low reserves of plant food so regular feeding is needed when the plants are in active growth. Dormant plants on the other hand take up very little plant food so feeding at this time is not necessary. Indeed it can lead to root damage due to the build up of chemicals in the growing medium.

INSPECTIONS
Keep a regular check on your plants for any sign of cultural defects or attacks by pests and diseases. These troubles are much easier to remedy if they are dealt with at an early stage.

CLEANING FOLIAGE

Dust Deprived of the natural cleaning effects of wind and rain the foliage of indoor plants inevitably becomes dusty. This deposit not only spoils the appearance of the plants but also restricts their growth and general vigour.

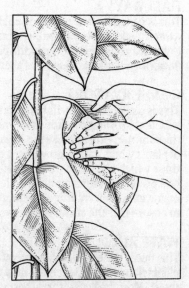

Light dusting with a soft cloth or with a feather duster will remove some but not all of the dust. Smooth and glossy leaves can be gently swabbed clean using a cotton wool pad soaked in water. When doing this it is important to support the leaf with your hand and to use minimum pressure on the pad. This technique must not be used with hairy-leaved plants or very young developing foliage as it might well cause damage.

LEAF-SHINE TREATMENT

Much of the attractiveness of plants such as ficus, philodendron and monstera is due to the glossy sheen of the young foliage. Unfortunately the older leaves gradually become duller. These plants therefore benefit from the application of a leaf-shine product. Many such cosmetic preparations are available. Some come in the form of creamy liquids which are applied to the leaves either with a cotton wool pad or with a special tissue. Others are presented as aerosols. Applied correctly as recommended either type restores the natural sheen and really brightens up the foliage. These products must, however, only be used on naturally glossy foliage and should never be applied to plants with hairy or fragile leaves.

HOLIDAY CARE

SUMMER HOLIDAYS

These pose serious problems for owners of houseplants. The plants certainly cannot be left untended for long periods at a time when their water requirements are at a peak.

One solution is to arrange for a relative or friend to visit your house at intervals to attend to the essential watering. This arrangement works very well provided that your plant caretaker is experienced in dealing with houseplants. There is, however, a risk of the plants being damaged by excessive water so these friendly helpers need to be carefully briefed as to what is required.

Automatic watering The only possible alternative to this arrangement is to provide some form of automatic watering. Self-watering pots are one answer but these are rather expensive and somewhat bulky for general use. Another approach is to rig up a supporting shelf for the pots over a large reservoir of water and use absorbent wicks to draw up water from the reservoir into the pots.

Capillary matting is much the easiest way of dealing with the problem. You simply lay a sheet of this in the bottom of the bath or in the kitchen sink and soak it with water. Then you stand the pots on the matting and leave the cold tap gently dripping. You must ensure that the plug hole is left clear to drain away any excess water.

WINTER HOLIDAYS

Low temperatures rather than water deficiencies are the most likely cause of damage at this time. Well watered plants will survive happily for a couple of weeks. Plants on window sills are most at risk and these should be moved towards the centre of the room.

CULTIVATION AND PROPAGATION

FEEDING

All potting composts contain a supply of essential plant foods, so newly purchased houseplants will continue to grow quite happily for some time provided that they are regularly watered. The amount of nitrogen, phosphate and potash in the growing compost, however, is limited and after a couple of months it will begin to run out. Indeed the plant food content of soil-less composts may well be exhausted in as little as five or six weeks. Regular feeding is therefore needed to keep the plant growing actively. Cacti are the one exception since they tolerate being short of food although their ability to flower may be reduced.

BASIC PLANT FOODS

The major plant foods are *nitrogen*, *phosphate* and *potash*. Each of these has its own special role in plant nutrition. Nitrogen encourages the growth of shoots and leaves whilst phosphate plays a dominant role in root development. Potash is important in the production of flowers but also helps to give sturdy shoot growth.

Trace elements In addition to these major nutrients, minute quantities of other elements are necessary to support healthy plant growth. Adequate supplies of these so-called trace elements are normally present in fertile soil whilst soil-less composts are artificially enriched with these key elements. Impoverished soil may need special feeding.

HOUSEPLANT FEEDS

Various brands of specially prepared houseplant feeds are readily available. These are convenient to use and supply the basic nutritional needs of the plants if they are used as directed. Most are applied as liquid feeds but some slow release solid fertilizers are also sold for this purpose.

Liquid feeding This is much the most popular way of supplying houseplants with essential nutrients. All you have to do is to prepare a dilute solution and then water it on to the compost. An alternative method of application, recommended for some products, is to add a few drops of the concentrate to the compost immediately before watering in the usual way. This approach is particularly economical when only a few plants have to be treated and it would be wasteful to make up a large volume of dilute solution.

Slow release fertilizers These are available as fertilizer sticks or pills. They are simply pushed into the growing compost where they slowly release plant foods over a period of about a couple of months. They are certainly convenient to use but have the disadvantage that the nutrients are not evenly distributed throughout the compost. Also, unlike liquid feeds, these fertilizers are not immediately available for uptake by the plant roots. Another difficulty is that these slow release fertilizers may still be acting when the plant has gone into its resting phase.

When to feed Plants only benefit from feeding when they are growing actively. This means from spring to autumn in the case of most houseplants. Plants that make a lot of growth will need more than those of more restrained habit. Bromeliads and cacti do not need much food. Applying fertilizer to dormant plants is not only wasteful, but can lead to a build-up of unused chemicals in the compost which could affect root growth with consequent ill effects on the plant as a whole.

POTTING ON

Most pot plants grow best if they are potted into containers which are only slightly larger than the existing root system. Consequently it is only a matter of time before the roots have penetrated the compost and reached the inside of the pot. From then on the roots are forced to grow laterally between the compost and the pot with the result that their ability to take up both plant foods and water becomes restricted. The plant is now said to be pot-bound.

Trouble symptoms The first indication that a plant is becoming pot-bound is that the growth is slowed down and more frequent watering is required. Roots may also appear through the drainage holes at the base of the pot.

This pot-bound diagnosis can be confirmed by removing the root ball from the pot for examination. You do this by spreading the fingers of one hand over the top of the compost and then inverting the pot before tapping its rim on the edge of a table. This should free the root ball and allow the pot to be lifted away. If there is a mass of roots on the surface of the root ball then the plant is clearly in need of being potted on into a larger pot. If, however, no surface roots are showing then the fault probably lies with the root system. This can be checked by carefully removing some of the compost when it is likely that browned and rotting roots will be seen. These should be removed before the plant is re-potted in a clean pot of the same size using fresh growing compost.

How to re-pot First ensure that the root ball is moist but not waterlogged. Then put a shallow layer of fresh moistened compost in the base of a clean new pot. The root ball is then placed on top of this layer and a check made to see that the base of the plant stem is about 2cm (¾in) below the rim of the pot. If it is not, the depth of the basal layer of compost should be adjusted. Now fill in the gap between the root ball and the pot with more compost, gently firming this either with your thumbs or with a blunt stick.

When to re-pot The best time to re-pot is in spring when active growth is beginning again after the winter rest period. Some houseplants benefit from annual re-potting whilst others need this

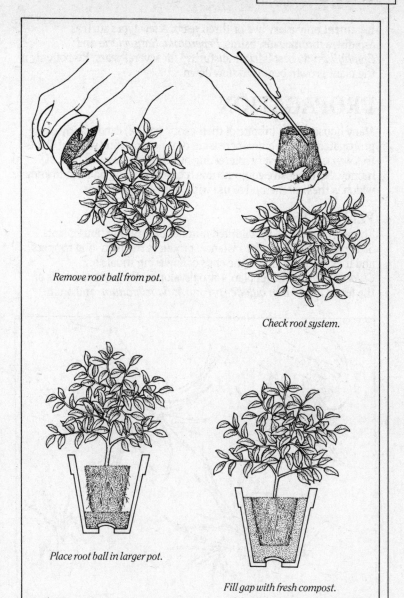

Remove root ball from pot.

Check root system.

Place root ball in larger pot.

Fill gap with fresh compost.

treatment only every two or three years. A few types such as aspidistra, bromeliads, palms, *Peperomia, Sansevieria* and *Epiphyllum* do best if left undisturbed for several years. Re-pot only if the plant growth begins to slow down.

PROPAGATION

Many houseplants, in spite of their exotic nature, can be fairly easily propagated in the home. Increasing or renewing your stock of plants this way is not only very interesting but can also save you a lot of money. No expensive equipment is required but you do need to know which is the best method to use with any particular plant.

PLANTLETS

These are produced by a limited number of common houseplants. *Saxifraga stolonifera*, for instance, produces them on long runners and they often develop at the ends of flowering shoots on *Chlorophytum*. Midget plants also develop on the mature fronds of the ferns, *Asplenium bulbiferum* and *A. flabellifolium*, and on the

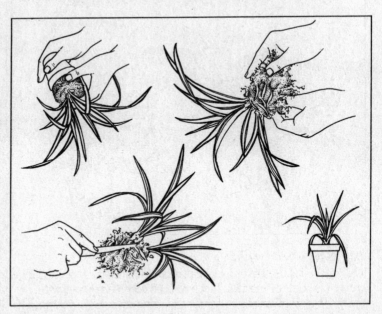

edges of the leaves of some species of *Kalanchoe Bryophyllum*. Plantlets root very easily in moist seed compost so it is very easy to increase your stock of these particular houseplants.

OFFSETS

These are the young plants which develop from the bases of mature specimen plants. They are found on bromeliads, *Sansevieria* and some types of succulents. Those on bromeliads usually have their own roots so all that is needed is to cut off the offset and plant it up in potting compost. More commonly, the offsets are not rooted so after being removed from the parent plant they should be immediately potted in seed compost. Offsets from succulents are the exception: they need to be left for a few days to allow the cut surface to heal before being inserted in the compost as otherwise they may develop basal rots.

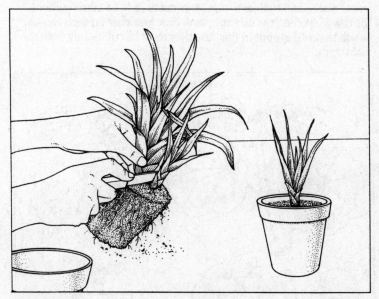

DIVISION

This method is used to propagate plants which naturally develop a clump of shoots or rosettes. It can be used very successfully with *Chlorophytum*, *Cyperus*, *Maranta* and some ferns. What you have to do is first of all knock the plant out of its pot and then carefully remove some of the compost to expose the connections between the clumps. Cut these with a sharp knife or a razor blade to give a number of separate plants, each with its own root system. These are then potted up separately in potting compost. This operation needs to be done carefully so as to avoid damaging the plant roots.

STEM CUTTINGS

Many kinds of houseplants can be propagated using this method. The basic procedure is to take a short piece of stem, cutting it cleanly just below a leaf joint. With woody plants, however, it is better to pull off a suitable side shoot together with a strip of bark from the main stem. Any ragged edges of this 'heel' are then trimmed off with a sharp knife or razor blade. With either type of cutting the lower leaves need to be removed at this stage. This is a good method for use with small-leaved plants and enables a number of cuttings to be taken without the risk of spoiling the original plant. Side branches on cacti can also be used as cuttings but in this case they must be cut cleanly from the main stem.

Stem Cutting.

When to take cuttings This procedure works well at almost any time of the year with plants such as *Impatiens* and *tradescantia* which root very readily. Cuttings from other plants are best taken during the period of active growth, preferably in late spring. Fuchsia and geranium (*Pelargonium*), however, can be propagated equally well in late summer or early autumn.

Rooting hormones The rooting of stem cuttings is generally improved by dipping the cut ends in a rooting powder or liquid but this treatment should not be given to geranium cuttings. It may be necessary to moisten the cut ends to enable the hormone rooting powder to stick to them.

Rooting cuttings The prepared cuttings are inserted in moistened seed compost and left to form roots. Since they survive best in a very humid atmosphere the pots of cuttings should be placed in polythene bags. Three or four sticks can be stuck into the compost to keep the bag off the cuttings.

Special treatment The cuttings are normally inserted in the compost as soon as they have been prepared. The soft basal tissue on cuttings of succulents and cacti, however, is liable to rot if treated this way. Instead the cuttings must be left to dry out for several days before they are put into the moist compost. Geranium cuttings also benefit from being left to dry out for a few hours.

LEAF CUTTINGS

Somewhat surprisingly, new plants can be induced to develop on leaf tissue placed in contact with moist growing compost. This method is commonly used with rosette plants where the leaves emerge directly from the crown of the plant. Some begonias can also be more easily propagated from leaves than from stem cuttings.

Whole leaf cuttings Succulents such as *Crassula*, *Echeveria* and *Sedum* are particularly easy to propagate from leaf cuttings. Indeed, in some species young plants develop naturally on fallen leaves left in contact with the growing compost. Whole leaves used for propagating succulents are allowed to dry out for two or three days. All that is then necessary is to push the stalk ends into moist compost and wait for the new plants to develop.

Whole leaf cuttings of Saintpaulia.

Gloxinia, Peperomia and Saintpaulia are also relatively easily propagated from semi-mature leaves. These should be cut off with as long a leaf stalk as possible and then inserted in the compost so that the leaf blade is just above the surface. Dipping the leaf stalk in a hormone rooting powder or liquid is to be recommended although it is not absolutely necessary.

Begonias A different technique is used to induce the formation of plantlets on the leaves of some begonias such as *B. rex*. Cuts are first made on the underside of the leaf across pairs of veins just above where they join. The leaf is then pinned down on the compost with its upper surface on top. In due course plantlets develop where the cuts were made. When the plantlets are large enough to be handled, the rooted plants can be potted individually.

Streptocarpus Leaf cuttings are also used for propagating *Streptocarpus*. Since, however, the leaves are rather large it is normal practice to cut off the top half of the leaf so as to reduce the loss of water by transpiration.

PLANT CARE

SECTIONS OF LEAVES

This type of leaf cutting is used for *Sansevieria* where a single leaf is cut into 5cm (2in) deep sections. The bottom half of each section is then buried in moist compost. This method is not, however, suitable for the propagation of variegated forms.

Small triangular sections cut from the leaves of *Begonia rex* and *B. masoniana* can also be induced to form plantlets if the inner quarter of the triangle is inserted in moist compost.

HOW TO ENCOURAGE ROOTING

Most cuttings and plantlets need to be kept in humid conditions if they are to survive and root. One way of ensuring high humidity is to put them in a plant propagator fitted with a transparent cover. Alternatively, single pots can be enclosed in a plastic bag which is kept clear of the plant foliage by being supported on three or four short canes stuck in the compost.

Exceptions to this general rule are cacti, succulents and geranium (*Pelargonium*), the cuttings of which are liable to rot if kept at high humidity.

All cuttings need plenty of light but they must not be exposed to direct sunlight. The time taken to form roots varies from species to species. It is important, however, not to disturb the cuttings till they have rooted so you should wait till new growth develops before attempting to pot them up.

AIR-LAYERING

This is a good way of producing new compact plants from tall growing houseplants such as *Ficus elastica* and *Monstera deliciosa*. The first job is to make a slanting upward cut halfway through the stem just below a leaf joint at a distance of not more than 50cm (20in) from the growing point. Then wedge the cut open with a matchstick and apply a rooting hormone powder or liquid to the cut surfaces. Moist sphagnum moss of the type used in hanging baskets should now be packed into and around the cut to act as a rooting medium. If necessary remove any leaves which would get in the way. Finally, encase the ball of moss with polythene, securing this firmly to the stem at both ends. No attention is then needed till roots are

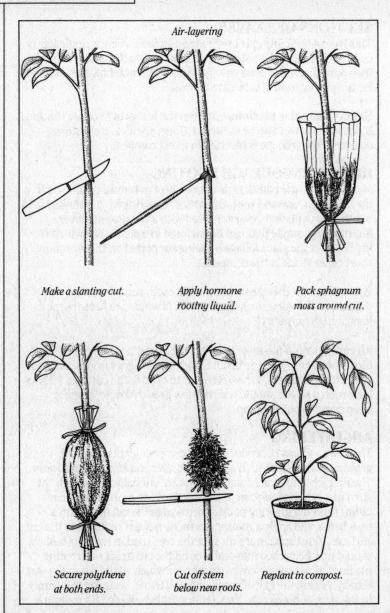

Air-layering

Make a slanting cut.

Apply hormone rooting liquid.

Pack sphagnum moss around cut.

Secure polythene at both ends.

Cut off stem below new roots.

Replant in compost.

seen to be emerging from the moss in a couple of months. The new plant should now be cut off just below the roots and planted up in potting compost. If the old plant is pruned down to a convenient height it will produce new side shoots which will give it renewed life.

Grafting

This method of propagation is necessary for the survival of the red and yellow forms of the cactus, *Gymnocalycium*. These contain no chlorophyll so they need to be grafted on to a normal green cactus such as *Tricereus* or *Harrisia*. You must first select suitably sized stock and scion plants. Then cut off the top of the green stock plant and the base of the coloured scion and press the cut surfaces of the scion and stock plant together. These can be held in contact by hanging a string, weighted at both ends, over the top of the *Gymnocalycium* knob, the string being left in position till the graft has taken, or they can be tied together, as below.

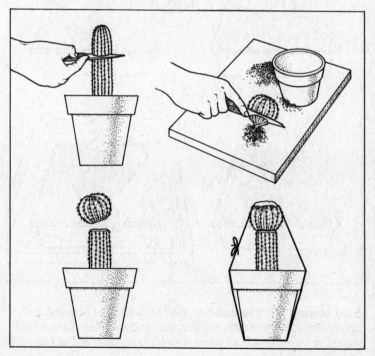

RAISING PLANTS FROM SEED

This is a simple and inexpensive way of extending your range of houseplants. Common bedding plants such as polyanthus (*Primula vulgaris*), cockscomb (*Celosia argentia cristata*) and butterfly flower (*Schizanthus pinnatus*) make splendid pot plants and are easy to grow from seed. Even exotic plants such as the bird of paradise flower (*Strelitzia reginae*) do not present too much difficulty. Foliage plants such as coleus, philodendron and aralia (*Fatsia*) can also be raised from seed as can a variety of cacti and succulents. Most good seed catalogues list a whole range of suitable varieties.

Seed sowing Fill a seed pan or small pot with seed compost and lightly firm it before scattering the seed on the surface. Larger seeds should be covered with a further sprinkling of compost but fine seed is left uncovered. Some seeds are best sown in small drills. It is usually best to water the compost first before sowing. Light can also be important – read the instructions on the packet.

Watering Soil composts can be watered after sowing. This is best done by immersing the pot in water to just below the soil level and leaving it there till the surface becomes moist. Seed pans can be watered before sowing, for fine seed, or after sowing when the seed is covered.

Aftercare Enclose the pot in a polythene bag or stand it in a covered plant propagator so as to prevent the compost drying out. Then leave it in a somewhat shady spot. Most seeds germinate readily at room temperatures but the more exotic species such as *Achimenes*, *Exacum*, *Cyperus* and *Strelitzia* need temperatures in the range 18°-21°C (65°C-70°F). These should therefore be kept in a heated cupboard or heated propagator till the seedlings emerge. Seedlings should be potted out separately into small pots of potting compost as soon as they are large enough to handle.

SAVING YOUR OWN SEED
This can be done but the results may be disappointing since many decorative plants do not come true from seed. Should you try this approach the first essential is to ensure that the seeds are completely ripe before they are harvested. So make sure that the seed pods or capsules have browned and begun to dry out before you remove them from the plants. To avoid loss of seed from natural shedding it is a good idea to enclose the young seed heads in bags made from an open nylon or cotton fabric. After harvesting, the seed heads should be left to dry out completely. The seeds are then separated from the chaff and stored in paper bags in a cool, dry, frost-free place.

RAISING FERNS FROM SPORES
Spores are the brown 'seeds' of ferns which develop on the undersides and edges of the fronds. All you have to do is to brush the spores off on to a sheet of paper with a paint brush and then sprinkle them thinly on to the surface of well-moistened seed compost. Cover the pot with a sheet of glass or enclose it in a polythene bag and place it in a shady spot. In time seedling ferns will develop and these should be pricked out into potting compost as soon as they are large enough.

FUN PLANTS

Citrus (Orange, lemon, grapefruit) Fresh pips are fairly easy to germinate and produce attractive evergreen pot plants even though there is no guarantee that they will flower.

Avocado pear (*Persea gratissima*) To germinate the large egg-shaped stone of this fruit, half bury it in moist seed compost in a 7.5cm (3in) pot enclosed in a polythene bag. The stone usually splits in half with the shoot and root emerging between the two halves. When it has germinated the young plant should be potted up in a larger pot using potting compost.

Pineapple (*Ananas commosus*) Cut across the top of the pineapple about 2.5cm (1in) below the crown and then pare away the flesh to the central core. Allow the cutting to dry for several days before planting it in seed compost. Stand the pot either in a heated propagator or in some other warm place to allow it to root. Pot up in potting compost as soon as renewed top growth indicates that rooting has taken place.

FORCING BULBS

Bulbs for indoor display are normally planted in moist bulb fibre which can be obtained ready mixed in garden shops and garden centres. First put a layer of the fibre in the base of the bowl and press it down firmly before spacing the bulbs evenly on top, taking care that they do not touch each other or the sides of the bowl. More fibre is then packed around the bulbs till the bowl is almost filled. Then after watering, it should be placed in a cool dark place for 8-9 weeks. Professional growers stand the bowls outside and cover them with a deep layer of peat but equally good results can be obtained by putting them in the garage or garden shed. This treatment ensures the development of a good root system, provided that the fibre is kept moist. The bulbs are now brought indoors where they should be placed in a shady position till the flower buds are seen when they can be moved into full light.

Hyacinth bulbs specially prepared for early flowering can be grown in special vases containing water. These vases are made so that the bulb rests at the top of the glass whilst the roots grow down into the water. They are filled so that the base of the bulb is about 6-7mm

(¼in) above the water. A few lumps of charcoal placed in the vase will keep the water sweet and prevent harmful substances developing. Bulbs grown in water need to be started into growth in a cool dark place for a few weeks to allow the roots to develop.

AFTER-CARE OF BULBS

When flowering is finished bulbs should not be thrown away. Instead they should be given a liquid feed and then planted out in the garden just as they are, leaving the bulb, root and compost intact. Here they will bloom freely the following year and for many years afterwards. Amaryllis is the exception to the general rule, since these bulbs should be retained indoors with regular feeding and watering until late August when the leaves begin to die back. Water is then withheld. When the leaves have finally withered, the bulb can be taken from the pot and stored in a warm dry place before it is potted up again in February for the next flowering.

PRUNING

Some of the more vigorous foliage plants need to be pruned from time to time if they are not to become straggly or outgrow their quarters. See examples on page 46.

TIMING OF PRUNING

Foliage plants are best pruned in spring. This is also the time for cutting back some perennial flowering plants including fuchsia, *Jasminum*, *Pelargonium* (geranium) and *Abutilon*. Pruning immediately after flowering is, however, recommended for *Dipladenia*, *Lantana* and *Sparmannia*. *Aphelandra* on the other hand should only be cut back when it has become too tall.

Euonymus japonica A close watch needs to be kept on the growth of the golden variegated form of this as it tends to revert back to the green form. Any green branches which may develop on this plant must be completely cut out as otherwise they quickly become dominant and spoil the appearance of the plant.

Hedera (ivy) plants often develop spindly shoots bearing small pale leaves during the winter. These should be cut out in spring to encourage the growth of normal side shoots.

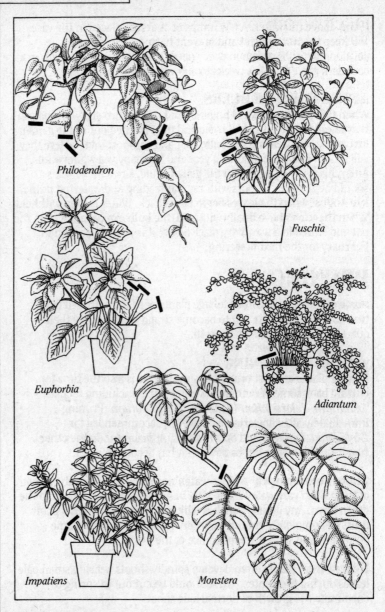

Philodendron

Fuschia

Euphorbia

Adiantum

Impatiens

Monstera

PINCHING OUT

This form of pruning is of value with flowering plants such as fuchsia and *Schizanthus* which tend to become leggy. Nip out the growing tips of the branches when a few inches long. This will encourage the growth of lateral branches, giving a bushier plant.

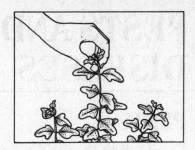

PLANT SUPPORTS

Climbing houseplants need to be supported and there are various ways in which this can be done. Ivies, for instance, can be tied to thin canes whilst the rather bushy vines, *Rhoicissus* and *Cissus* look better if they are supported on a framework made of either cane or plastic.

The vigorous growing but weak-stemmed Monstera and Philodendron on the other hand are shown to advantage if they are supported by a moss pole. This consists of a thick column of sphagnum moss which is either tied around a central cane or packed within a tube of plastic netting. Keeping the moss constantly wet ensures that the plants are growing in a favourably humid atmosphere. Furthermore the aerial roots of monstera are able to supply water to the foliage by absorbing it from the wet moss.

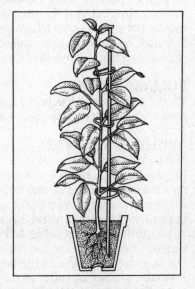

The flowering of climbing plants such as *Hoya*, *Passiflora* and *Stephanotis* is stimulated if the shoots are not allowed to grow vertically. Consequently, rounded wire hoops provide the best support for these plants.

PESTS AND DISEASES

PESTS

The warm protected atmosphere in a modern home provides the perfect environment for plant pests. So one has always to be on the look out for possible troubles and be prepared to take immediate countermeasures before the plants suffer serious damage. It is fairly easy to spot infestations of foliage pests at an early stage in the attack. Soil pests, however, are not usually detected till the damage to the plant is such that the growth of the plant has begun to suffer.

FOLIAGE PESTS

These can be dealt with either by spraying the plants using a small hand sprayer or by the use of an insecticidal aerosol.

APHIDS (GREENFLY)

Although these all too common pests are known as greenfly, they can be coloured black, reddish-brown, pink or yellow rather than green. Aphids usually congregate near to the growing points of the plants where they are easy to spot. Some species, however, feed on the undersides of the leaves where they are hidden from view. They feed by puncturing the plant tissues and sucking up the sap. This not only weakens the plant but also can cause the growth to become distorted. Furthermore, they excrete large quantities of a sweet fluid known as honeydew which is deposited on the foliage making it sticky and shiny. This is an ideal growth medium for black sooty moulds which further disfigure the plant. Apart from the harm done to the plants as a direct result of their feeding, aphids can be responsible for the plant becoming infected with diseases which enter through the pinpoint feeding punctures. Many aphids also act as carriers of plant viruses which they transmit from one plant to another. Female aphids produce six to eight live young daily for two to three weeks. These offspring start producing young within eight days so infestations build up at an alarming rate if the pests are not controlled.

Plants attacked Most types of houseplants are liable to attack but flowering pot plants are especially susceptible.

Control measures Aphids are readily controlled by general insecticides or by special greenfly killers.

WHITEFLY

Whitefly look like tiny white moths. They feed on the undersides of the leaves but flutter around the plant when they are disturbed. Both the adults and the larvae suck the sap of the host plants and disfigure the foliage with deposits of sticky honeydew which quickly become covered with sooty black mould growth. Whitefly infestations therefore spoil the appearance of the plants as well as weakening their growth.

Reproduction is by eggs which are laid on the underside of the leaf. Wingless larvae hatching from these eggs quickly settle down to feed on the plant sap and eventually pass into the short pupal stage before emerging as winged adults.

Plants attacked Most plants may be subject to attack but Abutilon, begonia, calceolaria, chrysanthemum, fuchsia and *Impatiens* are the most susceptible.

Control measures Whitefly are difficult to control because the larvae and pupal stages are resistant to most insecticides. They are best controlled by synthetic pyrethrins such as bioresmethrin or permethrin. Insecticides based on pirimiphos-methyl are also effective. Three or four repeat sprays at 4-7 day intervals are, however, needed to obtain complete control of the pests and care must be taken to spray the undersides of the leaves.

THRIPS

Thrips are minute, slender, winged insects which feed on the undersides of the leaves, on young stems and on flowers by scraping the surface tissues and sucking up the sap. Attacked leaves show a characteristic fine yellow or silvery mottling. Feeding areas on the flowers show up as white flecks. Severe infestations can lead to the plant growth becoming puckered and distorted. The plants are further disfigured by small blobs of liquid excreted by the insects and these often become covered with a brown mould. Attacked plants tend to become stunted and may lose their leaves. Young shoots may be distorted whilst attacked flowers are malformed and may fail to open fully.

Plants attacked Many types of houseplants are liable to be attacked, including chrysanthemums, cineraria, cyclamen and fuchsia.

Control measures Thrips are readily controlled by general insecticides.

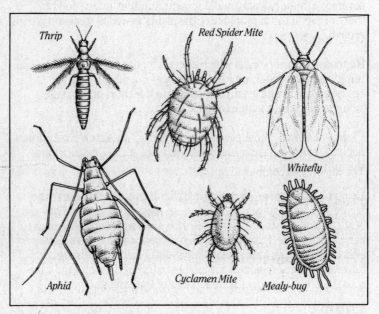

Thrip

Red Spider Mite

Whitefly

Aphid

Cyclamen Mite

Mealy-bug

RED SPIDER MITE

These tiny mites, which are only just visible to the naked eye, flourish in the warm, dry atmosphere of the modern home. They feed on the undersides of the leaves, causing a yellow speckling of the upper surface. Later the leaves lose their normal healthy colour, turning a sickly yellow and falling prematurely. The mites produce fine silky thread on the undersides of the leaves and, when infestations are severe, they spin webs from one part of the plant to another so that they can move on to new feeding areas. Infested plants become stunted and may even be killed by these pests. Some red spider mites leave the plants in September. One species, however, remains active throughout the year so one must be constantly on guard.

Plants attacked Most types.

Control measures Daily misting of the plants with water reduces the risk of attack since red spider mites thrive best in dry air. Attacks are best dealt with by repeat sprays with insecticides containing dimethoate, malathion or pirimiphos-methyl.

CYCLAMEN MITE

This close relative of the red spider mite is difficult to spot since it starts feeding in the folds of young leaves and in unopened buds. The damage it causes, however, shows up when the leaves expand. Infested leaves are distorted, hardened and covered with small brown scars. Flowers opening from infested buds are spoilt by streaks and blotches. In severe cases the buds may simply wither and die without opening. Cyclamen mites breed continuously throughout the year, the eggs being laid in young developing leaves and in flower buds. The life cycle is completed in 14-28 days.

Plants attacked These include azalea, chrysanthemum, cyclamen, fuchsia, gloxinia, *Impatiens, Hedera* (ivy) and *Saintpaulia*.

Control measures Daily misting of the plants with water reduces the risk of attack. Infestations of cyclamen mite can be controlled by spraying with insecticides containing dimethoate, malathion or pirimiphos-methyl. Two or three applications at 2-4 week intervals will, however, be needed to eliminate the pest. Care must also be taken to ensure that the spray penetrates into the folds of the young leaves.

MEALY BUGS

These soft, flat, wingless insects are covered with mealy white wax. Their bodies are also fringed with white waxy projections. Consequently they are easily recognisable when they are feeding on exposed parts of the plant. Unfortunately they have the habit of finding hidden corners such as curled up leaves, the sheaths of leaves and bud axils where they are difficult to detect. Both adults and young suck sap from the plant, weakening and stunting its growth. Mealy bugs also excrete masses of sticky honeydew which quickly becomes covered with sooty black moulds. Infested plants make poor growth and, in severe attacks, the leaves turn yellow and fall.

Plants attacked Mealy bugs feed on a wide range of plants but those most in danger of attack include azalea, cacti, citrus, *Codiaeum*, ferns and *Hedera* (ivy).

Control measures Light infestations can be wiped off with a moistened swab of cotton wool or with a moist paintbrush. Heavy infestations can be dealt with most easily by repeat sprays with an insecticide containing either malathion or pirimiphos-methyl. Ferns, cacti and succulents are sensitive to insecticides so these are best treated by the more laborious method of hand swabbing.

SCALE INSECTS

Adult females remain fixed to the plant in one position and can be readily recognised by their shell-like scaley covering. They feed by sucking up the plant sap from stems and leaves. This reduces the vigour of the plant and the leaves consequently turn yellow. The appearance of the plants is further spoiled by deposits of honeydew with their sooty black mould growth.

Reproduction is by eggs laid by the females shortly before they die. These eggs may be protected by white waxy 'wool' or they can be retained within the shells. After hatching the young larvae crawl over the plant till they find a suitable place to settle down and feed. These young scales are very small and inconspicuous so it is possible that a heavy infestation may build up before the trouble is spotted.

Plants attacked These include ornamental asparagus, cacti, citrus, croton, dracaena, ferns, *Hedera* (ivy), hibiscus, palms and succulents.

Control measures Scale insects are introduced into the home on infested plants so it is essential that new acquisitions are carefully checked over to ensure that they are completely free from this pest. Because of their close attachment to the plant and on account of their protective scaley covering they are resistant to most insecticides. It is a good idea therefore to first scrape off as many of the scales as possible. This job poses no difficulty with woody subjects. Softer tissues, however, need to be handled carefully. Here a plastic label makes a good scraper.

Insecticides containing malathion or pirimiphos-methyl are active against scale insects but repeat treatments are usually needed to obtain complete control. Some cacti, ferns and succulents can be damaged by pesticides so care is needed.

SOIL PESTS
These hidden enemies can be troublesome on most types of houseplants. They are particularly difficult to deal with because their presence is not suspected till signs of distress show up on the aerial parts of the plant. Root damage may then be well advanced and difficult to remedy.

The usual method of control is to apply heavy soil drenches of spray-strength insecticide. In some cases, however, it may be necessary to wash the roots free of compost before dipping them in insecticide solution and re-potting in fresh compost. Insecticides containing HCH, malathion or pirimiphos-methyl are recommended for use against these soil pests.

VINE WEEVIL
It is the larvae rather than the adult beetles which are so damaging to houseplants. Eggs laid in the compost hatch to give plump, whitish curved grubs with brown heads. These feed on the plant roots and also tunnel into the bases of bulbs, corms and tubers. The first sign of attack is that the plants tend to wilt even when well watered. Later, if no action is taken, the plants may well die. Since there are several possible causes of wilting it is necessary to knock the plant out of its pot to examine the root ball for the presence of these white grubs.

Plants attacked Most pot plants are liable to be attacked by these pests. Those which suffer most are azalea, begonia, cineraria, coleus, cyclamen, ferns, hydrangea, *Saxifraga* and *Sedum*.

Control measures Repeat applications of heavy soil drenches of spray-strength insecticide.

FUNGUS GNAT (SCIARID FLY)
The larvae of these small gnats are all too common pests of potted plants and they can cause serious damage. Eggs laid in the compost hatch to give tiny white maggots with shiny black heads. These larvae feed on the young roots and may also tunnel into the main roots, sometimes invading the base of the stem. Attacked plants make poor growth and tend to wilt in bright sunlight. Breeding can go on throughout the year so it is advisable to keep a constant watch out for the gnats flying around the plants. Should any be seen then it is good insurance to take immediate countermeasures. Alternatively you can knock the plant out of its pot and examine the root ball for the presence of the maggots. If you wait till the plant has begun to wilt, there is a risk of the roots being seriously damaged.

Plants attacked Most houseplants.

Control measures Repeat applications of heavy soil drenches with spray-strength insecticide.

ROOT MEALY BUGS
Some species of mealy bug feed on plant roots rather than on the aerial growth. Infested plants look as though they are suffering from drought, having dull wilted foliage, as a result of the damage done to the root system by these hidden pests. Here again the only way of positively identifying the cause of the trouble is to knock the plant out of its pot and examine the root ball. Colonies of mealy bugs are readily recognisable by their cottony wax wool covering.

Plants attacked A wide range of houseplants are attacked, including *Abutilon*, acacia, cacti, *Dracaena*, *Grevillea*, *Pelargonium*, *Stephanotis* and succulents.

Control meaures Root mealy bugs are difficult to eradicate. Ideally the root of infested plants should be washed free of compost and then dipped in an insecticidal solution. Repeat applications of heavy soil drenches of spray-strength insecticide are, however, reasonably effective.

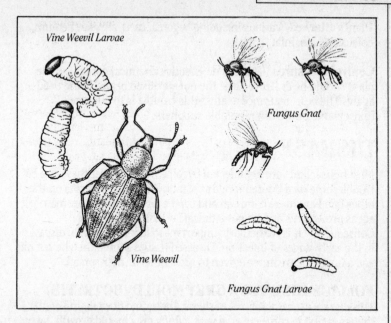

Vine Weevil Larvae

Fungus Gnat

Vine Weevil

Fungus Gnat Larvae

ROOT APHIDS

Root-feeding aphids can be troublesome out of doors but are rarely a problem with pot plants since the pests are usually carried to new hosts by ants. Some root aphids are readily recognisable as greenfly but others are covered with white powdery wax and so look like mealy bugs. Here again infested plants make poor growth and have a tendency to wilt.

Plants attacked Primulas are the most likely host plants.

Control measures As for root mealy bugs.

EELWORM

Eelworms are microscopic soil-borne pests which fortunately are not commonly found associated with houseplants. If, however, a plant suddenly collapses for no apparent reason it is worthwhile examining the roots for the presence of irregular-shaped corky swellings. These are the result of the reaction of the plant root cells to invasion by the eelworms.

Plants attacked Various including begonia, cacti, chrysanthemum, coleus and gloxinia.

Control measures There is no effective chemical control so the plant should be destroyed and the pot sterilised before being used again. The best insurance against this trouble is to buy one's houseplants only from reputable suppliers.

DISEASE

Most houseplants are not affected by foliage diseases yet these can be troublesome on a limited range of plants. Root and stem rots on the other hand are more common and can be lethal. Fungicides mainly act as protectants and do not eradicate established diseases. Consequently it is particularly important to identify possible diseases in the early stages of infection. Diseased tissues should then be cut off and a fungicide treatment given to prevent its further spread.

FOLIAGE DISEASES: GREY MOULD (BOTRYTIS)

This disease causes a soft rot of stems, leaves and flowers. Infected tissues at first become covered with a fluffy grey mould growth, later they tend to dry out and become a greyish-brown. Spores of this fungus are airborne so any damaged tissues are liable to become infected. Thus even the feeding punctures made by greenfly and mealy bugs are potential infection points as also are the scars left by detached leaves. Tender floral parts, even when undamaged, readily become infected with this disease. Grey mould is favoured by still air and by high humidity.

Plants attacked Most are susceptible but flowering plants with soft tissues such as begonia, cyclamen, gloxina and *Saintpaulia* are most at risk.

Control measures All infected parts should be cut off and destroyed before applying a protective fungicide such as benomyl. Removing leaves which have turned yellow or have been damaged in some way and cutting off dead flowers is one of the ways of preventing the disease becoming established. It is also important not to mist the plants late in the day as this can result in the foliage remaining wet overnight and so favouring infection by grey mould.

POWDERY MILDEWS

This type of disease shows up as a white powdery covering on the stems, leaves and flowers. Infected leaves later dry up and fall prematurely so the disease not only disfigures the plant but also reduces its vigour. Powdery mildews are favoured by high humidity and still air. Allowing the compost to become too dry also makes the plants more susceptible to attack by powdery mildews.

Plants attacked Only a very limited range of plants can become infected with powdery mildew. Popular favourites on this list are begonia, chrysanthemum, cineraria, *Euonymus* and *Kalanchoe*.

Control measures Remove all badly mildewed leaves and flowers before spraying with fungicides containing benomyl, bupirimate, propicazole or thiophanate-methyl. The risk of further attacks can also be reduced by improving the ventilation around the plants.

RUSTS

Rust diseases are only rarely found on houseplants but should this trouble develop it is easily recognised by the concentric rings of orange or brown powdery spores which appear on the underside of the leaves. The upper surface of the leaves may also develop a patchy yellowing.

Plants attacked chrysanthemum, cineraria and *Pelargonium* (geranium) are the only common houseplants subject to attacks by rust fungi.

Control measures Cut off any infected leaves and apply a protective fungicide spray based on propiconazole or mancozeb.

LEAF SPOTS

Leaf spot diseases can attack a number of different types of houseplants. The spots first appear as pinheads but later become larger. They are usually brown but are sometimes black. Normally this type of disease does not cause much damage but the spots may merge together, killing the leaf.

Plants attacked These include citrus, *Dieffenbachia*, *Dracaena*, ficus and palms.

Control measures Infected leaves should be removed and destroyed before the plant is sprayed with a fungicide based on benomyl. It is also good policy to keep the plants in rather drier conditions for some time as this helps to hold the disease in check.

AZALEA GALL
This fungal disease of evergreen azaleas shows up as rounded galls on the younger leaves and flower buds. These galls are reddish at first but later covered with a white bloom of fungal spores.

Plants attacked Azalea only.

Control measures This disease is introduced into the home on infected plants, so it is essential that you carefully examine any azalea before purchase to ensure that it is completely free from galls. Should galls appear later the affected leaves and flower buds must be removed and burnt before they start producing spores.

SOOTY MOULDS
These moulds commonly develop on the honeydew excreted by greenfly, whitefly, mealy bugs and scale insects. They are purely superficial growths and do not directly damage the plants even though they are unsightly. Sooty moulds, however, block out the sunlight from the affected leaves and thus reduce the vigour of the plants.

Plants attacked Any plants which become infested with sap sucking insects.

Control measures The mould growth can be removed by swabbing with a wad of moist cotton wool. The only way of preventing further mould growth is to control the insects which produce the honeydew.

ROOT AND STEM ROTS: ROOT ROTS
These killer diseases are brought about by various fungi. Some cause the roots to turn brown whilst others produce a black rot. The first sign of attack is a greying or yellowing of the foliage. Infected plants also tend to wilt because of the damage to the root system. Death of the plant then follows if remedial measures are not taken.

Plants attacked Most plants are liable to suffer from root rot troubles but begonias, cacti, palms, *Saintpaulia* and succulents are most likely to be attacked.

Control measures Any plant with unhealthy foliage, especially if it is showing a tendency to wilt, should be knocked out of its pot and a close examination made of the root ball. Any rotting roots must then be cleanly cut off and the plant re-potted in fresh compost in a clean pot. A spray-strength solution of benomyl should then be watered on and the plant kept out of direct sunlight till fresh growth appears. Waterlogging of the compost favours these diseases so care is needed to avoid overwatering.

CROWN AND COLLAR ROTS

The first sign of trouble with this type of disease is that the plant suddenly collapses because of the rotting of the base of the stem or crown of the plant. These diseases are usually associated with gross overwatering of the compost, coupled with rather low temperatures.

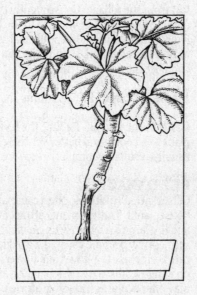

Plants attacked Mostly soft herbaceous plants with multiple stems or leaves arising from a central crown.

Control measures No remedial action is possible. Diseased plants should be discarded. The plant pot can be used again but only after it has been washed and sterilised.

BLACK LEG

This is a disease of stem cuttings, the bases of which become blackened and rot. The blackening is caused by fungal or bacterial infections and is most troublesome when the growing compost is cold and wet or has been allowed to become waterlogged through overwatering.

Plants attacked Geranium (*Pelargonium*).

Control measures The disease can be prevented by avoiding overwatering. Severely diseased cuttings should be destroyed but valuable plants may be saved by trimming the cutting back to clean healthy tissue and replanting them in fresh compost.

CORKY SCAB (OEDEMA)
This trouble, which takes the form of brownish corky scabs on leaves and other plant tissue, is a response by the plant to unfavourable growing conditions rather than because of attacks by pests or diseases. Oedema develops when the roots take up more water than is lost from the foliage. Consequently the plant cells swell up and some of these later burst giving rise to the brown scabs. Oedema is most likely to develop on susceptible plants when they are exposed to high temperatures and high humidity at a time when the growing compost is excessively moist.

Plants attacked Pelargoniums and succulents.

Control measures Reduce the level of watering and move the plant to a cooler and better ventilated situation. This simple remedy usually results in complete recovery.

PET DAMAGE
Cats, especially kittens, often cause a lot of damage to treasured houseplants. Trailing plants attract attention as suitable punch bags and the large leaves of *Ficus elastica*, *Dracaena*, *Yucca* and *Cordyline* species may become covered with disfiguring scratch marks. Some cats even chew the leaves and flowers of houseplants. Potted plants on window sills are at risk of being knocked over whilst large pots may offer scope as indoor lavatories.

Prevention One way of preventing this damage is to make sure, where possible, that the houseplants are placed out of reach of the cats. Much the best approach, however, is to spend time training young kittens.

THE SAFETY OF PESTICIDES

Houseplants are under constant threat of attack by pests and diseases so regular checks need to be made on the health of the plants. Small infestations of some pests such as greenfly and mealy bugs can be dealt with by brushing or washing them off the plant. Scale insects too can be controlled by lightly scraping them off the bark or foliage. It is, however, all too easy to miss some of the pests and infestations can quickly build up again. Other pests such as whitefly, thrips and red spider mites cannot be dealt with in this way. Nor can the various root pests. Consequently the sensible use of insecticides is the only answer to most pest problems on your plants. The control of fungus diseases also necessitates the use of fungicides.

Unfortunately some people are reluctant to use such chemical aids because they consider them to be dangerous. This attitude, although understandable, is quite unfounded since pesticides can only be marketed after they have been cleared for use by amateur growers under the Government's Pesticides Safety Precautions Scheme. This ensures that no new product or even a new formulation of an existing pesticide is approved until the results of extensive safety studies carried out over a period of years have been examined and accepted by the Advisory Committee on Pesticides. There are no industry representatives on this committee and it is composed entirely of independent scientists and officials chosen for their expert knowledge of all aspects of pesticides. Products are only cleared for sale when members are convinced that they pose no risks to the user, his or her family, domestic pets or wildlife, provided that the chemicals are stored and handled as directed on the label.

POINTS ON THE HANDLING OF PESTICIDES

1. Store the products out of reach of children and pets.
2. Read and follow the directions for use given on the label.
3. Use only the recommended dosage. Using higher rates is wasteful since it will not improve the efficiency of the spray and may well cause damage to the plants.
4. A simple trigger-operated hand spray of about 450 ml (1pint) capacity is ideal for use on houseplants.
5. The sprayer should be washed out thoroughly both before and after use.

6. Surplus spray solution should not be kept since these dilute solutions rapidly lose their efficiency on storage.
7. Any surplus solution, however, can be safely emptied down the outside sink drain or flushed down the WC.
8. The use of insecticidal aerosols is a particularly easy way of dealing with pests on houseplants since these products are prepared for immediate use. They must, however, be used exactly as directed since they can cause damage if wrongly applied. Visible wetting of the foliage with aerosol sprays is neither desirable nor necessary.
9. Sprays should not be applied in direct bright sunshine as this can result in scorching of the foliage.
10. Finally, remember to wash your hands after using pesticides. It is also advisable to wear rubber gloves.

CHOICE OF PESTICIDES

Readily available products containing the active chemicals mentioned in the section on pests and diseases are listed below. All show general activity against pests or diseases except products based on pirimicarb. This chemical is only active against greenfly and blackfly.

INSECTICIDES

Active chemicals	Products
dimethoate	Boots Greenfly and Blackfly Killer Murphy Systemic Insecticide
dimethoate with malathion and lindane	Fisons Greenfly and Blackfly Killer
dimethoate and permethrin	Bio Long-last
fenitrothion	Murphy Fentro PBI Fenitrothion
HCH with rotenone and thiram	PBI Hexyl

malathion	PBI Malathion Greenfly Killer
	Murphy Greenhouse Aerosol
	Murphy Liquid Malathion
malathion with dimethoate	Vitax Greenfly/Blackfly Spray
permethrin	Baby Bio Houseplant Insecticide
	Bio Sprayday
	Fisons Whitefly and Caterpillar Killer
	Synchemicals House Plant Leaf Shine plus Pest Killer
	ICI Picket
	ICI Picket G
	Boots Caterpillar and Whitefly Killer
permethrin with heptenophos	Murphy Tumblebug
pirimicarb	ICI Abol-G
	ICI Rapid Greenfly Killer
	ICI Rapid Aerosol
pirimiphos-methyl	ICI Sybol 2
	ICI Sybol 2 Aerosol
pirimiphos-methyl with synergised pyrethrins	ICI Kerispray Aerosol
pyrethrum with peperonyl butoxide	Synchemicals Py Spray Concentrate
	Synchemicals Py Spray Garden Aerosol
	Synchemicals Py Spray Whitefly Killer
pyrethrins with resmethrin	Synchemicals House Plant Pest Killer
rotenone with quassia	PBI Bio Back to Nature Insect Spray

FUNGICIDES

Active Chemicals	Products
benomyl	ICI Benlate plus Activex
bupirimate with triforine	ICI Nimrod-T
carbendazim	Boots Garden Fungicide
mancozeb	PBI Dithane 945
propiconazole	Murphy Tumbleblite
thiophanate-methyl	May and Baker Fungus Fighter
thiram with gamma HCH and rotenone	PBI Hexyl

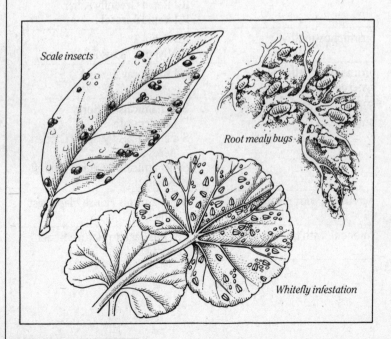

Scale insects

Root mealy bugs

Whitefly infestation

TROUBLESHOOTING

Attacks by foliage pests and diseases are fairly easy to recognise. Troubles caused by soil pests and diseases, however, produce identical symptoms to those induced by cultural failures. In this situation therefore the best approach is first to check in the *Troubleshooter Guide* what are the likely causes of the trouble showing up on your plants. By examining the growing compost you can then determine whether wilting of the foliage is due to under- or overwatering. If the compost is in good condition then the next step is to knock the plant out of its pot and examine the root ball for the presence of insect pests. If these are absent and the roots or base of the stem are beginning to rot then clearly disease organisms are to blame. Scorching of the foliage and premature drop of leaves and flowers are generally caused by cultural faults but may be due to incorrect use of aerosol sprays.

TROUBLESHOOTER GUIDE

SIGNS OF TROUBLE	POSSIBLE CAUSES
Poor growth	Underfeeding Overwatering Low lighting level Plant pot-bound
New growth pale coloured and spindly	Underfeeding Low lighting level Too high a temperature
Foliage wilting	Lack of water Overwatering Plant pot-bound Root pests Root diseases
Total collapse of plant with rotting at the base	Crown and collar rot
Base of cutting blackens and rots	Black leg disease
Tips of leaves turning brown and dry	Dry atmosphere

SIGNS OF TROUBLE	POSSIBLE CAUSES
Tip and edges of leaves yellow or brown	Lack of water Overwatering Dry atmosphere Sun scorch Draughts
Yellowing of new leaves	Effect of watering acid-loving plants with hard water
Yellowing of older leaves	Overwatering Draughts
Dry brown patches on leaves	Lack of water
Pale coloured patches on leaves	Sun scorch Water splashes Spray damage
Dark brown soft patches on leaves	Overwatering
Moist dark brown or black patches on leaves	Leaf spot disease
Yellow speckling of leaves	Red spider
Silvery streaks on leaves	Thrip
Leaves distorted and covered with brown scars	Cyclamen mite
Brown corky scabs on the underside of the leaves	Oedema
Concentric rings of spores on the undersides of the leaves	Rust disease
Black sooty mould on the upper surface of the leaf	Sooty mould
White powdery deposits on leaves, stems, flower buds and flowers	Powdery mildew
Grey fluffy fungal growth on leaves, stems, flower buds and flowers	Grey mould (Botrytis)

SIGNS OF TROUBLE	POSSIBLE CAUSES
White cottony masses on leaves and stems	Mealy bug
Tiny white moth-like insects on the undersides of the leaves	Whitefly
Colonies of yellow, green, pink, red, or black insects near the growing points and on the undersides of the leaves	Aphid (Greenfly)
Brown shell-like oval scales attached to leaves and stems	Scale insects
Loss of leaves	Movement shock Lack of water Overwatering Draughts Aerosol damage
Flower buds drop off	Lack of water Dry atmosphere Movement shock
Flowers fade quickly	Too hot Lack of water Dry atmosphere
White flecks on flowers which may turn brown	Thrip
Layer of roots on the outside of the root ball	Plant pot-bound
Roots with brown corky swellings	Eelworm
Roots brown and rotting	Root rot disease
Root system poor. Large fat, white grubs present	Vine weevil
Root system poor. Infested with tiny white maggots	Fungus gnat (Sciarid fly)
Insects feeding on the roots	Root aphid or root mealy bug

Contributor
Ron Menage

 Indicates plants that are on sale at Marks and Spencer (subject to availability).

A-Z OF FLOWERING AND FOLIAGE PLANTS

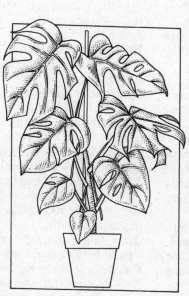

FLOWERING AND FOLIAGE PLANTS

ABUTILON HYBRIDS
(*Flowering maple*)

Description: Shrubby plants with maple-like leaves and large cup-shaped veined flowers in rich colours. The hybrid 'Belle' can be specially recommended. It grows to about 90cm (3ft) and the flowers face out – rather than drooping down as in other types.

Position: Give a cool position in good light or slight shade. Some of the hybrids, other than 'Belle', may grow tall and bushy, needing considerably more space.

Watering: Freely in summer, but keep only slightly moist in winter.

Propagation: Can be very easily grown from seed sown on a window sill in spring. Plants with good flower colours can be propagated from cuttings taken in spring.

Care: Feed when buds begin to form. Fully grown plants need 15cm/6in pot. Easy subject, very quick flowering. Old plants are often best discarded if they become straggly, but they can be pruned back in spring.

ACACIA ARMATA
(*Kangaroo thorn*)

Description: Shrubby, up to 3m (10ft) in height, with foliage in the form of narrow oblong leaves, the branches bearing spines. Mimosa-like blossom clustered along upper leaves in April.

Position: Give bright, airy, cool conditions. Can be grown in relatively small pots for some years, and young plants do not demand much space.

Watering: Moderate in summer, but keep only very slightly moist in winter – just enough water to prevent complete drying out.

Propagation: Can be grown from seed sown on a window sill. Take cuttings from side shoots, about a finger's length, with a 'heel' (a strip of the main stem they were attached to) in summer. They root readily in moderate warmth.

Care: Culture is much the same as for the popular mimosa. Young plants can be kept in 20cm (8in) pots for some time. Eventually, large pots or small tubs will be needed.

ACACIA DEALBATA
(*Mimosa*)

Description: The well-known mimosa of the florist. Makes a good foliage plant in young stages, but does not usually flower well until mature and established in tubs. Height 1.8m (6ft) or more, depending on size of container. Restricting the pot size to the minimum retards growth and is advisable where space is limited.

Position: Give a cool bright airy position. Can be stood outdoors in summer if desired. Hardy in mild areas. After some years plants need considerable space (in their natural habitat can reach 7.5m (25ft) in height), but may be useful for picture windows, porches, conservatories, and similar places where mature plants will be seen at their best.

Watering: Water freely from spring to early autumn, sparingly during winter.

Propagation: Very easy from seed sown on a window sill in spring and will quickly produce a useful foliage plant.

Care: Cut back plants in spring to restrict size if necessary, but mature plants that flower should be pruned back *after flowering*. Do not feed too much – this can discourage flowering. It is normal for the small leaflets to fold up at dusk.

ACACIA PODALYRIIFOLIA
(*Queensland silver wattle*)

Description: Silver-grey to whitish foliage with downy texture. Young shoots covered with thick white down. Rich golden-yellow mimosa-like flowers in winter on mature plants. Height 1.2-1.5m (3-4ft) depending on size of container.

Position: Give cool bright airy position. Hardy in mild areas outdoors. Plants ultimately need space, such as cool conservatory or porch, and large pots or tubs.

Watering: Freely from spring to autumn, sparingly in winter.

Propagation: Easily grown from seed sown on a window sill in spring.

Care: Fairly easy and much the same as for mimosa. If required as a foliage plant, delay re-potting for as long as possible to check size. Feed sparingly. With large pots and tubs the plant reaches considerable height and spread. Foliage may take on a bluish tint in winter – this is normal.

ACACIA VERTICILLATA
(*Prickly Moses*)

Description: Whorls of spiny-tipped leaves and a profusion of bright yellow fluffy catkin-like flowers in spring. Excellent for small pots.

A–Z

Position: Give a bright airy cool position. When grown in 15cm (6in) containers rarely exceeds about 90cm (3ft) in height and does not need much space.

Watering: Moderate from spring to autumn, sparingly in winter.

Propagation: Easy to raise from seed readily obtainable from specialist seedsmen. Can be grown on a window sill.

Care: Similar to other acacias. If given a free root run or put in large pots, it may become much larger, even tree-like. Feed sparingly. This species usually flowers more readily in small pots than others of this group.

ACALYPHYA HISPIDA
(*Red-hot cat's tail*)

Description: Shrubby habit with very striking long bright crimson dangling tails of velvety texture. Also popularly called Chenille Plant. Height 90cm-1.2m (3-4ft).

Position: Moderate warmth and humid atmosphere essential to success. Give good light to develop the best colour in the 'tails', but not direct sunlight.

Watering: This species is aquatic. Stand in a pan of shallow water and never allow to go completely dry. Spray with a mist of water daily in summer.

Propagation: Take cuttings and root in a warm place in spring. These should flower within 12 months if given warmth and humidity.

Care: This is a difficult plant without the conditions stated. Add some crushed charcoal to the potting compost to keep it sweet. Prune back in spring if growth is too vigorous – unlikely in the average home. Feed moderately during active growth.

ACORUS GRAMINEUS
(*Sweet flag*)

Description: Usually sold in the form 'Variegatus' which has creamy-white striped green grassy leaves about 18cm (7in) long. A dwarf tufted variety, 'Pusillus', is also sold.

Position: The plant is hardy. Give a cool bright position or slight shade.

Watering: The plant is aquatic and should be stood in a pan of water and not allowed to dry out at any time.

Propagation: Easily propagated by simple root division in spring.

Care: Very easy plant. Feed only sparingly. Add some crushed charcoal to potting compost to keep it from souring.

AGLAONEMA COMMUTATUM
(*Poison dart*)

Description: Feathery silvery-grey varied colouring on spear-shaped leaves that can be more than 20cm (8in) in length. Reaches 15cm (6in) in height. White leaves in July followed by red berries. A compact form, 'Treubii' is sometimes sold. 'Silver Queen', with brighter colouring, is popular but is a form of a different plant, *A. crispum*.

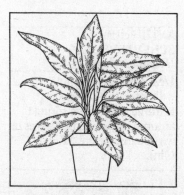

Position: Moderate warmth and humidity. Clean air. No draughts. Slight shade in summer, maximum light in winter. Does well in houseplant groups.
Watering: Keep moist but not waterlogged.
Propagation: From shoots at base of plant, or by dividing the whole plant when possible.
Care: In summer spray frequently with tepid water. Feed moderately during active growth. Good humidity is important. Should never be exposed to gas, oil, or coal-fire fumes.

AGLAONEMA MODESTUM
(*Chinese evergreen*)

Description: Spear-shaped green foliage with waxy texture and pale green leaves. Height 30cm (12in).
Position: Does well in a cool, but not cold, place. Does not mind shade.
Watering: Always keep moist but never waterlogged.
Propagation: Detach shoots from base of plant in spring and pot individually. Keep the pots in a warm place until the shoots are seen to be actively growing.
Care: Grows well in peat-based potting compost. Feed moderately during summer. Unlike many of the others in the same species, this is generally an easy plant, although the least attractive. Stems can be cut and last a long time in water.

ANTHURIUM ANDREANUM
(*Painter's palette*)

Description: Also called Wax flower or Oil-cloth flower

because of the texture of the leaves. These are bright red, or white and pink in colour. Leaves are heart-shaped. Height 45cm (18in).

Position: Needs plenty of warmth and humidity. No draught. Slight shade in summer, good light in winter. Not good in central heating, but does better in houseplant groups.

Watering: Always keep moist but not waterlogged. Spray with mist of water frequently in summer.

Propagation: By division of plants with two or more crowns.

Care: Repot when necessary in spring. Needs compost of fibrous peat, sphagnum moss and crushed charcoal added to the normal potting compost. Feed moderately during active growth.

ANTHURIUM CRYSTALLINUM
(*Crystal anthurium*)

Description: Large heart-shaped leaves, purplish when young, with a crystalline sheen. Height 45cm (18in).

Position: Must have good warmth and humidity. In cold positions leaves will brown around the edges. Give deep shade in summer, moderate light in winter.

Watering: Always keep moist but not waterlogged. Mist with tepid water frequently in summer.

Propagation: By division, but not easy.

Care: Aerial roots that form around the base must be well covered with moist compost as they grow. Use special compost as described for *A. andreanum*. Feed moderately during active growth.

ANTHURIUM SCHERZERIANUM
(*Flamingo flower*)

Description: A popular species with attractive red waxy-textured leaves from spring to autumn. Spear-shaped leaves on wiry stems. Height 22.5cm (9in).

Position: Warmth and moderate humidity. Slight

shade in summer. Does not need much space.

Watering: Water well from spring to early autumn, only just moist in winter. Mist from time to time during summer, but not in winter.

Propagation: Repot and propagate by division of the roots in spring.

Care: Do not set plants too deeply in the compost or the base may rot. Use compost as for *A. andreanum*. Make sure pots are well drained by putting a generous layer of broken pot or clean pebbles at the bottom. Do not overfeed.

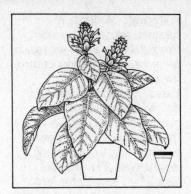

APHELANDRA SQUARROSA
(Zebra plant)

Description: Large spear-shaped glossy green leaves veined in cream. Yellow flower spikes. Usually sold as the cultivars 'Louisae' or 'Dania'. Height 22.5-60cm (9-25in).

Position: Despite tropical appearance often does well in cool position, but grows more rapidly in warmth. Give slight shade in summer. Can be kept compact.

Watering: Well during summer. If given cool position in winter, must then be given only enough water to prevent complete drying out.

Propagation: Cuttings taken from any new non-flowering shoots that may form, and rooted in warm place.

Care: Generally easy. After flowering, plants can be cut back to keep them bushy. Growth removed can be used as a source of cuttings. When cold, leaves may droop or drop off, but the plant usually recovers when warm again. Moderate feeding.

ARAUCARIA HETEROPHYLLA
(Norfolk Island pine)

Description: Characteristic fir with frond-like branches.

Position: Useful for cool airy parts of the home, but can grow to 2m (7ft) high in time, and then needs a large container. Does well in north-facing windows and out of direct sunshine. Can be stood outdoors in summer.

Watering: Moderate in summer, sparingly in winter.
Propagation: From seed sown in spring, or from shoot cuttings from cut-back plants.
Care: Mist occasionally to maintain humidity or foliage may be shed – a common trouble. Delay repotting and feed sparingly to prevent too rapid growth. Plants can be cut back if they become too large, but appearance may be spoiled for a time.

ASPARAGUS DENSIFLORUS 'SPRENGERI' (*Asparagus fern*)

Description: Well known for hanging basket foliage. Arching stems of fine needle-like leaves. Also used for cutting. Stem length 60-90cm (2-3ft).
Position: Cool shaded position. Can become large in time if repotted frequently. The form 'Myersii', much more compact and erect, can be grown where space is limited. A more compact form – 'Compactus' – also sometimes available.
Watering: Moderate in summer, sparingly in winter.
Propagation: Easy from seed sown on a window sill in spring, or by simple root division in early spring.

Care: Plants soon become potbound. To keep size in check, cut up and divide the root ball to propagate and keep the pots small, rather than repotting. Feed only moderately.

ASPARAGUS SETACEUS (syn. *A. plumosus*) (*Asparagus fern*)

Description: Very fine needle foliage and spreading habit like the Cedar of Lebanon. Can grow to 3m (10ft) in height.
Position: A favourite window sill plant, ideal for north-facing windows. Cool position out of direct sunlight. Can send out long climbing stems which can be cut off easily if space is limited.
Watering: Moderate most of the year, sparing in winter.
Propagation: Easy from seed sown on a window sill in spring, and by root division.

Care: Generally easy. Feed only moderately. Browning of the needles may be caused by hot dry conditions or dry roots.

ASPIDISTRA ELATIOR
(*Cast iron plant*)

Description: Well known glossy green foliage, lance-shaped and growing to points. The form 'Variegata' is the more attractive plant with cream-striped leaves. Height 30cm (12in).

Position: Suitable for places where it may be cool, draughty, shady, or even where there are fumes from gas, oil, or coal fires.

Watering: Sparingly at all times since the plant is a slow grower. Will survive considerable watering neglect, as well as overwatering.

Propagation: By simple division of the roots at almost any time.

Care: Although resistant to neglect and ill treatment, reasonable care results in far more handsome plants. Feed only moderately when active growth is being made. Treat leaves with a leaf-shine product and keep free from dust. Avoid brushing against them frequently or the edges may brown, so allow space if large.

AUCUBA JAPONICA
(*Spotted laurel*)

Description: Glossy spear-shaped rich green leaves flecked and spotted golden yellow.

Position: Hardy, suitable for the chilliest or draughtiest places, and even poor light. Plants may eventually reach a moderate to large size (about 2m (7ft) in height), and can then be used in cool spacious hallways or porches. Not suitable for warm stuffy situations.

Watering: Never allow to dry out completely or leaves may deteriorate. Water moderately in summer. Plants can be put outdoors to get washed by the rain.

Propagation: Cuttings usually root readily.

Care: Plants that become too large can be pruned back in spring. Keeping plants slightly pot-bound and avoiding feeding too generously also checks rapid growth. When plants outgrow their usefulness indoors they can be found a place in the garden or in outdoor tubs.

AZALEA

Description: Neat shrubby plants smothered in showy flowers in many colours. Height about 30cm (12in).

Position: Plants bought at about Christmas time cannot stand extreme cold, but should be kept in a cool place, neither chilly nor warm and stuffy. Plants bought as flowering specimens from early spring to early summer are probably

hardy azaleas, and should be given a cool position. In both cases keep in slight shade.

Watering: Keep moist at all times (this is important). Use clean rainwater if your mains water is hard or limey.

Propagation: From cuttings but not usually attempted for houseplants.

Care: Tender azaleas are usually best discarded after flowering unless you have greenhouse facilities. They are specially grown to flower out of season for the Christmas market. Hardy azaleas can be grown outdoors, but should be potted in a lime-free compost.

BEGONIA BOWERI
(*Eyelash begonia*)

Description: Similar to well known Rex begonia in habit, but very much smaller. Height 15-22.5cm (6-9in). Leaf edges fringed with lash-like hairs and chocolate-brown markings. Pretty pink-white flowers.

Position: Moderate warmth and humidity and slight shade in summer. Does not need much space.

Watering: Moderate in summer, sparing in winter. Mist from time to time in summer to improve humidity.

Propagation: Detach leaves with piece of stalk and insert in a cutting compost in summer, covering with a polythene bag. Rooting is usually easy.
Care: Easy provided there is good summer humidity. Feed moderately in summer. Avoid chill.

BEGONIA CATHAYANA
(*Chinese begonia*)

Description: Looks like a tall-growing Rex begonia with similar leaf colourings and markings, but has velvety textured foliage and reddish stems. A striking plant. Can grow to about 60cm (2ft) in height.
Position: Cool to moderately warm position, moderate humidity and shade.
Watering: Moderate in summer and sparingly in winter. Likes frequent misting in summer to maintain high humidity.
Propagation: Similar to *Begonia rex*, by slitting leaf vein and lying it on compost. Can also be divided when an old plant becomes straggly and overgrown.
Care: The stems of this plant can become extremely brittle – move about with great care or they may snap off. Feed when active growth is being made.

BEGONIA COCCINEA
(*Angel wing begonia*)

Description: Spear-shaped leaves with red margins. Panicles of bright red/pink flowers, spring to autumn. Hybrid 'President Carnot' has silver leaf spotting, grows well, but has paler flowers.
Position: Cool to moderate warmth, slight shade. Avoid placing where fallen flowers can be trodden into floor or carpet. Can eventually grow to considerable height (1.8m (6ft)) if given a large container.
Watering: Freely from spring to early autumn. Sparingly the rest of the year.
Propagation: Cuttings root readily during summer.
Care: Generally easy. Large plants are best housed in a cool conservatory where there is space. Feed moderately during active growth in summer. Will survive quite low temperatures if kept on the dry side.

BEGONIA CORALLINA
(*Spotted angel wing*)

Description: Most popular is the cultivar 'Lucerna' with bold ear-shaped irregular-edged foliage, olive green and silver spotted, purple red below, and with masses of pinkish flowers. Stout cane-like stems. Can

A–Z

reach 90cm (3ft) in height.
Position: Cool to moderate
warmth. Similar to *B. coccinea*.
Watering: Also similar to *B.
coccinea*.
Propagation: Usually
extremely easy from cuttings
which often root merely if
placed in water.
Care: A very easy plant which
will endure some neglect. Will
survive surprisingly low
temperatures if kept on the dry
side. Will deteriorate, but soon
recovers with return of warmth.
Feed moderately during active
growth.

BEGONIA FUCHSIOIDES
(*Fuchsia begonia*)

Description: Shrubby,
compact, with glossy oblong
leaves. Clusters of red/pink
flowers autumn to spring.
Position: Cool, airy, with
slight shade in summer. Bright
position in winter, but out of
direct sunlight. Can reach 1.2m
(4ft) in height when fully grown
and then needs large pots.
Watering: Moderately in
summer, sparingly in winter.
Propagation: Cuttings taken
in spring and rooted in warmth.
Care: Fairly easy, but do not
firm potting compost too much
since a friable texture is
preferred. Grows well in modern
peat composts. Feed moderately
during summer.

BEGONIA HAAGEANA
(*Elephant's ear begonia*)

Description: Dark green
foliage with whitish hairs and
red veins, and reddish below.
Pretty pink/white flowers in
summer. Height up to 1.2m
(4ft).
Position: A favourite plant on
Victorian window sills. Can be
grown in almost any conditions
within reason, but does better in
lighter position than most other
foliage begonias. Leaves can
reach 20cm (8in) in length, but
plants can be kept compact.
Colours of the leaves show up
better against the light.
Watering: Freely in summer,
much more sparingly in winter.
Propagation: Stem cuttings
taken early summer.

Care: To preserve compactness, cut back from time to time to encourage new growth at base. Feed moderately during summer.

BEGONIA MANICATA
(*Pink showers*)

Description: Leaves are at first arrow-shaped, pale green and smooth, with thin reddish edge. As the plant grows older, leaves become rounded and heart-shaped. Profusion of pinkish flowers on tall spikes in winter. Height up to 45cm (18in).
Position: Is happy in quite cool conditions, but flowers better in winter with moderate warmth. Otherwise similar to *B. haageana*.

Watering: Freely in summer, but only enough to keep compost moist in winter. If conditions tend to be chilly in winter, water less.
Propagation: By division when repotting in spring.
Care: Generally easy and not fussy. Much the same as for *B. haageana*.

BEGONIA MASONIANA
(*Iron cross begonia*)

Description: Similar to well known Rex begonia, but smaller and more compact and bristly. Striking feature is the bold chocolate brown central leaf marking – just like an iron cross. Height 22.5cm (9in).
Position: Much as for the Rex begonia. Will survive quite low temperatures if kept on the dry side over winter. Will deteriorate, but soon recovers with warmth. Slight to moderate shade. Needs little space.
Watering: Freely in summer, keep only slightly moist in winter.
Propagation: From leaf cuttings as for the Rex begonia, also by root division in spring.
Care: Generally easy. Likes moderate humidity in summer, but be careful that water does not remain on the bristly leaves too long as the droplets may cause spotting. Feed moderately when growth is active.

BEGONIA METALLICA
(*Metal begonia*)

Description: Branching habit. Leaves with metallic lustre, veined and crimson below, white to pink flowers in autumn. Can reach a height of about 1m (3½ft).

Position: Moderate warmth and humidity, and slight shade. Best not put too low, so beauty of underside of foliage can be enjoyed.

Watering: Freely in summer, moderately in winter. Do not waterlog. Mist with water from time to time during summer.

Propagation: Stem cuttings root well in the warmth of early summer.

Care: Take care that plant is watered as recommended. Chill is best avoided or leaves may tend to drop. Feeding can be generous in summer.

BEGONIA REX
(*Rex begonia*)

Description: Crinkled irregular-edged spear-shaped leaves. Variety of beautiful colours and markings with silvery variegation. Height up to 30cm (12in).

Position: Best in slight shade – leaf colours bleach in excessive light. Moderate humidity in summer. Does not need much

space. Will survive low temperatures if kept dryish over winter. Deteriorates, but recovers with warmth.

Watering: Water freely in summer, sparingly in winter especially where temperature is low.

Propagation: Slit leaf veins underneath at several points. Place flat on compost surface and cover with polythene. Plantlets form where the veins are slit and can be potted when well rooted. Can also be divided.

Care: Old plants can become a mass of rhizome-like stems at the base and should be re-propagated. The cut-off stems will often root if potted. Feed moderately during active growth in summer.

BEGONIA SEMPERFLORENS
(*Bedding begonia*)

Description: Popular for summer bedding but also excellent pot plants, often flowering in the winter on a sunny window sill. Height 15-22.5cm (6-9in).

Position: Bright position, sunny in winter if possible, airy cool conditions. South-facing window best.

Watering: Enough to keep compost just moist.

Propagation: Seed down on a

window sill from February to spring. Surface sow and do not cover seed with compost – just press into the surface. Late sowings give the winter-flowering plants. Seed is very fine. Water with a mist in the early stages.
Care: Seedlings are normally slow-growing at first but faster by late spring. Re-pot healthy seedlings in 10-13cm (4-5in) pots for flowering. Feed only when the plants are well established and flowering freely. Overfeeding will encourage leaves rather than flowers.

BEGONIA TUBERHYBRIDA
(*Tuberous begonia*)

Description: Showy flowers: single, double, or tassel-like on some pendular forms. Height 30-60cm (12-24in).
Position: Cool, shaded. Some are suited to pots on window sills. Pendular types for hanging pots or baskets. Flowers summer to autumn.
Watering: Keep moist.
Propagation: Cuttings in spring of shoots from started tubers, or tubers can be cut up with one shoot to each piece.
Care: Start tubers by immersion in bowl of moist peat in warmth early spring. (Top curves inwards.) Inspect frequently and pot into a potting compost as soon as signs of growth are seen. Plant pendular types about three to each basket. Support large-flowered exhibition types with cane. Remove buds carrying winged seed capsules so plant develops only showy 'male' flowers. Multifloras and pendulas can be left alone. Feed while buds are forming. Store tubers in dry sand, frost-free, over winter.

BELOPERONE GUTTATA
(*Shrimp plant*)

Description: Shrubby and usually compact. Salmon-pink decorative leaves borne over long period. Grows to about 60cm (2ft).
Position: Cool airy position in good light. Will tolerate full sunlight in summer if kept watered.
Watering: Must not be allowed to go dry in summer. Keep slightly moist in winter.
Propagation: Cuttings taken in spring.
Care: Mature plants can get straggly. Cut out any weak or unwanted growth February to March. Good light in summer develops richer colour provided adequate watering is not neglected. Feed from spring to late summer.

BOUGAINVILLEA GLABRA
(*Paper flower*)

Description: Shrubby climber with brilliantly coloured leaves. Height 1.5-2.4m (5-8ft).

Position: Cool, bright, and airy. Can be grown as wall shrub in a conservatory or porch, and as a pot plant if pruned.
Watering: Freely in summer with occasional misting. Rest in winter by keeping on the dry side. Resume watering in March.
Propagation: Take cuttings in summer.
Care: Where space permits train on wires against a wall or up canes. By frequent pruning back, plants can be grown bushy in 15-20cm (6-8in) pots. Feed during active growth.

BROWALLIA SPECIOSA
(*Bush violet*)

Description: Neat, bushy pot plants, about 45cm (18in) in height. Some new cultivars, such as 'Troll', are dwarf, with a profusion of blue or white cup-shaped flowers.
Position: Cool but not chilly position, in slight shade.
Watering: Keep moist all the time.
Propagation: Can be grown from seed sown on a window sill from February onwards. Pinch out top of seedlings to promote bushy growth and plant several to each 13cm (5in) pot.
Care: Late spring sowings give winter-flowering plants. After flowering plants are not usually worth saving, but they can be cut back in spring to encourage new growth. Feed when buds are forming.

BRUNFELSIA CALYCINA
(*Yesterday, today, tomorrow plant*)

Description: Popular name alludes to the changing colour of the flowers from purple to white as they age. Fragrant flowers year round. Glossy foliage. Height up to 60cm (24in).
Position: Cool, but not chilly or draughty. Slight shade in

summer. Can be grown in 13cm (5in) pot.

Watering: Keep moist all year round. Mist in summer.

Propagation: Cuttings taken in summer, rooted in a warm place.

Care: Moderate temperature is important – avoid both chill and excessive warmth, and sudden changes. Avoid unnecessary potting and disturbance of roots. Varieties with smaller flowers are easier than those with larger. Only feed during active growth.

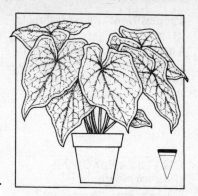

over winter in a temperature of about 13°C/55°F. Repot if necessary, in spring. Best leaf colours will not develop in too much shade or light. Avoid sudden changes of temperature.

CALADIUM BICOLOR
(Angel's wings)

Description: Large shield-shaped leaves, veined and patterned in a variety of glorious colours. Height 22.5-37.5cm (9-15in).

Position: Warm, out of draught, moderate humidity and slight shade. Does not need much space.

Watering: Keep moist during growing period, but completely dry during winter.

Propagation: When offsets from tubers formed, detach and pot in spring.

Care: Plants are grown from tubers started in spring in warm place. In autumn let pots go dry and store dry in a warm place

CALATHEA LANCIFOLIA
(syn *C. insignis*)
(Rattlesnake plant)

Description: Long narrow spear-shaped leaves, wavy edged, purple below, snake-like patterning above. Height 22.5cm (9in).

Position: Will tolerate cooler conditions than most calatheas, and more frequent changes of temperature, but ensure moderate humidity and slight shade.

Watering: Keep moist at all times and mist frequently in summer. Use clean rainwater if tap water is limey.

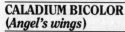

A–Z

Propagation: Division of roots in spring.
Care: Very easy. Can be grown in a 13cm (5in) pot for a long time. Repot in spring. Feed during summer.

CALATHEA MAKOYANA
(*Peacock plant*)

Description: Spear-shaped leaves marked with a feathery pattern on a silvery background and flushed red below. Height 45-60cm (18-24in).
Position: Warmth, moderate humidity and shade. Does well mixed with other houseplants. Full beauty is shown if leaves can be seen against the light. Happy in 13cm (5in) pot for a long time. Excellent in a bottle garden.
Watering: Keep moist with clean rainwater or soft water, and mist frequently in summer.
Propagation: Easily multiplied by division of the roots during late spring.
Care: Conditions of warmth and humidity are important – humidity especially in summer. Exposure to excessive light may bleach foliage and cause browning. Feed during summer.

CALATHEA ORNATA

Description: Spear-shaped leaves delicately lined, herringbone fashion, pink to white against dark green background, purplish below.
Position: Moderate warmth and shade. In large pots or tubs plants can reach 2m (7ft) in height and bear leaves 60cm (2ft) in length.
Watering: Keep moist at all times, using clean rainwater.
Propagation: Division of roots when repotting.
Care: The plant tends to vary in appearance and size according to conditions. Pink leaf colour may be lost with age and if exposed to too much light. Warmth and humidity are important for best results. Do not feed too generously if growth has to be restricted in limited space. Repot in same size or larger pots in spring.

CALATHEA ZEBRINA
(*Zebra plant*)

Description: Long leaves with velvety texture, zebra striped, purplish below, palm-like when well grown. In ideal conditions can reach about 60cm (2ft) in height with leaves 30cm (1ft) long.
Position: Good warmth, moderate humidity and shade.

Best effect of leaf colour obtained by viewing against the light.
Watering: Always keep moist with clean rainwater or soft water. Mist in summer.
Propagation: Division of roots when repotting.
Care: Not an easy plant unless conditions specified are kept to strictly. Never allow to go dry or plant may seriously deteriorate and not recover. Avoid draughts and erratic temperatures. Feed moderately during summer.

CALCEOLARIA
(*Slipper flower*)

Description: Compact plants smothered with pouch-like flowers, exotically marked and brightly coloured. About 30cm (12in) in height.
Position: Cool airy shaded position. Not stuffy hot room.

Watering: Keep moist, but not waterlogged.
Propagation: Can be grown from seed, but not usually done without a greenhouse. However, try an easy new cultivar called 'Anytime'. This will flower 14 weeks after sowing at any time.
Care: Plants are usually bought as short-term flowering pot plants. Too much warmth and exposure to sunlight may cause severe wilting. Transfer to cool and shade, but do not water unless compost is obviously dry. Not usually necessary to feed unless there are many more buds forming. Discard after flowering.

CALLISIA ELEGANS
(syn. *Setcreasea striata*)
(*Striped inch plant*)

Description: Spear-shaped leaves, close together and grasping stem, green lined in white, purplish below. Entire plant covered with fine hair. Trailing habit. (Often sold as a Tradescantia). Height 30cm (12in).
Position: Cool and where plant can trail. Good light (not direct sun) develops best leaf colour and contrast.
Watering: Moist at all times, but less so in winter.
Propagation: Easy from

cuttings taken spring to summer. These often root if merely stood in water.

Care: Plants can become straggly with age, so propagate frequently. Put several rooted cuttings in each container. Avoid excessive shade – the plants will grow but never look at their best. Feed in moderation during summer.

CAMPANULA ISOPHYLLA
(*Italian bellflower*)

Description: Popular trailing campanula, which is smothered with blue or white starry flowers, summer to autumn. Forms occur with cream variegated foliage. Height 15cm (6in).

Position: Happy in quite cool position, but should be kept frost free. Not suitable for warm stuffy rooms. Give slight shade and room for trailing.

Watering: Generous in summer, sparing in winter.

Propagation: Very easy from cuttings. Also by root division.

Care: Remove remains of blooms promptly as they wilt, otherwise plants become covered with brownish debris. Sometimes variegated leaf shoots form. These can be removed and rooted as cuttings. The flowers of variegated plants may be inferior or smaller. Feed moderately in summer.

CAPSICUM ANNUUM
(*Winter pepper*)

Description: Neat compact shrubby plants with bright berries, usually shades of red, often conical or shaped like chillies. About 45cm (18in) in height.

Position: Cool, airy, in good light.

Watering: Keep slightly moist. Avoid overwatering.

Propagation: Very easy to grow from seed sown on window sill in spring. Seedlings should not be potted in pots larger than 13cm (5in).

Care: Berried plants are often bought around Christmas time. In the cool the berries will be retained for a long time.

Overwatering may cause leaves to fall. Discard plants when they deteriorate and the berries begin to shrivel. Feeding is not necessary. Plants being grown from seed need feeding when they begin to flower from summer onwards. The flowers are of no decorative merit. Early sowing may yield berried plants from summer to autumn, but to guarantee berries for Christmas may need experiment.

CATHARANTHUS ROSEUS
(syn. *Vinca rosea*)
(*Madagascar periwinkle*)

Description: Neat shrubby plants with glossy leaves and starry flowers, white to magenta shades, sometimes with contrasting 'eye'. Height 30-37.5cm (12-15in).
Position: Moderate warmth and humidity, and slight shade.
Watering: Keep moist with misting from time to time in summer. Drier in winter.
Propagation: Very easy to grow from seed sown on a window sill in spring. Seed is sold under the former name, Vinca. Pot in 13cm (5in) pots. (Flowers same year as sowing.) Also from cuttings taken in spring.
Care: To save plants over winter, reasonable warmth is necessary or leaves will fall. To keep plants neat, prune back in early spring as new growth is about to start. After flowering, which may go on into winter, rest the plants by reducing watering, but do not allow to dry out. Feed during active growth. Often best grown as annuals which flower freely.

CELOSIA ARGENTEA

Description: Two forms are Plumosa or Prince of Wales feather with feathery plumes, and Cristata or Cockscomb which looks like a large velvety cock's comb. Various colours. Height 60cm (24in).
Position: Cool airy bright position. Most are of compact growth.
Watering: Keep moist, but avoid overwatering which can cause leaf yellowing.
Propagation: Very easy from seed sown on a window sill in spring. Pot in not larger than 13cm (5in) pots.
Care: Grown as annuals. Discard at end of year when plants deteriorate. Careful watering is important to preserve appearance of the foliage as well as the 'plumes' or 'combs'. Avoid overfeeding; little feed is needed once the decorative stage is reached.

CHLOROPHYTUM COMOSUM
(syn. *C. capense*)
(*Spider plant*)

Description: Long narrow arching leaves margined in cream in the cultivar 'Variegatum' or centrally banded cream in 'Mandrianum'. Arching stems of starry white flowers in summer which also bear plantlets. Height 15-25cm (6-10in).

Position: Cool but not draughty. Slight shade. Plants need space to hang. Very good for pedestals.

Watering: Generous in summer, sparing in winter.

Propagation: Easily propagated from little plantlets formed on stems. Detach and pot, or peg down to the surface of compost and detach when rooted.

Care: Plants will survive quite low temperatures but may deteriorate. Chill is best avoided. Also avoid brushing against the leaves – this may cause browning of the tips. Feed from spring to late summer.

CHRYSANTHEMUM

Description: Sold as houseplants, they are small and compact, usually several plants in each pot or bowl. About 30cm (12in) in height.

Position: Cool airy position. Bright but not in direct sunlight.

Watering: Keep moist but not waterlogged. Do not allow to go dry, or overwater.

Propagation: Not usually practical from plants sold as houseplants, but can be grown from seed in Spring or September.

Care: Plants are grown under specially controlled conditions by nurseries, usually for out-of-season flowering. If saved they will grow tall and flower at a different time, and may take a while to regain their normality. It may be worth planting them out in the garden. If kept cool and moist the potted plants will remain decorative for weeks, but are usually best discarded when they fade. Feeding is not necessary unless there are many buds forming. Best bought when they are in flower.

CISSUS ANTARCTICA
(Kangaroo vine)

Description: Shrubby climber with shiny spear-shaped leaves with toothed edges. Height 4.5-6m (15-20ft).

Position: Cool airy position in good light. Ideal for stair wells or hallways with plenty of height. If given large pot, it can soon reach ceiling height.

Watering: Water well in summer, sparingly in winter.

Propagation: Cuttings taken in summer.

Care: Although the plant enjoys the cool, severe cold and chill will cause deterioration. If growth is to be restricted do not be afraid to cut back. Keeping pot size to the minimum also slows development, but feeding should not be neglected. Canes or some other means of support will be necessary.

CISSUS DISCOLOR
(Begonia vine)

Description: Climber with extremely beautifully coloured and variegated leaves. Height 4.5-6m (15-20ft).

Position: Moderate warmth and humidity is essential, and good light – not direct sunshine. Although a climber it is best displayed as a trailer from hanging pot or basket; will trail to a considerable distance – 2m (6½ft).

Watering: Keep moist at all time and maintain humidity by frequent misting in summer.

Propagation: From stem cuttings rooted in warmth in early summer.

Care: This is a difficult plant for the average home, without year-round warmth and humidity. When cold, it quickly drops leaves. Good light develops the finest leaf colours. Feed from late spring to late summer. If winter conditions become cool, survival is more likely if kept drier.

CITRUS MICROCARPA
(syn. C. mitis)
(Calamondin orange)

Description: Charming miniature orange with starry scented white waxy flowers. Walnut-sized oranges. Height 45cm (18in).

Position: Cool, airy, in good light – not direct sunlight. Unsuitable for warm stuffy rooms and where the air is very dry, causing leaf fall.

Watering: Keep moist, slightly drier in winter. Use clean rainwater if tap water is limey. Mist in summer.

Propagation: From cuttings or from seed – the fruits usually contain very few 'pips', but they are of moderate size and easy to handle.

Care: Leaves tend to yellow. Try watering with one saltspoonful of aluminium sulphate (from chemist) dissolved in 500ml (1pt) of clean rainwater. Prune in March to maintain neat shape. Feed during active growth. For potting, use a lime-free compost.

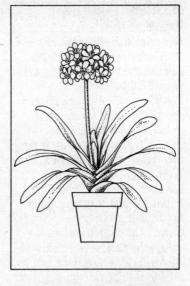

CLIVIA MINIATA
(*Kaffir lily*)

Description: Bold strap-shaped leaves, showy orange trumpet flowers in spring. Height 45cm (18in).

Position: Cool, airy, light shade. Tolerates chill, but is soon damaged at freezing. Needs moderate space for large pots.

Watering: Enough to prevent drying out in winter, plenty in summer.

Propagation: Division of clumps when repotting. Seed takes some years to produce flowers.

Care: Plants need large pots – at least 18cm (7in) – even so, they soon become pot-bound. Flowers are produced over a period of 2-4 weeks. Pots can be put outdoors the rest of the time, weather permitting – not during winter when it may be freezing. Cut stems right down after flowering. Feed lightly when the leaves are making active growth. Established plants in large pots will need more care over feeding. Incorporate a little fertilizer with the top of the compost in the pots each spring.

CODIAEUM VARIEGATUM PICTUM
(*Croton*)

Description: Foliage plants with a variety of different shaped leaves with various lovely colours and markings. Height up to 60cm (24in).

Position: Moderate warmth and humidity, and a bright position out of direct sunlight.

Does well in groups of similar houseplants.

Watering: Keep moist, using tepid water.

Propagation: From cuttings dipped in charcoal to absorb

exuding latex. They need brisk warmth for good rooting.

Care: Avoid buying plants when they may have been chilled in winter as they soon deteriorate after exposure to cold. Plants damaged this way may recover if cut back in spring, the cuts dusted with charcoal, and placed in the warm. New shoots may form. Feed moderately in summer. Will be happy in 18cm (7in) pots for some time.

COFFEA ARABICA
(*Coffee plant*)

Description: Neat bushy plant with glossy dark green spear-shaped leaves. Same species produce commercial coffee beans. Height 60-90cm (2-3ft).

Position: Moderate warmth, humidity and good light.

Watering: Freely in summer, moderately in winter. Mist occasionally in summer.

Propagation: Can easily be grown from fresh beans (available from seedsmen) sown on a warm window sill, spring to summer.

Care: Deteriorates in chill which soon causes leaf shedding. Best grown in a lime-free potting compost. The form usually grown is 'Nana' which is naturally dwarf, and the plants need little attention. The white flowers, followed by red berries, are rarely produced in home conditions. Feed during active growth in summer.

COLEUS
(*Flame nettle*)

Description: Popular foliage plants with exotic rich colours and markings and a variety of leaf forms. Height 45cm (18in) or more. Some varieties are extra dwarf – particularly useful if space is limited.

Position: Cool, airy and good light, but not direct sunlight behind glass.

Watering: Keep moist at all times, but avoid waterlogging which may cause leaf shedding.

Propagation: Very easy from seed sown on a window sill in early spring or from cuttings in spring or summer. Best grown as annual. Pot on to 13cm (5in) pots.

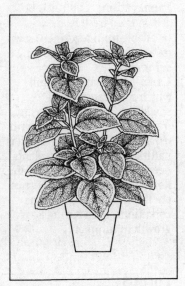

Care: Very easy plants for summer to autumn display. Not easy for keeping over winter without warmth and good light. Feed moderately when in final pots. Snip off the flower spikes at an early stage to direct plants energy to producing foliage.

COLUMNEA × BANKSII
(*Goldfish plant*)

Description: Trailer with dark green glossy leaves and reddish orange tubular flowers, autumn to spring, sometimes followed by pale violet berries.

Position: Warm position and moderate humidity at all times including winter. The stems can trail to about 90cm (3ft) so allow space. Best in hanging pots or baskets. Unsuitable for chilly houses.

Watering: Keep moist, not waterlogged, at all times, and maintain humidity by misting.

Propagation: By cuttings taken late spring. Good warmth for rooting.

Care: Use special potting compost: peat-based potting compost mixed with one-third of its volume of sphagnum moss, with a little crushed charcoal and bonemeal added. Feed only sparingly. With the right humidity conditions the plant is not too difficult.

COLUMNEA GLORIOSA
(*Goldfish plant*)

Description: Trailer with hairy leaves and tubular scarlet flowers with yellow throats, autumn to spring.

Position: Needs warmth and humidity. Plants can trail down to about 120cm (4ft), so must be given sufficient space. Best planted in wire basket or slatted orchid basket.

Watering: Moist, but not waterlogged, at all times.

Propagation: Cuttings taken in spring need moderate warmth for rooting.

Care: Needs same treatment and compost as for C. × *banksii*. There is a form, 'Purpurea', with purplish tinted foliage, said to be a little easier, needing less attention to temperature and humidity.

CORDYLINE AUSTRALIS
(*Cabbage palm*)

Description: Cluster of sword-shaped leaves in young plants, developing a short 'trunk' with maturity to present a palm-like appearance. Also in reddish to purple-leaved versions. Height 60-90cm (2-3ft).

Position: Give cool, airy, bright position. Useful for hallways, foyers and the like. Gives a 'tropical' look to chilly places. In pots can grow to 90cm (3ft) or more, depending on container size. Can be stood outdoors for summer if desired.

Watering: Moist in summer, less so in winter.

Propagation: Detach root suckers from base of plant when

formed to reproduce desirable colours. Can also be grown from seed in warmth in spring.

Care: A slow grower which can be kept in 20cm (8in) pots for some time. Generally easy. Feed only moderately.

CORDYLINE TERMINALIS
(syn. *C. fruticosa*)
(*Ti plant*)

Description: Similar to *C. australis*, but with large spear-shaped leaves, green and cream variegated, often with red or purplish tints. Young leaves tend to have the best colour and variation. Can reach about 90cm (3ft) in height.

Position: Moderate warmth and humidity, and slight shade. Not suitable for chilly or draughty positions.

Watering: Keep moist at all times.

Propagation: Usually grown from 'ti' log, see below.

Care: Frequently sold as 'ti' log. This is a stem cutting. Pot into potting compost plus some extra grit for drainage. Cover with polythene bag and place in warmth. When roots and leaves have formed transfer to larger pot. Warmth and humidity are important for success. Feed only sparingly.

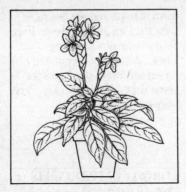

CROSSANDRA INFUNDIBULIFORMIS
(*Firecracker flower*)

Description: Neat plant with glossy spear-shaped, wavy-edged leaves, and spikes of orange-lobed flowers. Height up to 60cm (24in).
Position: Moderate warmth. Good light in winter, slight shade in summer. Not suited to chilly positions. Does not need much space, but may fail in dry central heating.
Watering: Only slightly moist in winter, generously in summer. Mist from time to time if the air tends to become dry.
Propagation: Cuttings late spring. Seed sown March/April.
Care: The plant likes a rich compost, such as John Innes No. 3. Keep well fed. Avoid sudden changes of any kind.

CTENANTHE OPPENHEIMIANA 'TRICOLOR'
(*Never never plant*)

Description: Neat plant with spear-shaped leaves banded each side of the central leaf vein with light green, and with white to pinkish splashing, pinkish below. Can grow 45-90cm (1½-3ft) tall, depending on pot size.
Position: Good warmth and moderate humidity. Does best in a case, or with other houseplant groups needing warmth and humidity. Give shade, but useful for areas of artificial lighting. Unsuitable for chilly or dry air conditions.
Watering: Moist, but not wet, at all times. Mist to maintain humidity.
Propagation: Root division when potting.
Care: Can be grown in a 13cm (5in) pot for a long time. Feed moderately. Will fail unless the conditions of comfortable warmth and humidity can be maintained.

CUPHEA IGNEA
(*Mexican cigar plant*)

Description: Neat sturdy shrubby plant with dainty foliage and a profusion of quaint small red tubular flowers. Height 30cm (12in).

Position: Cool, airy, bright or slight shade. Does not need much space.

Watering: Keep moist. Waterlogging may cause leaf and bud drop.

Propagation: Very easy to grow as an annual from seed sown on a window sill in early spring.

Care: Pot in 13cm (5in) pots. Seedlings are very quick to come into flower. Can be allowed to grow without interference. Can be saved over winter in frost-free conditions if kept on the dry side, but not really worthwhile.

CYANOTIS KEWENSIS
(*Teddy bear plant*)

Description: Usually grown as a trailer but can be trained as a short climber. Reddish-brown woolly coated small oval leaves, olive green above and purple below. Magenta flowers.

Position: Cool but not chilly and with moderate ventilation. Good light in winter, slight shade in summer. Can be used as a trailer for small hanging containers or pots on shelves.

Watering: Sparingly in winter, moderately in summer. Waterlogging can easily cause root or lower stem rotting.

Propagation: Cuttings taken in spring.

Care: Wide temperature changes cause leaf shedding, and so does uneven watering. For hanging baskets plant roots around the edge – there will usually be room for other plants in the centre. Feed moderately in summer.

CYPERUS ALTERNIFOLIUS
(*Umbrella plant*)

Description: Clumps of strong stems topped with long narrow leaves radiating like the spokes of an umbrella. There are some extra compact forms available and also a cream variegated cultivar. Height about 60cm (24in).

Position: Cool, airy, bright position. Does not take up space.

Watering: This is an aquatic plant and can be stood permanently in a pan of water so that the compost is always quite moist.

Propagation: By root division in spring. Also easy from seed sown on a window sill in spring.

Care: Seedlings must be kept moist. Old plants can soon become pot-bound and will need dividing. Generally very easy. Only modest feeding is necessary.

CYPERUS PAPYRUS
(*Egyptian paper reed*)

Description: Rather like a tall or giant form of *C. alternifolius*. Grows to about 90cm (3ft) in height; much more in large containers.

Position: Warm, bright, airy position. Large windows, porches in summer, conservatories and hallways.

Watering: This is an aquatic plant and the pots should be stood in a bowl or large pan of water so that the compost is always moist.

Propagation: Can be expensive to buy, but very easy to grow from seed, when available, sown on a warm window sill in early spring.

Care: The grass-like seedlings grow away very quickly in pots of moist compost and will need transferring to at least 20cm (8in) pots. Not easy to save such large specimens over winter, so plant is more conveniently grown as an annual. Not much feeding is required.

CYTISUS
(*Broom*)

Description: The plant is usually sold under the names *C. canariensis* or *C. racemosus*. It has masses of golden yellow pea flowers, winter to summer. Height 1.8m (6ft).

Position: Airy, bright position (but not in direct sunshine) where the fragrance may be fully appreciated. A good evergreen for a cool conservatory.

Watering: Moist in summer, less so the rest of the year.

Propagation: Cuttings with a 'heel' taken late summer.

Care: Like most members of the Pea family, rich compost is not required, and feeding should also be moderate. Overfeeding causes lots of leaves and stems and few flowers. To keep growth in check, cut back after flowering.

DIEFFENBACHIA MACULATA
(syn. *D. picta*)
(*Dumb cane*)

Description: Foliage plants extremely variable in form and

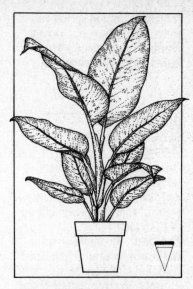

size but all with beautifully coloured and variegated foliage. Many versions with fancy names often labelled '*D. picta*'. Height 60cm-1.2m (2-4ft).
Position: Good warmth, and light but slight shade in summer, and high humidity. Space required varies – there are dwarf forms and others with leaves exceeding 30cm (1ft) in length.
Watering: Despite the need for high humidity, water carefully to avoid waterlogging which may cause rot around the stem base.
Propagation: From stem tip cuttings. Not easy in the home.
Care: A difficult plant for long term, in average home. If

bought early in the year it will usually give pleasure until autumn.
Special points: All parts of the plant are poisonous. The sap should be washed off the skin and not allowed to enter the mouth.

DIONAEA MUSCIPULA (*Venus fly-trap*)

Description: Famous for its touch-sensitive clam-like traps which catch and digest insects. Sometimes white flowers in summer. Height 1.2m (4ft).
Position: Moderate warmth in summer and high humidity usually achieved by covering with glass or clear plastic enclosure. Good light essential. Cool and drier in winter.
Watering: Plant is native to bogs and wet heaths. Stand pots in a tray of water.
Propagation: By division of root crowns, or from seed.
Care: Usually sold already planted. Use special compost: peat/sphagnum moss/charcoal to allow entry of both water and air to roots. Traps can be fed with *tiny* scraps of meat, fish, or other protein material. Avoid ordinary fertilizers, but foliar feeds may prove beneficial. Traps deteriorate or turn yellow in too much shade.

DIPLADENIA SPLENDENS
(*Pink allamanda*)

Description: Vigorous climber with lustrous, spear-shaped leaves. Rose-pink petunia-like flowers, summer to autumn. Height up to 4.5m (15ft)

Position: Warm and bright, out of direct sunlight. Can reach ceiling height. Not suitable for chilly or draughty places.

Watering: Generously in summer and spray with tepid water from time to time; sparingly in winter.

Propagation: Cuttings in spring need moderate warmth for rooting.

Care: To keep plants compact, cut back after flowering. Plants are best bought in spring and given 18cm (7in) pots. Do not overfeed or plants may produce leaves instead of flowers.

DIZYGOTHECA ELEGANTISSIMA
(*Spider plant*)

Description: Wiry stems carrying reddish to olive green, long, slender-fingered foliage of graceful appearance. Height up to 1.5m (5ft).

Position: Moderate warmth and reasonable humidity. Good light, but slight shade in summer. In large containers can reach a man's height, but foliage then loses some of its grace. Not

suitable for chilly and draughty places.

Watering: Generous in summer with frequent misting, sparing in winter.

Propagation: From seed when available.

Care: Will not grow vigorously unless temperature and humidity are maintained. In chill lower leaves may fall. If warmth can be restored the plants can be cut back and new shoots will form. Plants that have grown too tall can also be cut back: use warmth to encourage new growth. Feed only during active growth.

DRACAENA DEREMENSIS

Description: A number of cultivars are sold, with broad, pointed strap-shaped, palm-like foliage, beautifully striped or variegated. Well grown plants can reach about 120cm (4ft) in height and leaves can reach 45cm (18in) in length.

Position: Moderate warmth with humidity is essential.

Watering: Keep the compost moist, but waterlogging leads to leaf shedding and root rotting very easily.

Propagation: Tip cutting in spring. Not easy in the home.

Care: Not easy plants. Leaves are shed if temperatures fluctuate, if there is chill or draught, or if the atmosphere becomes too dry. Where the conditions are suitable the plants grow well in the usual potting composts and require little feeding until in the final pots.

DRACAENA DRACO
(Dragon tree)

Description: Foliage plant with palm-like, narrow, strap-shaped leaves with reddish margins. Height 90cm (3ft) or more.

Position: Cool, airy, bright position. Can be stood outside in summer. Sometimes used for sub-tropical bedding effects. Can reach considerable size in large pots or small tubs. Useful for cool halls or conservatories.

Watering: Plenty in summer, only just moist in winter.

Propagation: Easy from seed sown on window sill in spring. Fairly slow growing.

Care: An easy plant generally tolerating quite low temperatures. As plants grow, the lower foliage is naturally shed to create a palm-like appearance which is quite attractive. Very long-lived. Can be retained in small pots for a long time to retard development. Feed sparingly.

A–Z

DRACAENA FRAGRANS

Description: 'Massangeana', the type usually sold as a houseplant, has foliage remarkably like ornamental maize with colourful striping and variegation. Height 1.2m (4ft) or more.

Position: Much the same as for *D. deremensis*. If given a warm place with space for the plant to grow to maturity in large pot, fragrant yellow flowers followed by reddish fruits may be produced.

Watering: Keep moist at all times, slightly less so in winter.

Propagation: From base shoots in spring. (Not easy in the home.)

Care: Warmth plus moderate humidity is essential. Since the plant can grow to almost 2m (6ft), and has a fair spread, this may not be easy in the average home.

Watering: Generous in summer, sparing in winter.

Propagation: Tip cuttings. (Not easy in the home.)

Care: As for *D. draco*, although the plant will not tolerate such low temperatures. It grows slowly under cool conditions. A warmer environment speeds up development. Feed well only during periods of active growth.

DRACAENA MARGINATA
(*Madagascar dragon tree*)

Description: Similar to *D. draco*, but with narrower leaves. Lower leaves are shed earlier, so that the palm-like appearance comes sooner. Rarely exceeds 90cm (3ft).

Position: Much the same as for *D. draco*, but it tolerates more shade.

DRACAENA SANDERIANA

Description: Long narrow leaves, slightly waved, with contrasting silver to cream margins. Height 45cm (18in).

Position: Requires less humidity than most dracaenas, often doing much better than others in central heating. Slight shade.

Watering: As for other dracaenas.

Propagation: From base shoots. Not easy in the home.

Care: If potted on to a 20cm (8in) pot, a size of about 1m (3½ft) can be reached and the plant tends to branch at the base taking up more space – but then looking its most impressive. Although doing well in a drier atmosphere, misting in summer will hasten growth. It will then also respond to moderate feeding.

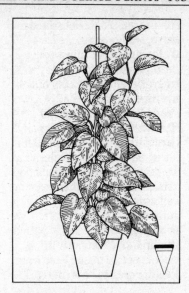

EPIPREMNUM AUREUM
(syn. *Scindapsus aureus*)
(*Devil's ivy*)

Description: Usually sold under the name scindapsus. Tall climber with broad spear-shaped leaves. There are a number of forms with different colourings and markings, such as 'Marble Queen', 'Golden Queen', and 'Tricolor', which is red, yellow, and green. Height 1.8m (6ft) or more.

Position: Similar to philodendrons. Young plants need little space, but they can reach a man's height eventually when well grown. They then also develop larger heart-shaped leaves up to 30cm (1ft) in length.

Watering: As for philodendrons.

Propagation: Cuttings rooted in warmth.

Care: Best grown up mossy pole as for *Philodendron domesticum*. Plants bought with large leaves have been grown from cuttings from mature plants. These plants will produce small leaves as they grow until they again reach maturity. If space is limited, plants can be cut back in early June.

ERICA HIEMALIS
(*Cape heath*)

Description: Neat heather-like plant with smothering of small pink and white tubular flowers, usually sold about Christmas time. Height up to 60cm (24in).

Position: Cool, bright, airy.

Popular gift plant. Not suited to warm, stuffy rooms.

Watering: Keep moist using clean rainwater if tap water is limey. Never allow to dry out at any time.

Propagation: Cuttings in March in warmth and humidity.

Care: Gift plants are forced for Christmas and may not flower at the same time if kept. Stand pots outside for the summer, keeping well watered. Plants forced by nurseries often deteriorate. Those that survive can be potted into lime-free compost. Bring indoors before frosts. Feed when buds are seen to be forming.

EUCALYPTUS CITRIODORA (*Lemon-scented gum*)

Description: Bristly spear-shaped leaves which emit strong lemon scent when pressed between the fingers. Height 1.2-1.8m (4-6ft).

Position: Cool to warm, with moderate humidity. In summer the leaves may scent the air in warm surroundings. Good light to slight shade.

Watering: Moderate in summer, with misting occasionally, sparing in winter, especially in cool surroundings.

Propagation: Easy from seed sown on warm window sill in spring.

Care: Pot on seedling to 13cm (5in) pots in which plants can be kept for some time. The species is tender, but will survive in temperatures almost down to freezing if kept on the dry side, though leaves may turn reddish and fall. Plants grow again with return of warmth and watering. Repotted plants need little feeding.

EUCALYPTUS GLOBULUS (*Tasmanian blue gum*)

Description: Bluish green leaves emitting the familiar fragrance of eucalyptus when bruised. Height 1.2-1.8m (4-6ft).

Position: Quick-growing and useful for decorating a large area of space that becomes cold and draughty – halls, stairways, porches, etc. – but with good light.

Watering: Generous in summer, sparing in winter.

Propagation: Easy from seed sown on warm window sill in spring.

Care: Seedlings are quick growing. Development can be retarded by restricting potting on if smaller plants are required. Old plants can be cut back, but it is best to start afresh from seed since young foliage is more attractive than mature.

EUCALYPTUS GUNNII
(*Cider gum*)

Description: Roundish leaves clinging to stems coloured bluish, silvery grey. Height 1.2-1.8m (4-6ft).

Position: Hardy. Excellent for cool or quite cold draughty positions with plenty of space and good light. Can reach considerable size before less attractive green leaves are formed.

Watering: Generous in summer, sparing in winter.

Propagation: Easy from seed sown on window sill in spring.

Care: Quick growing but can be potted on to stay in 13cm (5in) pots for a time. Can be cut back to encourage branching habit, but will ultimately need large pots or small tubs in which it will reach ceiling height. Feed sparingly. Grow from seed frequently, since the young foliage is the more attractive.

spreading habit, but most need little space. Will form larger plants if given large pots.

Watering: Keep moist at all times, winter included, so that roots never dry out.

Propagation: From cuttings or by root division.

Care: Generally easy – ought to be better known – and can usually be left to grow with little interference. Can be pruned back in spring. Feed sparingly, since the dwarf forms are not always rapid growers.

EUONYMUS JAPONICUS
(*Japanese spindle tree*)

Description: Several dwarf compact named forms with dainty variegated foliage make fine pot plants. Height 30cm (12in).

Position: Hardy; superb for chilly places that may also be shady. Some forms have

EUPHORBIA PULCHERRIMA
(*Poinsettia*)

Description: Popular Christmas gift plant with large showy coloured leaves. Height up to 60cm (24in).

Position: Warm room with no draughts and preferably where

A–Z

fragrant mauve flowers with yellow centres. Height 22.5cm (9in).

Position: Moderately warm room out of draught, slight shade. Should stay in flower for several weeks.

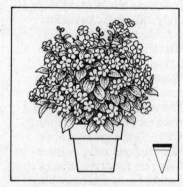

the air is not too dry. Mist with water in centrally-heated rooms. Shade from direct winter sunlight.

Watering: Keep moist, but never waterlogged.

Propagation: From cuttings, but not usually practical.

Care: Bought plants are specially treated with artificial light and dwarfing chemicals for the Christmas market. They are not usually worth trying to save. Moreover, plants are not at all decorative when not bearing the bright leaves – which can be most of the year. They will not recolour unless kept in the dark for 14 hours a day during the autumn.

EXACUM AFFINE
(*Arabian violet*)

Description: Compact little plant with a profusion of small,

Watering: Keep moist. Mist in central heating.

Propagation: Easy from seed sown on window sill in spring. Choose the variety 'Starlight Fragrance' which has a more pronounced scent or buy strains guaranteed to yield scented plants.

Care: Pot on to not larger than 13cm (5in) pots. Plants should be discarded after flowering. Plants bought from florists are not always scented as some varieties of seed have lost fragrance. No need to feed potted-on plants if a proper compost is used.

× FATSHEDERA LIZEI
(*Tree ivy*)

Description: Cross between a hedera and a fatsia. Five-lobed glossy cream variegated or plain green leaves. Can be trained as climber or bush. Height 1.2-2.4m (4-8ft).

Position: Hardy in frost. Ideal for cool shady positions. Can be grown to appreciable size.

Watering: Generous except in winter.

Propagation: Cuttings taken in summer.

Care: Generally a very easy plant. Can be grown as a short climber, but if cut back from time to time it will become more bushy. Exposure to sunlight is liable to cause wilting.

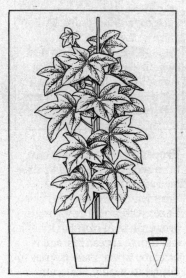

FATSIA JAPONICA
(syn. *Aralia sieboldii*)
(*False castor oil plant*)

Description: Large glossy palm-like leaves of tropical appearance. There is a cream variegated form. Height 2.4m (8ft) and over.

Position: Hardy and ideal for cold and draughty places – despite the 'tropical' look. Can be grown to considerable size if given large pots or tubs. Variegated form is a little more tender and slower growing.

Watering: Freely in summer, sparingly in winter.

Propagation: From seed sown on window sill in spring. Variegated form from cuttings.

A–Z

Care: Very easy, but often slow-growing at first. Appearance greatly enhanced by treating with a leaf-shine preparation. Can be kept in relatively small pots for some years. Feed only moderately.

FICUS BENGHALENSIS
(*Banyan tree*)

Description: Neat pot plant when young resembling popular 'rubber plant'. Height 90cm-1.2m (3-4ft) or more.
Position: In a cool place, little growth is made. In warmth growth is rapid and a plant may become inconveniently large. Otherwise culture similar to *F. elastica*.
Watering: Generous in the warm, sparing when cool, and in winter.
Propagation: Very easy, from seed sown on a warm window sill in spring.
Care: Generally easy. Pot on seedlings as required. They make attractive foliage plants in the young stages. To slow down rapid growth, keep the pot size to the minimum and feed sparingly. In its natural habitat this species is notorious for the size reached and its spreading habit, sending down enormous aerial roots which root into the soil.

FICUS BENJAMINA
(*Weeping fig*)

Description: Graceful tree-like plant with drooping slender-pointed leaves borne on long stems. Can exceed 1.8m (6ft) in height.
Position: Similar to *F. elastica*, but does better where temperatures are slightly lower.
Watering: As for *F. elastica*.

Propagation: Can be grown from seed, when available, sown on a warm window sill in summer.
Care: Often a more vigorous grower than *F. elastica*. It has a less formal appearance and is favoured where there is space to display its beauty. Watering

needs the most care where temperatures tend to be low. There is only need to feed when plants are in their final pots.

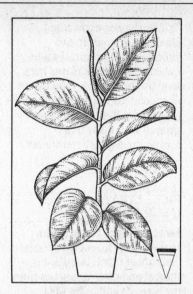

FICUS DELTOIDEA
(*Mistletoe fig*)

Description: Shrubby when in small pots, tree-like in large containers. Oval leaves on long stalks with berry-like fruits almost all year round. Height 30-60cm (12-24in).

Position: Cool, shady positions. Size depends on pot size. Large specimens are useful for cold porches, halls, conservatories and the like.

Watering: Generously in summer. In winter water according to temperature, keep on the dry side when cold.

Propagation: From cuttings in early summer. Root in warmth.

Care: Slow-growing but relatively easy to manage. Ultimate size depends on size of pots. Smaller, more bushy plants can be obtained by restricting pot size.

FICUS ELASTICA
(*India rubber plant*)

Description: Usually sold as *F.e.* 'Decora'. Large glossy oval leaves, young leaves and ribs red tinted, top leaf surrounded by reddish papery sheath. Height up to 1.2m (4ft).

Position: Warm, moderate humidity desirable, no draughts, out of direct sunlight but not too shaded.

Watering: Water freely and then let compost become almost dry before next watering. Extra care in winter to avoid excessive moisture. Mist with tepid water occasionally in summer.

Propagation: Can be grown from seed, but not easy in the home.

Care: Given conditions stated the plant is not difficult, but variegated forms, such as 'Black Prince', 'Doescheri' and

'Tricolor', need extra care. Shedding of lower leaves indicates chill or unsatisfactory watering. Cut-back plants may send up shoots from base if kept warm and humid, or new shoots produced if stems are frequently sprayed with foliar feeds containing a growth stimulant.

FICUS LYRATA
(Fiddle-back fig)

Description: Large violin-shaped shiny leaves with habit like rubber plant, but plant is shorter and rarely branches from the base. Height 1.2m (4ft).
Position: Same as for *F. elastica*.
Watering: Much the same as for *F. elastica* but need not be so careful.
Propagation: Cuttings taken from plants that have branched.
Care: This species is shorter than the rubber plant and rarely branches at the base. Should this occur the opportunity can be taken to use the shoots as cuttings for propagation, although this really requires a warm greenhouse for reliable results. The appearance of a plant is greatly affected by its environment. In unfavourable (cool, draughty) conditions the best leaf colours will not develop.

FICUS PUMILA
(Creeping fig)

Description: Grows as climber or trailer. Wiry stems, with dark green heart-shaped leaves with well defined veins. As a trailer can reach 1.2m (4ft) or more, but can also be trained up any suitable support.
Position: Hardy in mild areas outdoors. Ideal for cold parts of the home where light is poor.
Watering: Keep moist all year round, but avoid waterlogging. Plants in hanging containers may dry out quickly.
Propagation: Easy from cuttings.
Care: Very easy generally. If given large pot, it may become

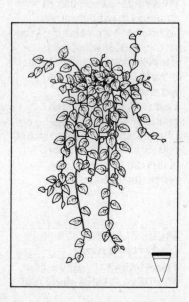

quite rampant and ramble or climb considerable distances. Make sure pots are well drained, since waterlogging is the most usual cause of deterioration. Feed sparingly unless you wish to encourage rapid and extensive development.

FICUS RADICANS
(*Trailing fig*)

Description: Usually sold as 'Variegata' with dainty, cream-edged spear-shaped leaves having slightly waved edges. Height 7.5-10cm (3-4in).
Position: Moderate warmth, humidity and shade. Suitable for small hanging pots, or pots on

shelves, or round the edge of hanging baskets. Trails only to about 10cm (4in). Not happy in draughty places.
Watering: Must be kept moist all the time including winter. Mist frequently in summer.
Propagation: Cuttings taken in early summer root easily if covered with polythene bag. Propagate frequently in case of losses.
Care: Can be a tricky plant in unsuitable surroundings. Too much light, such as direct sunlight, low humidity, and erratic watering, soon cause leaf shedding or deterioration, which may be difficult to save. Feed only moderately and during active growth.

FITTONIA VERSCHAFFELTII
(*Lace leaf*)

Description: Creeper, usually sold in the form *Argyroneura* with oval green leaves, delicately cream-veined.
Position: A favourite for bottle and case gardens, or in warmth coupled with humidity. Fails in chill and in dry air.
Watering: Needs care to ensure moist but never waterlogged conditions. Too much water soon causes rotting of roots and stems, particularly where conditions tend to be cool. Mist frequently in summer.
Propagation: Cuttings root easily if given warmth. Best rooted early summer.
Care and feeding: Can be a

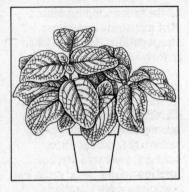

tricky plant. Grow from cuttings
when possible to provide
replacements in case of failure.
Best grown in shallow pots
(called half pots) or pans, as
used for alpines. Be careful not
to overfeed.

FUCHSIA
(*Lady's ear drops*)

Description: Well known,
with single to fully double
hanging flowers in many
colours. About 60-90cm (2-3ft)
in height.

Position: Should be seen as
temporary in the home; return
to a greenhouse or conservatory
after a few weeks of display. Give
cool, airy, bright conditions.
Space needed depends on how
plants have been grown.

Watering: Generous in
summer, sparing in winter.

Propagation: Easy from

cuttings in autumn or spring.

Care: Difficult as permanent
houseplants. In any case, they
are not decorative when out of
flower. With greenhouse
facilities, they can be trained in
various ways. It takes about 2
years to grow a standard, but
cuttings give useful plants for
baskets or pots very quickly. To

overwinter plants cut back and
keep in frost-free place with
enough watering just to prevent
drying out. Increase warmth and
resume watering when new
growth begins early in the year.

GARDENIA JASMINOIDES
(*Cape jasmine*)

Description: Famous for
white, waxy, strongly scented
flowers. Height 60cm-1.2m
(2-4ft).

Position: Warm, humid, good

light in winter, slight shade in summer. Not easy houseplants.

Watering: Moist at all times. Frequent misting in summer.

Propagation: Seed and cuttings, but not easy in the home.

Care: Some forms flower in summer; 'Veitchiana', more difficult, flowers in winter, needing more warmth. Remove any premature buds from winter flowers. Summer-flowering types need slightly less water in winter. Low and erratic temperatures cause bud drop. Feed carefully when buds are forming.

GERBERA
(*Barberton daisy*)

Description: Large daisy flowers in glorious subtle colours borne on stout stems. The new variety 'Happipot' is ideal for the window sill. Neat and compact and flowers in a few months after sowing. Height 30cm (12in).

Position: Cool, airy and bright, but not direct sunlight.

Watering: Free in summer, sparing in winter.

Propagation: Easily propagated from seed sown on warm window sill in spring.

Care: Pot on to 13cm (5in) pots, and feed when buds are

seen to be forming. No other attention is required. A first class, long-lasting houseplant.

GREVILLEA ROBUSTA
(*Australian silky oak*)

Description: Graceful ferny medium green foliage. Height 90cm-1.8m (3-6ft).

Position: Cool, airy, bright position or slight shade. Not suited to warm stuffy rooms. Can reach handsome proportions if well grown.

Watering: Generous in summer, sparing in winter. Use clean rainwater if tap water is limey.

Propagation: Very easy from seed sown on window sill in spring.

Care: Pot on as required using lime-free compost. When plants become too large they can be cut back, taking on a more bushy form of growth. Foliage is shed if conditions are extremely chilly.

GYNURA AURANTIACA
(*Velvet plant*)

Description: Erect to sprawling with toothed, spear-shaped velvety green leaves, with purplish hairs and reddish veins. Height up to 90cm (3ft).

Position: Warm, bright, airy, slight shade in summer. Leaf sheen shows up best in good light. Does not need much space. Can semi-climb and needs to be held upright with twiggy sticks.

Watering: Generously in summer but very sparingly in winter, especially when temperatures may fall.

Propagation: Very easy from cuttings taken in spring.

Care: Generally easy, but may deteriorate if exposed to excessive chill or low temperatures for long periods. Feed moderately when in active growth. This encourages orange flowers to form in winter.

GYNURA PROCUMBENS
(syn. *G. sarmentosa*)
(*Purple passion vine*)

Description: Similar to *G. aurantiaca*, but with slender trailing or climbing stems and narrower, jagged-toothed, more vividly coloured foliage. Height 1.2m (4ft) or more.

Position: The same as for *G. aurantiaca*, but the stems tend to twine and can reach as much as 2m (7ft) in good specimens.

Watering: As for *G. aurantiaca*.

Propagation: Very easy from cuttings.

Care: A fairly easy plant that can be kept in a 13cm (5in) pot for a long time.

HEDERA CANARIENSIS
(*Canary Island ivy*)

Description: Vigorous climber with boldly variegated cream and green leaves. Height 4.5-6m (15-20ft).

Position: Hardy in places outdoors on walls, but also suited to a warm environment where it will, however, tend to grow to considerable height and size. Useful for halls, foyers, and hallways, etc. Good light or slight shade.

Watering: Generous in summer, sparing in winter.

Propagation: Very easy from cuttings. Stems often send out aerial roots.

Care: A reasonably strong support is essential for large

used to climb and others to trail – some can do both. Climbing types should not be allowed to stray on to walls since the roots can cause marking.

Watering: Never allow to dry out completely.

Propagation: Cuttings root

specimens. Restricting pot size slows growth but, if space is limited, plants can be pruned back drastically without harm. Rapid temperature changes may cause leaf shedding. Feed moderately from late spring to summer.

HEDERA HELIX
(*Ivy*)

Description: Many versions of the common ivy make fine houseplants. Can grow over 6m (20ft) in height.

Position: Hardy outdoors. Ideal for cold, draughty and poorly lit places. Some can be

readily at almost any time.

Care: Easy generally. Overfeeding will encourage unwanted growth. The usual cause of deterioration is a hot dry atmosphere.

HELIOTROPIUM
(*Cherry pie*)

Description: Plant usually sold is 'Marine', a cross between

H. peruvianum (syn. *H. arborescens*) and *H. corymbosum*: large flattish heads of purple flowers with intense characteristic fragrance. Height 30-45cm (12-18in).

Position: Bright cool window sill where the lovely scent can be enjoyed. Does not take up space. Not suitable for hot stuffy rooms.

Watering: Keep moist, but not waterlogged or foliage may deteriorate.

Propagation: Very easy from seed sown on window sill in spring.

Care: Pot on seedlings to 13cm (5in) pots. A thin cane may be needed for support. Flowers from summer to autumn. Can be saved over winter in frost-free conditions, but not usually worthwhile where seed can be managed. Feed when buds begin to form.

HIBISCUS ROSA-SINENSIS
(*Chinese rose*)

Description: Bush shrub with glossy green leaves and handsome large flowers, summer to autumn. In tubs it can reach about 1.8m (6ft).

Position: Warm, moderately humid, out of direct sunlight and draughts.

Watering: Freely in summer

and sparingly in winter. Erratic watering causes leaves to fall especially in types with variegated foliage. Mist frequently, but keep water off buds and petals.

Propagation: Cuttings in summer need good warmth.

Care: The flowers are naturally

short-lived, but well grown plants always have plenty of buds to ensure daily colour. In low temperatures both leaves and buds fall, and if the plants survive they may look scruffy. Cut them back; they will make new growth with the return of warmth. Feed while buds are forming.

HOYA BELLA
(*Hanging wax plant*)

Description: Shrubby with pendulous stems. Glossy spear-shaped foliage, sometimes variegated. Clusters of starry, waxy white flowers with reddish/purplish eye, spring to autumn. Height 22.5-30cm (9-12in).

Position: Cool to warm, well shaded in summer. The plant is best displayed in a large hanging basket, in a pot on a pedestal, or raised in any way so that the flowers can be viewed from below.

Watering: Very well in summer but sparingly in winter.

Propagation: Cuttings taken in summer.

Care: Grows well in a peat compost. Can flower in 13cm (5in) pots, but is more impressive in a hanging basket. If winter temperature falls, plants are less likely to be set back if kept virtually dry. Feed when buds begin to form.

HOYA CARNOSA
(*Wax plant*)

Description: Climber with fleshy, glossy spear-shaped leaves, sometimes variegated. Clusters of starry waxy flowers similar to *H. bella*, but larger. Height up to 6m (20ft).

Position: Hardy in mild places outdoors. Survives considerable chill, and ideal for cold draughty places: stair wells, halls, etc. Also tolerates some shade. Given a large pot, it can go to ceiling height. It can also be trained up tall bamboos or similar.

Watering: Generously in summer, sparingly in winter, especially during low temperatures. Keep almost dry if very cold.

Propagation: Easy from cuttings.

Care: Very easy subject. A slight disadvantage is that it tends to send out long leafless unattractive stems before foliage and flowers form on them. This is normal; on mature plants they can be obscured by leading them among or behind existing growth. Feed only moderately.

HYDRANGEA

Description: Huge globular heads of usually blue to pink flowers: sold mid-winter to early summer. Height up to 1.2m (4ft).

Position: Gives a display for many weeks in a cool, airy, shaded place. Young plants do not need much space.

Watering: Keep moist at all times. If blue flowers are wanted, use clean rainwater if the tap water is limey.

Propagation: Easy from cuttings: not usually practical in the home.

Care: The plants are usually

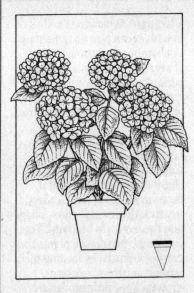

summer. Height 30cm (12in).
Position: Moderate warmth
out of draught. Shade in
summer, good light in winter.
Watering: Keep moist, but
overwatering soon causes
deterioration.
Propagation: Easy by division
when repotting, and from
cuttings taken after flowering.
Care: Pots should be well
drained; add extra grit to ensure
free drainage. Wet conditions
and/or chill yellows the foliage.
Pinch out the tips of young
plants to encourage neat bushy
growth. Feed moderately as
buds form.

nursery-forced for out-of-season
flowering. After flowering they
are best transferred either to
borders or large pots outdoors
and left to regain their normal
flowering which is summer to
autumn. They grow to form
large shrubs. Potted plants may
have been treated with a
'blueing compound' (from
garden shops). In all cases acid
soil or compost is needed for
best blue flower colour.

HYPOCYRTA GLABRA
(*Clog or pouch flower*)

Description: Dainty,
succulent glossy green foliage.
Orange-red pouched flowers in

HYPOESTES
PHYLLOSTACHYA
(*Polka dot plant*)

Description: Semi-trailer with
small spear-shaped leaves in
shades of green, spotted or
speckled in pink. Can reach
60cm (24in) in height.
Position: Moderate warmth
and slight shade in summer.
Erect and bushy when young,
but may sprawl with age. Does
not need much space.
Watering: Keep moist at all
times.
Propagation: Easy from seed
sown on window sill in spring.
Can be grown as an annual:
young plants are more attractive

with better colouring and habit.
Care: When bought, this plant
may have been treated with
dwarfing chemicals to keep it
compact. In time it can become
straggly. Frequent cutting back
to encourage new shoots helps

to prevent this, provided feeding
is not neglected. Colours are
variable. Good ones can be
preserved by propagation from
cuttings taken in spring.

IMPATIENS
(Busy lizzie)

Description: Popular compact
plants with fleshy stems
covered with bright flowers.
Height about 60cm (24in).
Position: Warm and airy, good
light or slight shade.
Watering: Keep moist:
overwatering causes leaf/bud
drop.

Propagation: Choose seed of
dwarf varieties. Finest plants are
grown from seed sown on
window sills in spring, for plants
that flower summer to winter.
Special types or colours must be
reproduced by cuttings taken
almost any time.
Care: Give final 13cm (5in)
pots and feed only after plants
have been in these for some
weeks. Overfeeding causes
leafiness but meagre flowering.
Plants grown as annuals can be
discarded when they deteriorate.
Young plants are usually most
attractive. Other exotic perennial
species need warmth and
humidity year round.

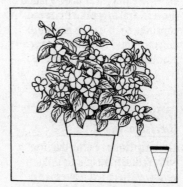

IPOMOEA TRICOLOR
(syn. *I. rubro caerulea*)
(Morning glory)

Description: Popular annual
climber with large flowers,

A–Z

usually glorious blue, that open during the morning. Can reach 2.4m (8ft) in height.

Position: Warm, moderately humid. A bright window is ideal. Will not flower well in shade.

Watering: Keep moist. Overwatering may cause yellowing and bud drop.

Propagation: From seed sown in spring.

Care: 'Heavenly Blue' is still a favourite, but there are other colours including red. Soak seed in warm water overnight before sowing. Pot on to about 18cm (7in) pots and provide canes for plants to twine up. Seedlings can be stopped to encourage branching and discourage excessive height. Pick off faded flowers and any attached seed capsules each day to promote constant bud formation. Discard plants at end of year.

IRESINE HERBSTII
(*Beefsteak plant*)

Description: Semi-trailing with reddish purple or golden yellow variegated leaves with paler veins and reddish stalks. Height 60cm (2ft).

Position: Airy. Good light for best colour development. Does not need much space. Useful for displays on shelves and in wall pots. Sometimes used for outdoor summer bedding.

Watering: Keep moist; moderate humidity is an advantage. Drier in winter.

Propagation: Cuttings taken in spring.

Care: Fairly easy. Grows well in most potting composts. Propagate frequently: old plants tend to become straggly. Remove any flowers to direct plants' resources to leaf production. Feed moderately spring and summer. Keep reasonably warm over winter. Can be cut back in early spring if growth has become untidy.

JASMINUM POLYANTHUM
(*Pink jasmine*)

Description: Vigorous climber often bought trained around wire hoop. Pink-budded, white, tubular, highly scented flowers

during winter and spring.
Height 1.5-3m (5-10ft).
Position: Cool and bright.
Shade in summer. Place where
the lovely scent can be enjoyed.
Watering: Moist the year
round.
Propagation: Easy from
cuttings in spring.
Care: Very quick grower.
Hoop-trained plants soon need
canes or more room to spread,
but plants can be pruned back
after flowering to keep a
convenient size. Plants can also
be trained up a tripod. Overfeeding and over-potting will
encourage leafy growth and
fewer flowers. Propagate from
time to time so that old plants
can be replaced.

LANTANA CAMARA
(*Shrubby verbena or yellow sage*)

Description: Neat shrubby
evergreen with verbena-like
flowers in various colours that
change as they age. Height
45cm-1.2m (18in-4ft).
Position: Bright, cool, airy.
The dwarf forms are not space-
demanding.
Watering: Generous in
summer, sparing in winter.
Propagation: Easy from seed
sown on window sill in spring,
but choose dwarf forms.

Cuttings root easily in summer.
Care: Give 13cm (5in) pots of
rich compost, such as John
Innes No. 3, or feed well.
Flowers spring to winter, same
year as sowing. Prune back
saved plants in late winter to
keep them neat and compact.
Do any repotting or potting on
at the same time.

MARANTA LEUCONEURA
(*Prayer plant*)

Description: There are three
types with neat habit and oval
leaves: 'Kerchoveana' (bold
brown-green spots domino
fashion); 'Massangeana'
(herringbone pattern with
black-green blotches);
'Erythophylla' (similar but very
beautiful rose-pink vein
pattern). Leaves fold up like
hands in prayer at night. Height
15-20cm (6-8in).

Position: Warm, humid, shade. Very compact.

Watering: Keep moist. Humid in summer, dryish in winter chill.

Propagation: Division when repotting in spring.

Care: Will survive quite low temperatures – not freezing – if kept almost dry. Leaves will brown and deteriorate, but new foliage soon appears with return of warmth and watering. Any scruffy vegetation can then be removed. Roots form tubers which help plants survive. Feed well when in active growth. Grow in 13cm (5in) pots.

MIMULUS HYBRIDS
(*Monkey flower*)

Description: Compact annual plants smothered with colourful musk flowers, often brilliant and exotically marked. Cultivars of *M. variegatus* are best, e.g. 'Queen's Prize', also used for bedding out of doors. Height 30cm (12in).

Position: Cool, airy, bright or slight shade. Good plants for bright window sill.

Watering: Stand in shallow pan of water, or keep very moist.

Propagation: Very easy from seed sown on window sill in spring.

Care: Pot on to 13cm (5in)

pots placing three seedlings to a pot. A few twigs may be needed to keep the plants neat, but some of the hybrids will cascade beautifully. Feed during summer to keep the flower buds forming, but not too generously. Discard after flowering.

MONSTERA DELICIOSA
(*Swiss cheese plant*)

Description: Huge glossy leaves 'lobed' or 'slashed' on young plants. Holes form in mature leaves – hence common name. Can grow up to 3m (10ft) or more.

Position: Warm, good light or

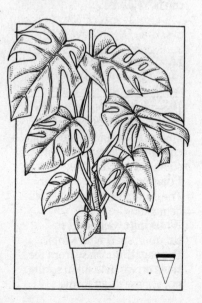

slight shade. Will survive cool winter conditions if then sparingly watered. Needs plenty of space where its impressive appearance can be appreciated.

Watering: Generously in warm conditions, sparingly in cool.

Propagation: From cuttings (stem tip or leaf bud) or fresh seed sown in June.

Care: The plant does well in pots that appear far too small. Feeding must not be neglected. Plants need careful support, ideally a moss stick. As they grow, long aerial roots may decend and enter the pots. Mature plants may form arum-like flowers followed by fruits like elongated pineapples – edible but unpleasantly fibrous. Too-large plants can be cut back in spring. Polish leaves with a leaf-shine product.

MUSA ENSETE
(Abyssinian banana)

Description: Enormous leaves typical of banana. Largest to be seen on a houseplant. Height 1.8m (6ft).

Position: Warm, good light. Hardy on Isles of Scilly. Used for sub-tropical outdoor bedding. Needs lots of space to display its impressive leaves.

Watering: Generously, except in cool conditions.

Propagation: From seed which *must* be fresh, sown in the maximum warmth of summer.

Care: Once germinated, plants grow with amazing speed if kept warm. Keep in minimum-sized pots the first year and over winter. In winter keep warm, but not above 18-21°C (65-70°F) and water only enough to prevent drying out. In chill the leaves brown and shrivel, but plants survive if watered sparingly. In the second year pot on to 25cm (10in) pots. The plants will then be at their best. Start again from seed.

NERIUM OLEANDER
(Oleander or rose bay)

Description: Shrub with evergreen spear-shaped glossy leaves. Masses of rose-pink, red or white single or double flowers summer to autumn. Height 1.8m (6ft) and over.

Position: Airy, bright or slight shade. Space needed according to age of plant and pot size. Neriums are almost hardy. Useful for quite chilly places.

Watering: Very generously in summer, very sparingly in winter.

Propagation: Easy from cuttings, also from seed.

Care: Remove shoots that form at base of flowers as soon as possible to prevent straggly development. Size can be controlled by cutting back after flowering. When cold keep roots almost dry. Feed moderately when buds are forming.

Special points: All parts are poisonous.

NERTERA GRANADENSIS
(syn. *N. depressa*)
(*Bead plant*)

Description: Mat-like growth covered with shiny brilliant orange-red berries like glass beads. A form with yellowish berries is *N. balfouriana*. A form with more vigorous growth and vivid red berries is probably a hybrid. Spreads 15cm (6in) or more.

Position: Cool and airy. Bright in winter, slight shade in summer. Not much space needed.

Watering: Keep the compost moist, but avoid spraying or allowing top growth to remain wet for too long otherwise there may be rotting or attack by moulds.

Propagation: By division or from seed.

Care: Best grown in well drained pans such as used for alpine plants. When flowers appear, stand the plants outdoors until the berries form and become attractive. The berries should last at least 3 months. Feed only very sparingly.

NICANDRA PHYSALODES
(*Shoo fly plant*)

Description: Compact and shrubby, with deep green irregularly-lobed crinkled leaves. Beautiful blue flowers followed by globular fruits inside a lantern-like seed-pod. Height up to 90cm (3ft).

Position: Hardy. Cool, airy, bright, not space-demanding. Reputed to repel flies.

Watering: Keep moist.

Propagation: Very easy from

seed sown on window sill in spring. Flowers the same year.
Care: Very easy. Pot seedlings on to 13cm (5in) pots. Do not feed too generously. The greenish to purplish seed-pod can be cut and dried for floral decoration – like the garden plant, 'Chinese Lantern'. Grow as an annual and discard plants at the end of the year.

NOLINA RECURVATA
(syn. *Beaucarnea recurvata*)
(*Pony tail or bottle plant or elephant-foot tree*)

Description: Stem with swelling at base bearing at the top a cluster of long thin leaves curving downwards. Height 90cm (3ft).
Position: Warm, bright – even some direct sunlight. Not suitable in chill or draught. Particularly good for centrally-heated homes where air tends to be dry. Grows palm-like in pots – naturally it is a small tree.
Watering: Always water thoroughly – but allow to go almost dry before watering again. Withstands some watering neglect, since it can store moisture.
Propagation: From seed sown on a warm window sill in spring.
Care: Pot on seedlings to 13cm (5in) pots the first year. From

then on pot on as the roots fill the pots. Grows well in most potting composts. Feed only when in final pots.

PACHYSTACHYS LUTEA
(*Lollipop plant*)

Description: Glossy spear-shaped crinkled leaves. Tall columns of yellowish leaves surrounding tubular white flowers, spring to autumn. Can grow to about 1m (3½ft).
Position: Cool to warm. Good light.
Watering: Keep moist and mist from time to time, but leave slightly drier in winter.
Propagation: From non-flowering tips of stems, rooted in warm place.
Care: To encourage branching and check height, take off tips of stems late winter/early spring. These can be used as cuttings. Avoid erratic temperatures and chill in winter, otherwise foliage may be shed. Feed during active growth.

PASSIFLORA CAERULEA
(*Passion flower*)

Description: Vigorous climber with strange blue and white flowers, the structure of which has been given religious significance. Often sold trained around a wire hoop. Height up to 6-9m (20-30ft).

Position: Hardy. Very bright airy position with plenty of room to climb – conservatory wall or some tall canes.

Watering: Generously in summer, sparingly in winter.

Propagation: Very easy from seed or from cuttings.

Care: Plants bought with a wire hoop will soon need more space. To prevent developing too fast keep the pots to the minimum size and do not feed too generously – this often gives more flowers and less leafiness too. Plants can be pruned back drastically after flowering. Large mature plants may produce golden-yellow egg-like fruits – too seedy to be edible.

PELARGONIUM PELTATUM (IVY)
(*Ivy-leaved geraniums*)

Description: Ivy-shaped leaves and 'geranium' single or double flowers in shades of pink, red, purple and white on longish stalks, usually grown in hanging containers. Height 90cm (3ft).

Position: Cool, bright and airy, where the plants can be viewed from below – but best not set too high.

Watering: Moist during growing period, just enough to prevent complete drying out during resting in winter.

Propagation: Easy from cuttings as for 'zonal' types.

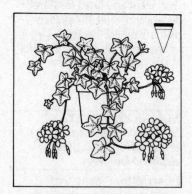

Care: The average basket will take about three plants. Stop shoots early on to encourage branching growth to cascade over the edge. At the end of the year cut back the plants and store in frost-free conditions. Plenty of new flowering stems will form when growth begins again in early spring. Feed while buds are forming. The new 'Harlequin' types are less vigorous.

PELARGONIUM × DOMESTICUM

Description: Best known as regal or show pelargoniums.

Neat bushy plants with great clusters of large-petalled blossoms in brilliant showy colours. There are many named cultivars. Height 37.5-60cm (15-24in).

Position: Cool, airy, bright. Good window sill plants in such conditions, but not stuffy rooms. However, flowering is less continuous than in the zonals or ivies and tends to be spasmodic.

Watering: As for 'ivy' types.

Propagation: As for 'zonals'.

Care: Basically much the same as for 'ivy' and 'zonal' types. However, the plants can become quite large, needing at least a 20cm (8in) pot by the second year after growing from a rooted cutting. To restrict growth where space is limited, more drastic pruning back may be necessary. Feed moderately while buds are being formed.

Old plants may become 'woody' and not flower so well. Propagate frequently to have a constant supply of young stock.

PELARGONIUM (SCENTED LEAVED)

Description: Bushy to shrubby plants with strongly fragrant leaves, especially when bruised, often used for making pot pourri. The plants of this group are usually given fancy names descriptive of the scents: rose, nutmeg, lemon, orange, pine, eucalyptus, apple, pimento and various other spices. Height up to 90cm (3ft).

Position: Cool, airy, bright and where scent can be appreciated. Porches, conservatories, bay windows, bright hallways, are good places for summer. Not suited to chilly positions in winter. Old plants need considerable space if they have been allowed to grow unchecked.

Watering: As other pelargoniums.

Propagation: As others.

Care: Much the same as for other pelargoniums. Old plants can become very straggly and woody and may need drastic cutting back unless large shrubby specimens are wanted for display.

A–Z

PELARGONIUM ×
HORTORUM
(*Geranium*)

Description: Well known for long-lasting flowers and often decorative variegated foliage. Height up to 1.8m (6ft).

Position: Cool, bright, airy. Often continue to flower in winter on a bright window sill – but unsuitable for warm humid rooms (these are really outdoor plants).

Watering: Moderate most of the year. Just enough to prevent complete drying out when resting in winter.

Propagation: Named cultivars from cuttings. F1 hybrids from seed, sown in March will flower the same year.

Care: Cut back plants severely at end of year to encourage new shoots and prevent lanky, tall, untidy growth so often seen. Over-winter in frost-free conditions with good ventilation and dry air. Avoid high temperatures. Feed during the production of buds.

PELLIONIA REPENS
(syn. *P. daveauana*)
(*Water melon begonia*)

Description: Trailer with spear-shaped wavy-edged leaves patterned with light and dark green suffused with bronze tint. Pink to purple below. Spreads about 30cm (12in).

Position: Warm, moderate humidity. Good for bottle and case gardens. Not suitable for cold, draughty places or erratic temperatures.

Watering: Plenty the year round, winter included.

Propagation: Cuttings from spring onwards, rooted in warmth.

Care: Very decorative when young. Old plants become leggy at the centre. They can be cut back but take a while to regain decorative appearance.

PEPEROMIA ARGYREIA
(syn. *P. sandersii*)
(*Water melon plant*)

Description: Neat clump of broad spear-shaped leaves patterned like some water melons with silver and green bands. Height 15-22.5cm (6-9in).

Position: Warmth and humidity essential. Not easy, but does well in bottle and case gardens. Unsuitable for cold places or erratic temperatures.

Watering: Moist most of the time, but be careful in winter if temperature tends to be low.

Propagation: By division.

Care: Overwatering and chill are the main causes of failure. Where the air is too stagnant, there is also risk of mould or mildew attack and rotting at base.

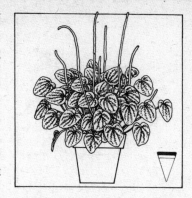

Watering: Keep moist but be careful not to waterlog. Moderate humidity is important during summer, but drier air is better for winter.

Propagation: By careful division.

Care: Very liable to attack by mould and rot in winter, especially where temperature is low and humidity high. Variegated forms are less vigorous and more sensitive to cool conditions. Feed moderately only when obvious active growth is being made.

PEPEROMIA CAPERATA
(*Emerald ripple*)

Description: Neat compact clump of small heart-shaped crinkled leaves, usually dark green but sometimes cream variegated. Pinkish stems. Height up to 25cm (10in).

Position: Warm, moderately humid. Useful for bottle and case gardens. Well grown plants produce erect catkin-like flower spikes.

PEPEROMIA GLABELLA
(*Wax privet*)

Description: The form 'Variegata' is usually sold. This is similar to *P. scandens* but with smaller foliage. Height up to 30cm (12in).

Position: Moderate warmth

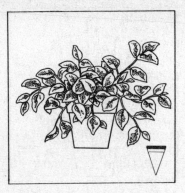

Leaves less crinkled and with attractive metallic sheen (nothing like ivy despite popular name). Height 1.2-1.8m (4-6ft).
Position: Similar to *P. caperata*, but less suited to case and bottle gardens.
Watering: Similar to *P. caperata*.
Propagation: Easy from leaf cuttings. Take leaves with short piece of stalk attached during spring and insert in the usual peat/grit mixture in warmth and humidity.
Care: Same as *P. caperata*. Is again liable to rotting at base if cold for long.

and humidity, out of draught. Slight shade. Usually grown as a trailer for walls and shelves.
Watering: Not easy since both under- and overwatering can cause leaf shedding. Aim to have the compost *moist* at all times.
Propagation: Easy from cuttings rooted in warmth.
Care: Generally rather difficult unless conditions can be kept very steady. To get as much branching as possible, snip off stem tips at an early stage. In well grown plants a rich red stem colour develops instead of usual pale pink. Feed cautiously in active growth.

PEPEROMIA GRISEOARGENTE
(*Ivy or silver leaf peperomia*)
Description: Similar to *P. caperata* in habit but larger.

PEPEROMIA MAGNOLIIFOLIA 'VARIEGATA'
(*Desert privet*)
Description: Neat bushy pot plant with oval fleshy leaves variegated emerald green and cream. Another cultivar, 'Green Gold', has richer colouring and pinkish leaf stems. Height up to 30cm (12in).
Position: Warm, moderate humidity. Slight shade. Not too fussy, does not need space.
Watering: Generous in summer, just moist in winter.
Propagation: Cuttings in spring.
Care: Less difficult than some peperomias, but even so liable to

base rot of stems if overwatered. To encourage spreading and more bushy growth, nip off tips of shoots in spring. These can be used as cuttings for propagation.

PEPEROMIA MARMORATA
(*Silver heart*)

Description: Resembles both *P. argyreia* and *P. caperata*: brownish green leaves with metallic sheen. Height up to 30cm (12in).
Position: Cool to warm. Moderate humidity and slight shade. Not too fussy. Clump-forming. Not space demanding.
Watering: Moderately in summer. Just moist in winter.
Propagation: By careful division.
Care: This is a good species to use as a test for conditions in your home. If it grows well, it is worth trying some of the more difficult peperomias. Useful for replacing *P. argyreia*, should it fail.

PEPEROMIA OBTUSIFOLIA
(*Baby rubber plant*)

Description: Looks like a miniature branching rubber plant. Leaves have reddish edge; there is a variegated form. Whitish flower spikes, summer to autumn. Grows only to about 20cm (8in), but may spread out.
Position: Cool, slightly shaded. Not so fussy as other peperomias.
Watering: Less watering than other peperomias. Water freely, then leave to become just slightly moist before watering again.
Propagation: By careful division.
Care: Easy compared with other peperomias, and much less liable to be affected by rots, moulds and mildews. However, in winter more care is needed if the temperature is low. Feed only moderately in summer.

PEPEROMIA SCANDENS
(*Cupid peperomia*)

Description: Trailer, but may be trained as a climber. Form usually grown is 'Variegata': spear-shaped leaves with green/cream variegation and with pinkish stems. Stems may trail to about 120cm (4ft), but can be trained upright on canes or similar if desired.
Position: Moderate warmth and humidity. Slight shade.
Watering: Must not be allowed to dry out completely, but must not be overwatered.
Propagation: From cuttings in spring.

A–Z

Care: This species is more temperamental in the young stages. Care is needed to keep temperature and conditions fairly steady, and protect from draught, otherwise leaves are quickly shed. Mature plants are easier to manage and will be happy in slightly lower temperatures. Feed sparingly in summer.

PERSEA
(*Avocado pear*)

Description: Tall shrubby habit with large dark green glossy foliage. Normally an evergreen tree. Can reach 1.8m (6ft) in height when well grown in large pots.
Position: Happy in little more than frost-free conditions. Airy. Good light. Resistant to considerable neglect.
Watering: Generous in summer. Sparingly in winter, especially in chill.
Propagation: Usually grown from stones after the pears have been eaten. These will germinate if immersed in a bowl of moist peat in a warm place – there is no need for the elaborate methods often suggested.
Care: Very easy. Can be stood outdoors in summer provided it is kept watered. Appearance is

enhanced by treating leaves with a leaf shine preparation. Keep potting on to a minimum to discourage rapid development and excessive size. Feed cautiously for the same reason.

PHILODENDRON BIPENNIFOLIUM
(syn. *P. panduriforme*)
(*Fiddle leaf*)

Description: Climber. Lobed leaves – more ivy-like than fiddle-shaped, with four upper lobes and a long central one. Dark green, leathery, and with slight gloss. Height 60-90cm (2-3ft).
Position: Needs similar conditions to *P. domesticum*.
Watering: Generous except in winter when the compost should be kept just moist.
Propagation: Cuttings in summer, rooted in warmth and humidity.
Care: Much the same as for *P. bipinnatifidum* and *P. domesticum*.

PHILODENDRON BIPINNATIFIDUM
(*Tree philodendron*)

Description: Erect, almost palm-like habit with very large lobed leaves. Height up to 1.2m (4ft).

Position: Moderate warmth and humidity. Good light – not direct sunshine. Needs moderate space owing to wide, spreading large leaves.

Watering: Never allow to go completely dry including winter. Water well and mist frequently in summer.

Propagation: Can only be propagated from seed. (Not practical in the home.) Cannot be divided.

Care: As for most philodendrons, a reasonably steady warmth and humidity is necessary for best results. Tends to be expensive – so see whether conditions suit it before purchase. Feed during active growth.

PHILODENDRON DOMESTICUM
(syn. *P. hastatum*)
(*Elephant's ear*)

Description: Climber with shiny spear-shaped leaves borne on long stalks – nothing like an elephant's ear. Height up to 1.8m (6ft).

Position: Moderate warmth and humidity. Good light. Not direct sunlight. Needs space.

Watering: As for *P. bipinnatifidum*.

Propagation: Cuttings of one to three leaf nodes (joints) in summer. Needs moderate warmth and humidity to root.

Care: To train climbing philodendrons cover a stout bamboo with sphagnum moss (moss stick), wiring it securely. Keep moss moist by spraying. Aerial roots penetrate giving support, also absorbing moisture. Liquid foliar feeds can be applied to the moss with advantage. Will ultimately need large pot, but do not be in a hurry to pot on.

PHILODENDRON ERUBESCENS
(*Arrowhead or blushing philodendron*)

Description: Vigorous climber with arrow-shaped leaves, pinkish young, maturing to bronze-green. Leaf stalks are purplish. The similar form 'Burgundy' (hybrid) has copper-red leaves. Height up to 1.8m (6ft).

Position: Similar to *P. domesticum*, but more tolerant of a drier atmosphere than most philodendrons. Can reach a man's height given good growing conditions.

Watering: Always keep moist. In summer misting will speed up growth. Beware of over-

A–Z

watering which will cause the roots to rot.

Propagation: As for *P. domesticum* but leave growing tips uncut.

Care: Despite its very attractive appearance, it is not very difficult to look after. However, it will not make much progress in a constantly dry atmosphere. Extra humidity helps it reach an appreciable size.

PHILODENDRON MELANOCHRYSUM
(syn. *P. andreanum*)
(*Velour philodendron*)

Description: Climber. Spear-shaped velvety leaves, pinkish below, dark green with golden iridescence above. Height up to 1.8m (6ft).

Position: As for *P. domesticum*. Can reach a man's height.

Watering: Keep moist at all times, but do not overwater in winter or roots may rot.

Propagation: Cuttings in summer need warmth and humidity.

Care: The same as for *P. domesticum*, but extra care should be taken. The leaves of this species are naturally hanging – do not mistake this for wilting and overwater.

PHILODENDRON SCANDENS
(*Heart leaf*)

Description: A popular species that can trail or climb: dark green, pointed, heart-shaped leaves. Height up to 1.8m (6ft).

Position: Will be happy in quite cool conditions – but will not then grow well. Survives in centrally-heated homes where air is dry. Not usually space-demanding unless well grown in warmth and humidity. Good light or shade.

Watering: Keep moist, regulating water according to temperature. Not as fussy as other philodendrons.

Propagation: Cuttings may root just placed in water.

Care: For best results, train up a moss stick support like *P. domesticum*. In warmth and humidity it becomes a vigorous grower, otherwise it is slow, but this may be desirable where space is limited. Variegated form is less easy, owing it is thought, to a virus. Leave sometimes naturally distort.

PHILODENDRON SELLOUM
(*Lace tree philodendron*)

Description: Similar to *P. bipinnatifidum* in the young state. Matures to form thicker stems and waved undulating leaf edges. Height up to 1.2m (4ft).

Position: As for *P. bipinnatifidum* but needs more space since leaves are larger. Often seen in public buildings – but not suited where heating is shut off for weekends or long periods, nor to draughty places.

Watering: Keep very well watered in summer with misting. Keep moist in winter where a moderate warmth is maintained – cautious watering in lower temperatures.

Propagation: As for *P. bipinnatifidum*.

Care: Exactly the same as for *P. bipinnatifidum*. (Some botanists believe that *P. selloum* is a form of *P. bipinnatifidum*.)

PILEA CADIEREI
(*Aluminium plant*)

Description: Neat, shrubby, with slightly puckered, spear-shaped leaves, variegated light and dark green with silvery metallic sheen. Height up to 30cm (12in).

Position: Cool, airy, slight shade or good light, but out of direct sunlight.

Watering: Keep moist always, winter included. Overwatering in cool conditions can cause base of stem to rot.

Propagation: From cuttings in spring.

Care: Old plants may become leggy. Propagate from cuttings every other year, so that such plants can be replaced. Also prone to magnesium deficiency – leaves become pale and distorted. Water with one teaspoonful of Epsom salts per 600ml (1pt) water from time to time or use a tomato feed.

PILEA INVOLUCRATA
(*Friendship plant*)

Description: Habit similar to
P. cadierei. Leaves broadly oval,
slightly hairy, bronze-green
above and purplish below.
Height up to 30cm (12in).
Position: Moderate warmth
and humidity. Good light – not
direct sunlight. Low-growing
and best displayed in a shallow,
wide pot so that it can spread
out.
Watering: Generously in
summer, misting occasionally;
sparingly in winter.
Propagation: From cuttings
taken in spring.
Care: Needs more warmth and
humidity than *P. cadierei*. Older
plants may shed foliage during
winter in cool conditions. Take
cuttings frequently to have
young replacement plants,
should any deteriorate.

PILEA MICROPHYLLA
(syn. *P. muscosa*)
(*Artillery plant*)

Description: Neat bushy plant
with 'ferny' foliage. Tiny
greenish flowers, spring to
autumn, emit clouds of smoke-
like pollen when disturbed.
Height up to 22.5cm (9in).
Position: Cool but not too
chilly in winter; airy, slight

shade. Does not need much
space.
Watering: Keep moist but
avoid overwatering which can
cause the foliage to turn yellow.
Excessive humidity, especially in
winter, can cause mould attack.
Propagation: Cuttings in
spring.
Care: Plants may deteriorate
after about three years, so take
cuttings every two years or so to
have young replacements.
Although tropical in origin,
seems happy in quite cool
temperatures if not exposed to
chill for too long.

PILEA MOLLIS
(*Moon valley plant*)

Description: Neat and
compact with golden-green
leaves like *P. cadierei* and with
deeply inset veins, coloured
contrasting chocolate brown,
making a lace-like pattern.
Height up to 30cm (12in).
Position: Easy in moderate
warmth and humidity, and good
light, especially in the winter. In
summer avoid direct sunlight.
Watering: Keep moist all year
round – but more sparingly in
winter.
Propagation: This species is
easy to grow from seed sown on
a warm window sill in spring.
Care: Pot on seedlings three to

each 13cm (5in) pot. They can then be left to grow without interference or further disturbance. There is no need to feed until plants have been established for some time. Plants that become crowded can be root-divided and repotted in spring.

PILEA NUMMULARIFOLIA

Description: Dainty creeper with almost circular small leaves with undulating surface and reddish stems.
Position: Moderate warmth. Does well even where light is quite poor. Best displayed in hanging pots, or wall pots, and cascading from shelves.
Watering: Reasonable care, since overwatering can soon lead to rotting at the base. The trouble is most likely when the temperature falls for long periods. In cooler conditions watering should be done sparingly.
Propagation: Easy from cuttings.
Care: Generally an easy plant but problems are frequently encountered in winter when a home, or a room where the plant has been growing well, becomes cold for long periods. A year-round moderate warmth is necessary.

PIPER ORNATUM

Description: Beautiful climber with spear-shaped leaves intricately patterned and coloured with green, cream, and pink marbling. Undersurface reddish, and young leaves entirely so. Height 90cm (3ft) or more.
Position: Needs steady moderate warmth and humidity to succeed. Best leaf colours develop in good light, but not direct sunlight. Not suitable for where there are drastic temperature changes or draughts. Does not usually need much space unless surroundings encourage quick growth.
Watering: Moist at all times. Frequent misting in summer.
Propagation: Cuttings in summer. Give warmth and humidity.
Care: This plant needs similar treatment to the climbing philodendrons and is best trained up a moss stick support (see *Philodendron domesticum*). Feed in same way.

PLECTRANTHUS COLEOIDES
(*Candle plant*)

Description: Form usually grown is 'Marginatus' with bushy habit, roundish to triangular leaves with irregular

edges. Green with white border, sometimes with grey to silvery sheen. White to purplish flowers similar to *P. oertendahlii*. Height up to 30cm (12in).
Position: Needs moderate warmth, humidity and slight shade. Usually easy – but more demanding of the conditions stated than *P. oertendahlii*, which it resembles, but less tolerant to chill and neglect. Not space-demanding.
Watering: Generous in summer, just enough to prevent complete drying out in winter.
Propagation: From cuttings, spring to summer.
Care: Can be grown in 13cm (5in) pot for a long time. Use a loam-based compost. When well grown it will tumble over the side, covering the pot. Overfeeding will encourage plenty of leaves but fewer flowers.

PLECTRANTHUS OERTENDAHLII
(*Brazilian coleus*)

Description: Rambler or trailer with roundish bronze-green leaves veined silvery white. Erect spikes of purplish/white flowers summer to autumn. Height up to 30cm (12in).
Position: A very easy plant:

cool to warm, and will survive temperature drops almost to freezing for short periods, as well as some watering neglect. Useful too where light is quite poor. Does not need space, and makes a good shelf or wall pot plant.
Watering: Generous in summer, sparing in winter – but not fussy.
Propagation: Easy from cuttings at almost any time – may root in water.
Care: Few plants could be easier to manage. Will survive even if allowed to remain dry for long periods, but wet conditions coupled with chill can be fatal. Feeding as for *P. coleoides*.

PLUMBAGO AURICULATA
(syn. *P. capensis*)
(*Cape leadwort*)

Description: Shrubby. Masses of blue or white phlox-like flowers spring to autumn. Height can exceed 3m (10ft).
Position: Cool but frost-free, airy in good light. Makes a superb wall shrub for a porch, foyer, or conservatory, but can also be grown as a shrubby pot plant.
Watering: Generous in summer, sparing in winter, especially when cold.
Propagation: From seed sown

in spring; should flower second year. Also from cuttings in summer.

Care: Plants ultimately need about 25cm (10in) pots, but young plants will flower in much smaller containers and then take on a bushy appearance. To restrict growth, plants grown as wall shrubs should be pruned back after flowering, reducing all shoots by at least a third. Do not feed too generously, which will encourage lots of growth but not flowers.

PRIMULA × KEWENSIS
(*Kew primula*)

Description: Whorls of fragrant yellow flowers, stems and buds coated with whitish floury surface. There are some extra fine named forms. 'Sungold' is notable for scent, and 'Yellow Perfection' for rich flower colour and size. Height 37.5cm (15in).

Position: Cool, airy, slight shade. Flowers from winter to late spring.

Watering: As for the other primulas described here, but clean rainwater is particularly recommended if tap water is limey.

Propagation: From seed as for *P. malacoides*. Needs greenhouse facilities to be successful.

Care: If young plants are bought needing potting on, use a lime-free compost. Final 13cm (5in) pots should be given for flowering. Plants can be saved but are not often long-lived.

PRIMULA MALACOIDES
(*Fairy primrose*)

Description: Numerous stems bearing whorls of dainty flowers, one above the other, arising from rosette of attractive foliage. Many delicate colours. Height 30-45cm (12-18in).

Position: Cool, airy, slight shade. Flowers usually in spring. Unsuited to warm stuffy rooms. Discard after flowering.

Watering: Keep moist. Overwatering may cause rotting at base.

Propagation: Must be grown from seed, but best not attempted without greenhouse facilities.

Care: To keep plants flowering as long as possible, snip off faded blooms promptly, encouraging more flower stems to arise from the leaf rosette. If plants are bought as seedlings, do not set too deeply in the compost when potting or the base may rot. Excessive humidity may encourage mould attack also at base of the leaf rosette. Feed as buds continue to form.

PRIMULA × POLYANTHA (syn. *P.* × *tommasinii*) (*Polyanthus*)

Description: Large heads of flowers borne well above the foliage on stout stems. Many lovely colours, often fragrant. Height up to 37.5cm (15in).
Position: Hardy. Same as for *P. vulgaris*.
Watering: Same as for *P. vulgaris*.
Propagation: F1 hybrid seed is available as for *P. vulgaris* and can be grown similarly.
Care: Again much the same as for *P. vulgaris*. A common pest that can cause serious trouble in summer is red spider mite. This causes yellowing of the foliage and sometimes greyish patches. Unless immediate action is taken

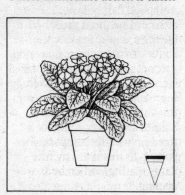

the plants are usually ruined. Spray with a systemic pesticide known to be effective against this pest – e.g. malathion – even if its presence is only suspected. It can usually be seen if the undersurface of the leaf is inspected with a powerful lens.

PRIMULA PRAENITENS (*Chinese primrose*)

Description: Large flowers on strong stems above the foliage. Some very bright colours. 'Dazzler' variety has vivid orange-scarlet flowers. Height 22.5cm (9in).
Position: Unsuitable for warm, stuffy rooms. Excellent window-sill plant.
Watering: As for other primulas, but again overwatering is liable to cause rotting at base.
Propagation: Easily grown from seed. Needs greenhouse facilities.
Care: Much the same as for other primulas described here. Seedlings are sometimes available and should be given 13cm (5in) pots. Discard after flowering.
Special points: It is not generally known that this species also may cause an allergic skin reaction, sometimes quite severe. Keep out of the reach of young children.

PRIMULA VULGARIS
(*Primrose*)

Description: Primroses are now available in many exciting, brilliant colours. Height 15cm (6in).

Position: Hardy and suitable for the chilliest places, and where slightly shaded. Unsuitable for warm stuffy rooms. Keep indoors only for the flowering period.

Watering: Never allow to dry out at any time – particularly in summer.

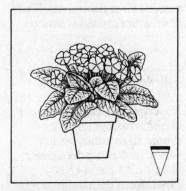

Propagation: Excellent plants are obtained from F1 hybrid seed, but the sowing and growing is best done in a frame outdoors. Plants can also be divided.

Care: After plants have flowered put them outdoors in a shaded place and keep watered and fed. The pots should preferably be plunged in moist peat or sand. Sow seed in May and pot on to 13cm (5in) pots. Flowering should be following spring. After flowering, plants can be planted out in the garden or in a window box.

PUNICA GRANATUM 'NANA'
(*Dwarf pomegranate*)

Description: Neat shrubby plants with tiny leaves. Large brilliant red flowers with crumpled petals, followed by walnut-sized inedible decorative fruits like miniature pomegranates. Height 90cm (3ft).

Position: Cool, airy, out of direct sunshine but good light and air circulation needed.

Watering: Keep moist at all times, water more sparingly in winter.

Propagation: Easy from seed sown on window sill in early spring. Flowers and may fruit the same year.

Care: Pot on seedlings to 13cm (5in) pots. Can be kept in these for some time. No special attention is needed since the plants are naturally neat, compact growers. In chill over winter the leaves may be shed. Keep drier then. In spring, growth will start again quickly and a little light pruning to maintain neat shape can be given if desired. Feed mature plants sparingly when buds are forming.

REINWARDTIA TRIGYNA
(*Yellow flax plant*)

Description: Shrubby habit with spear-shaped leaves, but prized for bright yellow primrose-like flowers produced all winter. Height up to 60cm (24in).

Position: Cool airy room in winter. Not chilly, or flowering will be poor. Good light. Can reach about 60cm (2ft), but can be given 13cm (5in) pots for some time.

Watering: Keep moist.

Propagation: Cuttings in spring.

Care: Old plants may not flower well – take cuttings frequently for replacements. To ensure good flowering stand the plants outdoors in a sunny position during summer. Plunge the pots in moist peat or sand and mist frequently when the sun is not shining. Do not allow to dry out. Prune back after flowering to maintain neat habit. Feed during summer.

RHOEO SPATHACEA
(*Boat lily*)

Description: Rosette of sword-shaped leaves, sometimes variegated, purplish below. White flowers surrounded by purplish bract about 5cm (2in) long – has inspired another common name 'Moses in the cradle'. Height up to 30cm (12in).

Position: Warm, moderate humidity, slight shade or good light – not direct sunshine.

Watering: Moderate in summer, sparing in winter.

Propagation: Base shoots taken from old plants when they are formed and when about 7.5cm (3in) long. Root in good warmth.

Care: Plants deteriorate with age, so take cuttings when possible for replacements. Feed when active growth is obvious.

RHOICISSUS CAPENSIS
(*Cape grape*)

Description: Very similar to *R. rhomboidea*, but leaves are simple, large, pentagonal in outline, and glossy deep green. Height 1.2-1.8m (4-6ft).

Position: Cool, similar to *R. rhomboidea*. Less tolerant of shade but should not be put in direct sunlight.

Watering: As for *R. rhomboidea*.

Propagation: Cuttings late spring, as for *R. rhomboidea*.

Care: Much the same as for *R. rhomboidea*, i.e. needs strong support, and should be fed sparingly. Pinch out growing tips for a better shaped plant.

RHOICISSUS RHOMBOIDEA
(*Grape ivy*)

Description: Climber with simple tendrils. Glossy dark green leaves made up from three diamond-shaped irregular-edged leaflets coated with fine brownish hair when young. Often confused with *Cissus rhombifolia* which has forked tendrils. Height 1.2-1.8m (4-6ft).

Propagation: Cuttings in spring. Also pieces of stem removed during pruning and cut with about two leaf nodes (stems) to each piece.

Care: Needs strong cane or similar for support. Remove to encourage branching and discourage fast upward growth. Check growth of large plants by cutting back in spring. Feed sparingly.

Position: Cool, airy. Particularly useful for where light is poor. Halls, stair wells, foyers but not where temperature can fall excessively.

Watering: Generous in summer with occasional misting, only slightly moist in winter.

ROSA CHINENSIS 'MINIMA' AND HYBRIDS
(*Fairy or miniature rose*)

Description: Neat shrubby plants with miniature rose flowers in proportion. 'Sunblaze' is a popular variety. Height 30cm (12in).

Position: Hardy. Bring into the home for a time during flowering only. Cool, airy, bright position. Unsuitable for warm

A–Z

stuffy rooms or in poor light for long periods.

Watering: Moist year round, never waterlogged.

Propagation: Named types from cuttings.

Care: Should be grown outdoors most of the time with pots plunged in moist peat in bright position. 10-13cm (4-5in) pots usually adequate. Culture similar to ordinary roses. These are popular plants to display on a coffee table or sideboard. There are many varieties to choose from with every colour one could want. Some have scarlet hips in Autumn.

RUELLIA MACRANTHA
(*Brazilian trumpet flower*)

Description: Shrubby habit. Spear-shaped rough-textured leaves. Large trumpet-shaped rose-purple flowers January to spring. Can reach 90cm (3ft) in height if containers large enough (20cm (8in)).

Position: Warmth and humidity. Shady. Does well under artificial lighting. Unsuitable in chill or draught, or dry central heating.

Watering: Keep moist all year round.

Propagation: From seed or cuttings in spring. Both need warmth. Division in autumn.

Care: Grow in a peat-based compost with some crushed charcoal added to keep it fresh – always keep well watered. Not an easy plant unless a moderate level of warmth and humidity can be maintained the year round. Feed during bud formation.

RUELLIA MAKOYANA
(syn. *Dipteracanthus makoyanus*)
(*Monkey plant*)

Description: Low-growing with a tendency to ramble. Spear-shaped leaves, purple below, olive green above, with contrasting creamy-green veins. Solitary deep rose-pink flowers.

Position: Moderate warmth, humidity and shade. Avoid draughts. Not space-demanding. Useful for shelf or wall pots if not sited too high above eye level when plants are grown enough to tumble over pot edge.

Watering: Moist the year

round, but only very slightly in winter.

Propagation: Cuttings rooted in moderate warmth in spring. Root division in spring.

Care: Best displayed in alpine

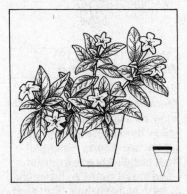

pots or pans so that it can spread and tumble over the edge. A peat-based compost is ideal, but some added grit for perfect drainage should be added and pots must be well drained. Feed during spring and summer.

SAINTPAULIA IONANTHA
(*African violet*)

Description: Neat small plants with velvety leaves, sometimes variegated. Single to double flowers almost all year round. Shades of blue, purple, or red, and white. Height 7.5-10cm (3-4in).

Position: Steady warmth and humidity. Good light – not direct sunlight. Unsuitable in chill, draught, erratic temperature, dry heating.

Watering: Freely in summer, sparingly in winter. Avoid wetting upper parts. Best watered by standing pots in a saucer of water until enough is absorbed, then removing. Overwatering causes rot at base. Keep water droplets off foliage (especially cold water). This may cause spotting and brown patches in direct light. Clean rainwater is best.

Propagation: From leaf cuttings, best taken in spring.

Care: Winter-bought plants must not have been chilled. Thin old plants by removing side crowns and suckers, which may interfere with flowering, with fine-tipped scissors. Feed moderately with special African violet feeds (obtainable from garden centres).

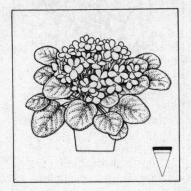

SALPIGLOSSIS SINUATA
(Painted tongue)

Description: Strong stems bearing many erect trumpet flowers exotically coloured and veined, summer to autumn. Height about 60cm (2ft).

Position: Cool, bright, airy in good light.

Watering: Keep moist, but avoid waterlogging.

Propagation: From seed sown on window sill in spring.

Care: Choose F1 hybrid 'Splash'. Pot three seedlings to each 13cm (5in) pot and pinch off tips when about 7.5cm (3in) tall to encourage bushiness. Give thin cane for support. Plants are easily grown as annuals, but can also be sown in autumn to flower following spring – best done with greenhouse facilities. Feed when buds begin to form. Pick off faded flowers and seeds to encourage continuity of blooming.

SANCHEZIA NOBILIS
(Humming bird flower)

Description: Resembles *Aphelandra* but with leaves more finely veined. Spikes of tubular yellow flowers make a spectacular display, emerging from purplish bracts in autumn – and are attractive to humming birds in native habitat. Can grow 90cm (3ft) in height with leaves up to 30cm (1ft) long.

Position: Moderate warmth coupled with humidity and bright place out of direct sunlight.

Watering: Generously in summer with frequent misting, sparingly in winter.

Propagation: From stem cuttings provided adequate warmth for rooting.

Care: Not an easy plant without constant warmth and humidity. Potting or potting on is best done in spring. Cutting back to maintain a neat shape can also be done then. Feed during obvious active growth period.

SANSEVIERIA TRIFASCIATA (*Mother-in-law's tongue or bowstring hemp*)

Description: Stiffly erect sword-shaped, sharply pointed leaves banded with light and dark green; 'Laurentii' is also bordered creamy-yellow. Can exceed 60cm (2ft) in height.

Position: Cool to warm. Good light to slight shade. Survives cool winter conditions if kept almost dry. Does well in central heating.

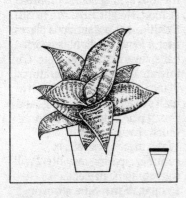

Watering: Generous when in active growth in summer. Very slightly moist in spring and autumn. Dry in winter. Most plants are lost through overwatering, causing root rot. Good drainage is essential.

Propagation: By root division. Given large pots it will send out runners producing leaves a short distance from the main clump. Runners can be severed with a sharp knife and potted for propagation. Leaf cuttings of 'Laurentii' do not reproduce the attractive cream leaf border.

Care: An easy plant provided it is not overwatered in winter. Feed during summer.

SAXIFRAGA COTYLEDON (syn. *S. pyramidalis*) (*Silver saxifrage*)

Description: Rosettes of narrow leaves coated with silvery encrustation along margins. Graceful sprays of numerous white flowers in summer. Height up to 60cm (24in).

Position: Hardy. Cool, bright, airy. The sprays of flowers rise well above the foliage.

Watering: Keep moist.

Propagation: From rosettes.

Care: Cut off flower stems from base after flowering. Stand pots outdoors, sheltered and shaded. Keep moist, and new leaf rosettes should form. During April/May young rosettes can be removed and treated like cuttings if desired – rooting may take months during which watering must be cautious to avoid rotting. This plant likes an alkaline compost, and some crushed limestone or chalk can be added to the potting compost with advantage.

SAXIFRAGA STOLONIFERA
(syn. *S. sarmentosa*)
(*Mother of thousands*)

Description: Trailer. Almost circular velvety leaves, green with whitish veining and purplish below. Plantlets form on the long red stems. Height 22.5-30cm (9-12in).

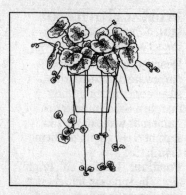

Position: Shady, airy, and cool – but not below freezing. Good for wall or shelf pots.
Watering: Generous in summer, sparing in winter.
Propagation: Detach well grown plantlets that form along the stems, complete with roots, and pot separately.
Care: Add extra grit to potting compost for perfect drainage. The form 'Tricolor' has foliage variegated with yellow and pink but is not so happy in cold conditions and is less vigorous. Although suited to shade, constant gloom causes weak growth. Conversely, excessive light bleaches the leaf colours and markings. Feed moderately in summer.

SCHEFFLERA ACTINOPHYLLA
(syn. *Brassaia actinophylla*)
(*Umbrella tree*)

Description: Tall-growing evergreen with glossy green oblong leaflets radiating from the tops of long stalks, umbrella fashion. Height 1.8-2.4m (6-8ft).
Position: Cool spacious places, useful for where light is poor: halls, foyers, stair wells, etc. Can tolerate quite low temperatures. Plants in large pots can reach a man's height, but seedlings and young plants do not need so much space.
Watering: Generous in summer, sparing in winter. Will tolerate some neglect.
Propagation: Seed sown on window sill in spring.
Care: Generally easy. Pot on seedlings as required. Young plants have only about three leaflets to each leaf stalk. Delaying potting on holds back development, but plants tend to become pot-bound quickly and so do not forget to feed.

SCHEFFLERA ARBORICOLA (syn. *Heptapleurum arboricola*) (*Green rays*)

Description: Similar to *S. actinophylla* but with smaller leaves, more bushy habit and lower-growing. Height up to 1.8m (6ft).

Position: Same as for *S. actinophylla* but needs far less space. Best displayed where there is reasonable light owing to the very dark green leaf colour. The extra gloss of the foliage will also be better appreciated in good light, but not direct sunlight.

Watering: Generous in summer, sparing in winter. Survives some neglect.

Propagation: From seed sown on window sill in spring.

Care: Much the same as for *S. actinophylla*. The number of leaflets on each stem increases much more quickly and quite young plants are rather more decorative.

SCHEFFLERA DIGITATA (*New Zealand umbrella tree*)

Description: Similar to the other schefflera species described here, but leaflets toothed and less pointed. Height variable according to potting on and pot size – can grow to size of a small tree.

Position: Almost hardy. Ideal for chilly and draughty places but prefers more light than the other scheffleras though not in direct sunlight.

Watering: As for other scheffleras.

Propagation: Seed sown on window sill in spring.

Care: As for the others. Potting greatly affects size. By restriction and delaying potting on, the plants can be kept relatively low for some time. Large pots or small tubs will produce large handsome specimens if there is space to display them and if they are given a free root run. Can be grown outside in mild areas.

A–Z

SCHIZANTHUS PINNATUS
(*Poor man's orchid or butterfly flower*)

Description: Bushy plants with ferny foliage, covered with orchid-like flowers in many colours with exotic markings. Dwarf cultivars are best – compact with sturdy stems and large flowers. Height about 30cm (12in).

Position: Cool, airy, slight shade. Unsuited to warm stuffy places. Flowers late spring to autumn. Discard after flowering.

Watering: Keep moist.

Propagation: From seed sown on a window sill late winter to spring. Can be sown in autumn for spring flowering, but then best with greenhouse facilities.

Care: Choose seed of compact types such as 'Hit Parade', 'Dwarf Bouquet' and the very compact 'Star Parade'. Pot three seedlings to each 13cm (5in) pot. These cultivars need no stopping or supports, and quickly come into flower. By staggering sowing, plants can be raised to flower over a very long period. Feed while buds are forming. They do not need stopping or pinching out as with taller varieties.

SCINDAPSUS AUREUS
see EPIPREMNUM AUREUM

SENECIO BICOLOR
(syn. *S. maritimus and Cineraria maritima*)
(*Dusty miller*)

Description: Popular foliage bedding plant with graceful silvery-grey 'ferny' foliage. Height 60cm (24in).

Position: Hardy. Useful for cold, draughty places, provided there is reasonable light. Space needed depends on cultivar.

Watering: Keep moist in summer, water sparingly in winter.

Propagation: From seed sown on window sill in spring.

Care: Pot on seedlings to final 13cm (5in) pots. Old plants become straggly and are best discarded. The yellow flowers are pretty but also untidy, and can be removed if desired when they form. Plants do not usually flower the first year from seed. Feed during summer.

SENECIO × HYBRIDUS
(syn. *S. cruentus*)
(*Cineraria*)

Description: Compact and bushy, and covered with a mass of large daisy-like flowers, often in rich dramatic colours sometimes obscuring the foliage. Height up to 45cm (18in).

Position: Cool, shaded, out of

direct sunlight. Unsuitable for warm, stuffy rooms. Not space-demanding. Discard after flowering which should continue for some weeks if plants are bought when buds are just beginning to show colour.

Watering: Keep moist. Waterlogging may cause wilting, owing to root rotting.

Propagation: From seed. Grown as biennial – but not

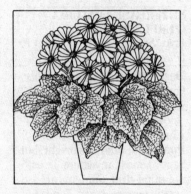

usually undertaken without access to greenhouse or frame facilities.

Care: In sunlight or too much warmth, cinerarias are very prone to wilting. Should this happen do not water unless plant is obviously in need. Place in cool shade and it should recover – may take overnight. Feed while buds continue to form. Remove faded flowers promptly to encourage more buds to develop.

SENECIO MACROGLOSSUS
(*Cape ivy*)

Description: Usually sold as 'Variegatus'. Vigorous climber. Ivy-like leaves with waxy sheen and green and gold variegation. Small clusters of yellow or yellow and white flowers in winter and spring. Similar to *S. mikaniodes* but can exceed a man's height.

Position: Moderate warmth and humidity. Unsuitable for draughty places and wide temperature change.

Watering: Keep moist year round, but water more carefully in winter. Mist frequently in summer.

Propagation: From cuttings in spring.

Care: Avoid letting the roots become too dry, since this may cause dramatic leaf shedding and the plants take a long time to grow new foliage. However, waterlogging must also be avoided. Best given reasonably large pots, but this does encourage considerable height. Grow up stout cane or similar. Feed sparingly.

SENECIO MIKANIODES
(syn. *S. scandens*)
(*German or parlour ivy*)

Description: Vigorous climber. Fleshy, ivy-like leaves,

but with more lobes sharply pointed, borne on very long stalks. Yellow scented flowers in large clusters in winter. Height up to 1.8m (6ft).
Position: Good light – not direct sunlight – to slight shade.
Watering: Similar to *S. macroglossus*.
Propagation: Cuttings in spring.
Care: Similar to *S. macroglossus*. Grow up stout cane or similar. Erratic conditions of all kinds are liable to cause sudden leaf shedding; low temperatures must also be avoided. May not flower unless the ideal conditions can be provided.

SENECIO ROWLEYANUS
(*String of beads*)

Description: Trailer with mat-like habit and long thread-like stems bearing spherical bead-like leaves. Brush-like scented white flowers in autumn. Height 5cm (2in).
Position: Cool, very bright, even a little direct sun. Useful for hanging pots, wall pots, and trailing from shelves.
Watering: Generously in summer and sparingly rest of year. Ensure good drainage.
Propagation: Stems usually send out roots spontaneously

and pieces can be cut off and potted. Also by root division when repotting.
Care: Easy generally – especially to propagate – but should not be subjected to cold. Add extra grit to the potting compost for perfect drainage if a modern all-peat compost is used. Feed sparingly.

SETCREASEA PALLIDA
'PURPLE HEART'
(syn. *S. purpurea*)
(*Purple heart*)

Description: Vigorous trailer. Lance-shaped foliage, green suffused with purple above, red below. Height 30-37.5cm (12-15in).
Position: Cool and bright, but happy almost anywhere. Does not mind chill, draught, or erratic temperatures. Tends to become leggy in too much shade. Useful for wall pots and shelves, but can be grown to be erect.
Watering: Generous in summer, sparing in winter. Survives considerable neglect.
Propagation: Easy from cuttings.
Care: Very easy; can survive almost any conditions. Old plants can become straggly and leggy, so propagate frequently from cuttings. Pinching out tips

will give bushy, more erect habit for a time. Place about three rooted cuttings to each 13cm (5in) pot. Feed moderately. Temperature should not fall below freezing.

SOLANUM PSEUDOCAPSICUM
(*Winter cherry*)

Description: Neat bushy plants with yellow to red cherry-like berries. Usually sold about Christmas time (but may not be widely available). Height 30-45cm (12-18in).
Position: Cool, airy, slight shade. Colour of berries changes from green through yellow-orange-red as they ripen, remaining decorative for weeks. Discard when berries shrivel.
Watering: Keep moist, but overwatering may cause leaf shedding.
Propagation: From seed sown on window sill in February.
Care: Pot on seedlings to 13cm (5in) pots. Stand outdoors when flowering for pollination by insects, or mist with water. Water occasionally with Epsom salt solution (see *Pilea cadierei*) as plants are liable to leaf yellowing.
Special points: Berries are poisonous and should be kept away from small children.

SOLEIROLIA SOLEIROLII
(syn. *Helxine soleirolii*)
(*Mind your own business*)

Description: Vigorous mat-forming creeper with tiny green leaves. There are also silvery-leaved and golden-leaved forms.
Position: Hardy in mild places outdoors. Cool, airy, good light or slight shade. Can be grown to form a 'carpet' on the compost of pots in which taller plants are growing. Grows well with other plants and can be used to create natural 'landscape' effects in conservatories, especially when used in conjunction with bark, cork, or natural stone. Will soon creep over a pot to cover the sides.
Watering: Keep moist, but overwatering quickly causes rotting and mould attack.
Propagation: Self-propagating since the stems send out roots as they creep. Pieces can be detached and potted.
Care: Generally easy. Where humidity is excessive and ventilation poor there is risk of mould attack. Feed sparingly.

SPARMANNIA AFRICANA
(*African hemp*)

Description: Tall shrub with large leaves, and white St. John's wort-like flowers, May-June. These have showy yellow and purple clusters which are touch-sensitive and spring outwards and back. Grows to about 90cm (3ft).

Position: Hardy in very mild areas outdoors. Bright, airy position. Unsuited to warm, stuffy rooms.

Watering: Generous in summer and sparing in winter.

Propagation: Easy from seed sown on a window sill in spring, or from cuttings in late spring or summer.

Care: Pot on seedlings to final 18cm (7in) pots. Cuttings flower within 12 months; seedlings may take longer. Old plants can be cut back and send up new shoots in spring. These make the best cuttings. Feed when flower buds begin to form.

SPATHIPHYLLUM × 'MAUNA LOA'
(*White anthurium*)

Description: Hybrid of obscure origin. Similar to *S. wallisii*, but taller, longer, with narrow foliage and larger flower spathes. Grows about 60cm (2ft) tall.

Position: Good warmth and humidity important. Slight shade. Not suitable for fluctuating temperature and draught.

Watering: As for *S. wallisii* but more frequent misting in summer.

Propagation: Division of roots in spring.

Care: Not easy unless warmth and humidity can be maintained, otherwise similar to *S. wallisii*. Misting with one of the modern foliar feeds containing vitamins and hormones tends to 'harden' the plant, making it easier to grow in less favourable conditions. Extra care is worthwhile owing to its impressive nature when well grown.

SPATHIPHYLLUM WALLISII
(*Peace lily*)

Description: Neat with shiny spear-shaped green leaves, slightly corrugated in herring-bone pattern, borne on long stems. White arum-like flowers from May to August. Grows about 30cm (12in) tall.

Position: Warmth and humidity, and slight shade. Unsuited to chill or draught. Will tolerate some fluctuation of temperature but not extremes.

Watering: Keep moist and mist frequently in summer.

Propagation: Division in spring.

Care: Use peat-based compost with some sphagnum moss and crushed charcoal added to prevent souring. Potting or repotting is best done in spring. Feed sparingly. Responds well to foliar feeds. An easier plant than 'Mauna Loa'.

STENOCARPUS SINUATUS
(Queensland firewheel tree)

Description: Evergreen shrub of variable height. Glossy lobed green leaves, reddish when young. Height 90cm-1.2m (3-4ft).

Position: Hardy outdoors in very mild areas. Cool, airy, good light, but does not like direct sunlight. Enormous tree in native habitat, but in pots needs little space in early stages. Makes an impressive plant if allowed to grow on in large pots or tubs. Useful for halls, porches, foyers and the like.

Watering: Generous in summer, sparing in winter.

Propagation: Easy from seed sown on a sunny window sill in spring.

Care: Generally easy. Pot on to 13cm (5in) pots in which plants can be kept for some time. Delay potting on if growth needs to be slowed down, but feed if the plants become rather pot-bound. Although this tree is famous for its glorious red flowers, these are unlikely to be seen on pot plants.

STEPHANOTIS FLORIBUNDA
(Wax flower or Madagascar jasmine)

Description: Climber, often sold trained around a hoop. Spear-shaped evergreen foliage. Clusters of waxy white tubular flowers, May to October, intensely fragrant. Height 3m (10ft) or more.

Position: Warm and moderately humid in summer. Survives cool winter conditions if kept dryish. Site where the scent can be enjoyed.

Watering: Generous in summer, sparing in winter.

Propagation: From seed sown on window sill in spring (flowers third year), or from cuttings rooted in warmth and humidity.

Care: Survives at little more than freezing if kept dryish. Foliage is shed, but recovery is quick with return of warmth and watering. Grow up stout canes. Plants trained around a hoop soon need to be given canes. If growth needs checking, prune back after flowering. Feed moderately while buds are forming.

STRELITZIA REGINAE
(Bird of paradise flower)

Description: Large oval leaves on long strong stalks borne in fan-shaped clumps. Large showy

A–Z

orange and blue flowers like head of exotic bird. Reaches about 1m (3½ft) but can spread.
Position: Cool, airy, bright or slight shade. Survives slight frost in winter if kept dryish. In year-round warmth will flower around Christmas and in summer. Impressive for halls, foyers, porches, picture windows, etc.

Watering: Generous in summer, very sparing in winter.
Propagation: Clump division when potting. Seed takes some years to yield flowering plants.
Care: Easy. Flowering plants need at least 25cm (10in) pots. Plants grown from seed are sometimes reluctant to flower – incorporate a little superphosphate (from garden shops) in top compost and water in. Plants eventually become pot-bound and need more feeding attention then.

STREPTOCARPUS
(*Cape primrose*)

Description: Clumps of long puckered leaves. Clusters of showy trumpet-shaped flowers in various colours, borne on strong stems well above the foliage for much of the year. Height up to 45cm (18in).
Position: Warm, moderate humidity, slight shade. Neat plant.
Watering: Generous in summer, very sparing in winter.
Propagation: By division when repotting or from seed sown on window sill early spring. Numerous named hybrids are available from specialists. From seed, choose F1 hybrid 'Concord' which is exceptionally easy to grow and manage under window sill conditions – unlike most other seed strains.
Care: Flowers same year as sowing. Plants can be saved over winter in little more than frost-free conditions if kept on the dry side. Feed during bud

formation. Remove faded flowers promptly. Repot or pot on in spring.

STROMANTHE AMABILIS
(*Brazilian arrowroot*)

Description: Oval leaves banded herringbone fashion in dark green and silvery green. Grey-green below. Similar to maranta. Grows up to 30-45cm (12-18in).

Position: Same as maranta – but more fussy regarding temperature and humidity. Moderate shade – avoid exposure to sunlight at any time.

Watering: Must never be allowed to dry out even in winter since, unlike maranta, foliage may be reluctant to grow again once it deteriorates severely.

Propagation: Same as maranta.

Care: Grows well in modern peat composts and can be kept in 13cm (5in) pots for some time. More sensitive to changes of temperature, watering, sunlight, etc. than maranta, and may develop browning of the leaf edges.

SYNGONIUM PODOPHYLLUM
(syn. *Nephthytis afzelii*)

Description: Climber. Young plants have arrow-shaped leaves but mature plants larger leaves with several lobes. Colours change from deep green to paler shade, but there are named variants with variegated foliage. Height 60-90cm (2-3ft).

Position: Moderate warmth and humidity. Very similar to philodendron which is closely related. The form 'Green Gold' can be grown as a trailer if desired, but is sensitive to

draught and changes of temperature.

Watering: Same as for philodendron.

Propagation: Cuttings rooted in warmth in spring.

Care: Fairly easy and much the same as philodendron with the exception of the variegated form 'Green Gold'. This has a reputation for being unreliable – it can suddenly wilt and shrivel for no obvious reason.

TETRANEMA ROSEUM
(syn. *T. mexicanum*)

Description: Dainty little plant somewhat resembling a miniature streptocarpus, but with purplish tubular flowers. Height 10cm (4in).

Position: Cool to warm, moderate humidity, and slight shade. Good window sill plant where there is little space. Flowers at intervals the year round, including winter in moderate warmth.

Watering: Always keep moist, but never waterlogged.

Propagation: Easy from seed sown on window sill in early spring. Flowers same year.

Care: Best as young plants and usually grown as annuals. Pot on seedlings to 10cm (4in) pots in which they will flower. Discard old plants when they stop flowering. Feed while buds continue to form. Pick off faded flowers promptly.

THUNBERGIA ALATA
(*Black-eyed Susan*)

Description: Climber or trailer with large orange, cream or white flowers, many with striking dark chocolate-purple 'eye'. Height up to 3m (10ft).

Position: Cool, airy, bright or slight shade. Can be grown up supports, such as fan of canes, or used to trail in baskets or wall and shelf pots – prefers to climb. Flowers from summer to autumn. Discard after flowering.

Watering: Keep moist, but overwatering causes leaf yellowing and shedding.

Propagation: Easy from seed sown on window sill early spring.

Care: Pot on seedlings according to how they are to be grown. A single plant will flower well in a 13cm (5in) pot. For baskets use several seedlings. They need no interference. A recommended seed strain is 'Susie'. Seedlings flower quickly and some people throw out those without the dark 'eye'. Feed while buds are forming.

THUNBERGIA GRANDIFLORA

Description: Vigorous perennial climber with large purple-blue flowers, summer to autumn. Height 6m (20ft) or more.

Position: Warm and moderate humidity, slight shade. Not suitable in chill or draught, or dry central heating. Can grow to an enormous height in suitable conditions.

Watering: Generous in summer and sparing at other times, but never let compost dry out.

Propagation: Cuttings taken in spring, rooted in good warmth and humidity.

Feeding: With the right conditions of warmth and humidity this can become a rampant climber. It can be kept in check by restricting potting on and by drastic pruning back after flowering. However, the latter does tend to result in fewer flowers being formed. Feed sparingly.

THUNBERGIA GREGORII
(*African sun vine*)

Description: Vigorous perennial climber with large dazzling orange flowers. Much like *T. alata* but flowers lack dark 'eye'. Height 3m (10ft) or more.

Position: Similar to *T. grandiflora*, but does not need so much space. If grown as an annual, as for *T. alata*.

Watering: As for *T. grandiflora* and *T. alata*.

Propagation: From cuttings, but also from seed sown on a window sill in early spring – will flower same year.

Care: Pot on seedlings to 18cm (7in) pots and provide cane for support. Mature plants need same treatment as for *T. grandiflora*. Many people prefer to grow it as an annual. This is a better proposition when it is not possible to maintain the warmth and humidity necessary for mature plants in winter.

THUNBERGIA LAURIFOLIA
(*Laurel-leaved thunbergia*)

Description: Glossy green laurel-like foliage. Large lavender-blue flowers with white or yellowish throats on mature plants. Height 1.2-1.8m (4-6ft).

Position: Much as for *T. grandiflora* but more particular regarding temperature. Grows well in large windows, if given bamboo canes for support. Not direct sunshine.

Watering: As for *T. grandiflora*.

Propagation: Cuttings rooted in warmth and humidity.

A–Z

Care: Young plants as usually sold may take at least 3 years to flower. In the meantime the foliage is quite attractive. This is fairly new as a houseplant so it will be some time before the best treatment for home conditions can be assessed.

TIBOUCHINA URVILLEANA (syn. *T. semidecandra*) (*Glory bush*)

Description: Tall shrub with a profusion of glorious purple-blue saucer-shaped flowers, summer to autumn or all year in warmth. Height up to 4.5m (15ft).

Position: An ideal conservatory plant. Cool, airy, slight shade. Needs moderate space. Can be grown as a wall shrub, but also compactly trained in such places as 'picture' windows.

Watering: Generous in summer, but just sufficient in winter to prevent roots drying out.

Propagation: Cuttings taken in spring and rooted in warmth.

Care: Pinch off tips of young plants bought in spring to encourage bushiness. Pot on to 18cm (7in) pots. Use rich compost such as John Innes No. 3. Give canes for support. Feed while buds form. Leaves may fall

in cool conditions or in winter, in which case be cautious with watering. Prune back plants during February to maintain compact size and neat shape.

TOLMIEA MENZIESII (*Piggy-back plant*)

Description: Clump-forming, with maple-shaped leaves covered with bristly hair. Tiny plantlets grow at the junction of leaf blade and stalk. Height up to 15cm (6in).

Position: Hardy. Useful for the chilliest places and moderate shade. Can be grown in shelf and wall pots, or have the pots raised by standing on inverted pots, or similar, so that the leaves can hang over. Do not need much space. Good hanging plant.

Watering: Keep moist at all

times, slightly less so in winter.
Propagation: Detach the plantlets that form on the leaves and pot individually.
Care: Very easy, especially to propagate. If given large pans or alpine pots the plant will soon spread over the surface, often propagating itself when the plantlets meet the compost surface. Well grown plants produce long stems of greenish-purple flowers in summer. Feed from spring onwards.

TORENIA FOURNIERI
(*Wishbone flower*)

Description: Neat bushy plant with profusion of oddly patterned flowers summer to autumn. Flowers are pale blue, with deep blue velvety lower lobes, and yellow throats. Height 30cm (12in).
Position: Cool, airy, slight shade. Good window sill plant for where space is limited. Not direct sunshine. Discard after flowering.
Watering: Keep moist, but overwatering causes leaf yellowing and bud drop.
Propagation: From seed sown on window sill in early spring.
Care: Pot on seedlings, several to each 13cm (5in) pot. No interference is usually necessary, but if they tend to

straggle give a few twiggy sticks for support. Quick-flowering annual. Feed while buds are forming.

TRADESCANTIA BLOSSFELDIANA

Description: Trailer or semi-erect. Stems and undersurface of foliage purple. Upper surface green with purple tinting and covered with fine hair. There is also a cream variegated form. Flowers more showy than those of most other species: rose purple with a white 'eye' about 12mm (½in) across from March to July.
Position: Fine basket plant. Warm and moderate humidity. Good light. Not direct sunshine.
Watering: Keep moist at all times, slightly less so in winter. Mist frequently in summer.
Propagation: Very easy from cuttings, which root readily when stood in water.
Care: Rooted cuttings can be inserted around the edge of a hanging basket to give quick cascading effect. Check baskets carefully as growth proceeds to prevent drying out, which can cause quick deterioration from which recovery is usually slow. If a more upright growth is desired remove the growing tips regularly during spring.

A–Z

TRADESCANTIA FLUMINENSIS
(*Wandering Jew*)

Description: Popular trailer with spear-shaped leaves, and a number of named forms having attractive colouring and markings. Some excellent names to look out for are 'Variegata' (white or cream striped), 'Quicksilver' (silver stripes), and 'Tricolor' (pink/green/white stripes).

Position: Cool. Good light brings out the best colour contrast and brightness. Ideal for shelf and wall pots, or hanging containers. Can also be grown more bushy.

Watering: Should be watered sparingly – but not allowed to dry out – which also produces better leaf colour and contrast.

Propagation: Well known for ease; cuttings root if merely placed in water.

Care: The plants are too often put in dim places and overwatered, which results in poor colour and leggy development. By grouping cuttings in a pot and taking off the tips neat bushy growth can be developed for a time. Feed sparingly.

TRADESCANTIA ZEBRINA
see ZEBRINA

YUCCA ELEPHANTIPES
(*Spineless yucca*)

Description: Stiff, sharply pointed narrow leaves, borne on short trunk-like stem on mature plants. Height 1.8m (6ft) or more.

Position: Cool, airy, bright. Happy in dry air. Useful for halls, foyers and the like where there is plenty of space – can reach ceiling height and branch out to form a large clump.

Watering: Generously in summer, very sparingly in winter.

Propagation: Suckers removed from base of plant when formed, and rooted in spring.

Care: Plants develop the trunk-like stem as they develop, but growth is naturally slow. Ensure

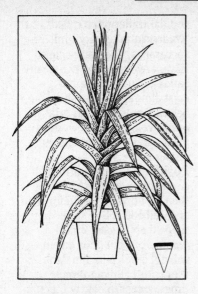

Along the leaf edges there are also long curly threads at intervals. Height 60-75cm (2-2½ft).

Position: Hardy. Suited to the coldest places in the home provided light is good. This species is compact and does not rise in height like *Y. elephantipes*. It may also produce tall creamy-white flowers.

Watering: Generous in summer, sparing in winter.

Propagation: As for *Y. elephantipes*. Plain-leaved form from seed.

Care: Much the same as for *Y. elephantipes*, but may flower. The common belief that yuccas flower only every seven years is not true: this may flower when only two years old.

compost is well drained when potting; peat types should have some sharp grit added. Tall central growth can be cut out of mature plants if they are growing too big for their position. Small plants can stand outdoors for summer provided they are kept watered. Slow growth means that feeding should be well moderated.

YUCCA FILAMENTOSA
(*Adam's needle*)

Description: The form grown as a houseplant is 'Variegata', which has the usual sharply pointed yucca leaves boldly margined with creamy-yellow.

ZANTEDESCHIA AETHIOPICA
(*Arum lily*)

Description: Well known arrow-shaped foliage and characteristic white lily flowers. Height 45-90cm (18in-3ft).

Position: Hardy outdoors, especially in ponds, provided roots do not freeze. Cool, airy, slight shade or good light. Not space-demanding.

Watering: Aquatic. Can stand in water.

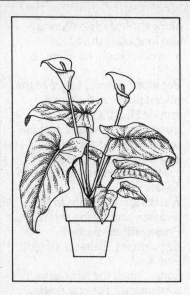

Propagation: Division of tuber-like roots when repotting.
Care: Buy named types if possible; 'Crowborough' can be specially recommended as a houseplant. Use pot just large enough to take the roots. Add some crushed charcoal to the potting compost to prevent souring. Stand the pots in shallow water. Plenty of water is important when the foliage is growing vigorously. After flowering (usually May/June) the pots can be moved outdoors.

ZEBRINA PENDULA

Description: Common

popular trailer often called 'Tradescantia' as very similar in appearance. The spear-shaped leaves are marked by two silvery bands and have a shining crystalline sheen, purplish below. One variety has bright purple colouring below the foliage and purple and green stripes above.
Position: Cool to warm. Will survive very cool conditions if then kept dryish. Useful for shelf and wall pots. More suited to shade than *Tradescantia fluminensis*, but good colours will not develop in dim light.
Watering: Freely at most times, except in cold winters.
Propagation: Extremely easy from cuttings – root in water.
Care: Generally easy. Neglected plants that have lacked water and lost top growth often grow again when care is resumed. Culture much the same as for tradescantia.

Contributor
Jock Davidson

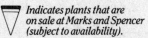 *Indicates plants that are on sale at Marks and Spencer (subject to availability).*

A-Z OF SPECIALIST PLANTS

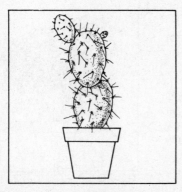

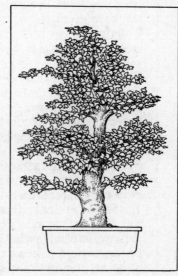

PALMS AND FERNS

ADIANTUM CAPILLUS-VENERIS
(*Maidenhair fern*)

Description: Very graceful fern, hardy outdoors in some mild climates, that also makes an excellent pot plant. Height 15-25cm (6-10in).
Position: Shaded, cool and airy, but not too dry atmosphere. Winter minimum 7°C/45°F. Will not stay evergreen if cold. Does not require much space.
Watering: Keep moist. Good drainage is essential to prevent waterlogging.
Propagation: Root division in spring. Cut out pieces having a growing point and pot.
Care: Preferably pot into a fibrous peat compost. Add extra grit for drainage. Keep containers as small as possible, but take care not to starve them by failing to repot them in time. This fern in a suitable climate will often root naturally into moss or leaf debris among rocks. Do not overfeed. A dressing of bonemeal in spring is usually adequate.

ADIANTUM RADDIANUM
(syn. *A. Cuneatum*)
(*Maidenhair fern*)

Description: Evergreen fern. Fronds composed of a multitude of little leaves, curving gracefully as they mature. The form 'Fragrantissima' is scented. Height 30-45cm (12-18in).
Position: Airy, shaded, cool but free from frost. Makes a splendid hanging basket fern. Unsuited to dry air.

Watering: Always keep moist but make sure it does not become waterlogged. Fine mist in summer. Do not let plants in baskets dry out.
Propagation: Division of the mature clumps in March.
Care: Grows well in John Innes No. 2 compost with fibrous peat added. Ensure good drainage. Feed sparingly and with caution. Small amount of bonemeal added to the compost surface

each March is beneficial. Bright sunlight must be avoided. Should plants deteriorate, cut them back in spring. New fronds usually replace the old.

ARECA LUTESCENS
(*Butterfly palm*)

Description: Clump-forming palm with bamboo-like stems and glossy yellowish-green leaves. Can reach ceiling height in ideal conditions, but is slow-growing.
Position: Warm and moderately humid. Good light.
Watering: Generous in summer. Keep slightly moist in winter.

Propagation: Can be grown from seed. Needs good warmth for germination. Best sown in summer on warm window sill.
Care: If grown in relatively small pots can be kept compact for many years, but care must be taken that small pots do not dry out. As for most palms, keep root disturbance to a minimum. Grows well in John Innes No. 2 compost. Feed moderately in summer.

ASPLENIUM NIDUS
(*Bird's nest fern*)

Description: Large, handsome fern with glossy leaf-like fronds forming rosette-like clump. Can reach 90cm (3ft) or more.
Position: Warm, moderate humidity, and good shade. Unsuited to cold or draughty areas.

Watering: Keep moist, but do not overwater in winter. Compost must be well drained.

Propagation: From spores, sown March to August.

Care: A fibrous peaty compost should be used for potting, with extra grit added for efficient drainage. Choose 18cm (7in) final pots. Handle with care, as fronds are brittle and easily snapped off. Best time to purchase is spring. Avoid overfeeding.

BLECHNUM GIBBUM
(*Cycad fern*)

Description: Fern with long fronds borne in clump formation on a short trunk. Can reach about 90cm (3ft) in height. Slow growth.

Position: Warm, and moderate humidity. Moderate shade. Happy in cool but not cold conditions if watered carefully.

Watering: Generous at all times in warm surroundings. In winter and in cooler conditions, keep the roots just moist. Use clean rainwater if tap water is limey.

Propagation: Spores, sown in July.

Care: At one time considered a 'stove' plant, it can be kept in cool conditions if sparingly watered. Young plants should be given moderate warmth to hasten development. Use fibrous peat compost with extra grit added for good drainage. Short trunk-like stem develops with growth. Feed sparingly.

CHAMAEDOREA ELEGANS BELLA
(syn. *Neanthe bella*)
(*Parlour palm*)

Description: This is the neat, more compact form of the palm sold as a houseplant. The small clump of stems bears fronds with wide leaflets. Mature plants may produce sprays of yellow flowers. Can reach 1m (3½ft).

Position: Warm, moderate

humidity, slight shade and good light, but not direct sunlight. Space needed depends on age of the palm, which is slow-growing.

Watering: Keep moist all year round.

Propagation: Dwarf form comes true from seed. Sow in summer.

Care: Two or three seedlings can be put in each pot for enhanced decorative effect. Does well in pots larger than usually given to palms. Use peat compost with grit and a little charcoal added. Can be fed more generously than most palms. Old plants lose attractiveness. Start afresh from seed from time to time.

CHAMAEROPS HUMILIS
(*Dwarf fan palm*)

Description: Palm, eventually forming clump of stout stems topped with fan-shaped fronds. Base of plant covered with mat-like fibre. Can reach man's height, depending on pot size.

Position: Hardy outdoors in mild climate. Cool, bright and airy conditions indoors with some direct sunshine. Can be stood outdoors in summer.

Watering: Generous except in winter, when compost should be kept just moist.

Propagation: Seed sown in warmth in early summer, or by rooting suckers at the base of the plant in spring in warm conditions.

Care: Easy. Pot using John Innes No. 2 compost with grit added for good drainage. Plants will grow more quickly and larger if given large pots. Feed moderately during active growth.

CYRTOMIUM FALCATUM
(*Holly fern*)

Description: Fern of unusual appearance. Fronds glossy and holly-like. Can reach 60 to 90cm (2 to 3ft). The form 'Rochfordianum' is larger.

Position: Cool, airy, and with moderate shade. Likes north-facing windows.

Watering: Generous during active growth, sparingly at other times.

Propagation: By division in spring, or by sowing spores (see page 43).

Care: A fairly easy and robust plant, it often survives quite harsh conditions. Grows well in most non-acid potting composts. Add extra grit to give efficient drainage. Is suited to 15cm (6in) pots. Can also be grown in hanging baskets where it is shown to best advantage.

DAVALLIA CANARIENSIS
(*Hare's foot fern*)

Description: Evergreen fern with feathery fronds and creeping underground stems (likened to a hare's foot). Height 30-45cm (12-18in).

Position: Moderate shade. Keep well free of frost in winter. Suitable for a shaded window sill. Does not require much space.

Watering: Moderate in summer. Never allow to dry out completely, but water sparingly in winter.

Propagation: Very easy by root division in April. Also from spores.

Care: Use a fibrous peat compost. Best grown in pans so that the underground stems have room to creep over the surface. Can also be grown in hanging baskets. A well planted basket can become a 'ball' of fronds in time. Feed in moderation during summer.

DIDYMOCHLAENA TRUNCATULA
(*Cloak fern*)

Description: Fern having thickish green fronds suffused with brown. Acquires tree-like habit with maturity. Fronds can exceed 1.5m (5ft) in length in ideal conditions.

Position: Moderate warmth, humidity and shade throughout the year. Not suited to dry, centrally-heated rooms.

Watering: Never allow to become too dry, and be sure compost is well drained.

Propagation: Best from spores sown in spring.

Care: Not easy without adequate warmth and humidity. Pot in a fibrous peat compost with added grit and charcoal. If the compost becomes too dry the leaflets of the fronds will be shed, leaving bare stalks. Feed moderately in summer.

HOWEIA BELMOREANA (KENTIA)
(*Sentry palm*)

Description: Palm with tall stems bearing fronds with numerous long leaflets. Can exceed a man's height and spreads considerably.

Position: Cool to warm, moderate humidity. Shade in summer, but good light in winter. Needs plenty of space.

Watering: In spring and summer water generously, but sparingly at other times.

Propagation: Seed sown in warmth in spring.

Care: Will survive cool winter temperatures, not less than 7°C/45°F, if cautiously watered. Seedlings and small plants can be retained in small pots for a long time, but at least 20cm (8in) pots will eventually be required. Use John Innes No. 2 compost. Feed moderately during summer.

HOWEIA FORSTERIANA (KENTIA)
(*Kentia palm*)

Description: Similar to *H. belmoreana* and more popular, but with fronds of drooping habit. Less formal, more graceful appearance. Height up to 3m (10ft).

Position: As for *H.*

belmoreana – cool to warm. Moderate humidity. Shade in summer, good light in winter. Fine subject for spacious foyers, hallways and the like, provided there is adequate warmth. Needs plenty of space to grow well.

Watering: Generously from spring to autumn, sparingly in winter, but care should be taken not to overwater.

Propagation: From seed sown in warmth in spring or summer.

Care: Can be grown in much the same way as *H. belmoreana*, but take care that the temperature does not fall too low in winter. Any fronds that deteriorate should be cut out cleanly low down.

NEPHROLEPIS EXALTATA 'BOSTONIENSIS'
(*Boston fern*)

Description: Vigorous fern with very long, rich green arching fronds, borne as a dense clump. Reaches about 75cm (2½ft) and spreads vigorously.

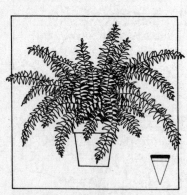

Position: Cool to moderately warm, moderate humidity. Slight shade or good light but not direct sunshine. Unsuited to draughts. Excellent for display on pedestals and in hanging baskets. Needs space to be seen to advantage.

Watering: Keep moist at all times.

Propagation: The fern spreads by producing runners. The young plants that grow from these can be separated and individually potted.

Care: Fairly easy. Pot using a peat-based compost with extra grit to ensure good drainage. Vigorous grower. When grown in baskets do not allow to dry out. Feed moderately in summer.

NEPHROLEPIS EXALTATA 'WHITMANII'
(*Lace fern*)

Description: Similar to *N. e.* 'Bostoniensis' in habit. The fronds have a distinctive feathery appearance.

Position: As for 'Bostoniensis', but more shade. Makes a beautiful basket plant.

Watering: Keep moist at all times.

Propagation: From plants that grow from runners, as for 'Bostoniensis'.

Care: Much the same as for 'Bostoniensis', although this fern is less vigorous and does better in larger baskets or pots.

In small containers the fronds tend to yellow. Feed moderately, but keep liquid fertilizers off the fronds as they may cause damage.

PELLAEA ROTUNDIFOLIA
(Button fern)

Description: Fern with low creeping habit. Fronds have roundish leathery leaves.
Position: Hardy outdoors. Can be grown indoors to creep over shallow pots or pans. Useful for cool to cold shady places. Does

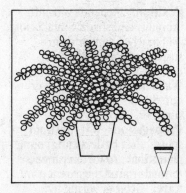

not need much space.
Watering: Keep moist throughout the year but slightly less so in winter and when temperatures drop markedly.
Propagation: Division of the creeping roots in spring or by sowing spores (see page 43).
Care: Easy. Grows well in most types of potting compost. Best given large but shallow containers, such as those used for alpines. Feed generously in summer. Exposure to bright light may cause yellowing.

PHOENIX CANARIENSIS
(Canary Islands date palm)

Description: Palm with large fronds composed of long, narrow, sharply pointed leaflets. Trunk forms as plant matures. Can grow to tree size.
Position: Most attractive as it matures, but can then demand enormous space. Plants kept in check give a tropical look to cool or chilly spacious places in the home, provided there is good light.
Watering: Generous in summer, sparing in winter. Do not allow to become waterlogged.
Propagation: Seed sown in the warmth of summer.
Care: Easy. Repot seedlings using any approved potting compost. For a year or so they will not look very decorative. Size can be restricted by delaying repotting, but the roots soon become pot-bound and feeding is required. Grows to handsome height in final 30cm (12in) pot or small tub. Can be stood outdoors for summer.

PHOENIX ROEBELENII
(*Pigmy date palm*)

Description: Small palm with arching fronds composed of feathery, glossy green leaflets. Can reach a man's height.

Position: Moderate warmth and humidity. Good light. Needs much less space than *P. canariensis* and is more graceful in the young state. Not suited to cold, draughty or dry conditions.

Watering: Generous in summer with misting, sparing in winter.

Propagation: Seed sown in summer, or by rooting suckers at the base of the plant.

Care: Can be difficult where temperatures fluctuate a lot.

Potting procedure same as for *P. canariensis* but use smaller pots. The palm does not usually form a trunk in pots, even when fairly old. From time to time cut out suckers that form at the base to deter clump formation, which is not attractive in these pot-grown plants.

PLATYCERIUM ALCICORNE
(*Staghorn fern*)

Description: Fern with strange fronds shaped like antlers. Height 45-75cm (1½-2½ft).

Position: Moderate warmth, humidity and shade. Suitable for wall or when supported in suspended containers. See below.

Watering: Never allow to dry out. Spray frequently in summer.

Propagation: Not easy from spores. Best by detaching young plants that grow from runners formed around the parent plant.

Care: Grow by wiring the plants to clumps of sphagnum moss and fixing them to pieces of bark that can be fastened to a wall or suitable support above ground. Slatted orchid baskets also make good containers. A little bonemeal mixed with the moss is advantageous. The plants also respond well to

modern foliar feeds, which
should be well diluted and used
only during active growth. Can
also be grown like bromeliads on
pieces of tree branch covered
with sphagnum moss.

PTERIS CRETICA 'ALBOLINEATA' (*Ribbon fern*)

Description: Fern with wiry
stems bearing long, ribbon-like
fronds with a central white band.
Height 30-45cm (12-18in).

Position: Cool, but not cold,
moderate humidity in summer,
moderate shade.

Watering: Generous except in
winter, when slight moistness
only is required.

Propagation: Root division
when repotting.

Care: Fairly easy, but the
minimum winter temperature
should not drop below 7°C/45°F.
Grows well in most potting
composts and can be kept in
13cm (5in) pots for a long time.
Feed moderately during
summer. Avoid direct sunlight
or bright conditions for too long
or the leaf variegation will
deteriorate.

BROMELIADS

AECHMEA CHANTINII
(*Amazonion zebra plant*)

Description: Bromeliad with
rosette of spined green leaves
banded silver-grey.
Multicoloured flowers held high
above leaves. Reaches about
90cm (3ft) in height.

Position: Moderately humid in
summer, slight shade. Tolerates
moderate fluctuations but
minimum temperature is 10°C/
50°F.

Watering: Keep moist. Ensure
that 'urn' (centre of leaf rosette)
is always filled with water.

Propagation: Remove offsets
(side shoots) attached to the
parent plant, allow to dry for a
few days and set firmly in the
same type of compost.

Care: Easy. Grows well in
almost any potting compost.
Seems to prefer a firmer rooting
medium than most bromeliads.
Use 13cm (5in) pots. Feed with a
foliar feed during summer.

AECHMEA FASCIATA
(*Urn plant*)

Description: Bromeliad with
funnel-shaped rosette of grey-
green spined leaves banded
silver-grey. Cone-shaped head
with small pink flowers growing
from a pink surround. The
flowers die comparatively soon
but the surrounding leaves
remain colourful and make a
good display by themselves.
Grows to about 60cm (2ft).

Position: Very tolerant and
happy in quite low temperatures
in winter. Not freezing. Slight
shade.

Watering: Keep moist and the
'urn' filled. Drier roots in winter
where temperatures falls.

Propagation: From offsets
which are produced freely, as for
A. chantinii.

Care: Probably the easiest of all
bromeliads. Needs very little
attention. Plants grown from
offsets should be supported if
necessary until well rooted.

AECHMEA FULGENS
(Coral berry)

Description: Bromeliad usually sold in the form 'Discolor': green loose rosette of broad leaves purplish below with whitish downy bloom. Stems carrying waxy purple flowers followed by long-lasting red berries. Height 37.5cm (15in).

Watering: More careful watering, to keep roots moist, than the other aechmeas described. The 'urn' is less watertight.

Propagation: From the plantlets arising from the offsets as for the other aechmeas.

Care: This is also a very easy bromeliad, but extra care is needed to see that the roots do not dry out. In centrally heated homes some misting the year round – winter included – may be beneficial. Feed with foliar feeds in summer. See *A. chantinii*.

ANANAS BRACTEATUS
'STRIATUS'
(Variegated pineapple)

Description: Bromeliad forming rosette of spined, cream-margined sword-shaped leaves. Stems bearing miniature pineapple fruits (inedible). Height 90cm (3ft).

Position: Moderate warmth and humidity. Good light. Remains reasonably neat and compact. Not suited to chilly rooms or where it is draughty.

Watering: Keep moist. There is no central 'urn' in this bromeliad, so watering needs greater care. During winter, allow to become almost dry before re-watering.

Propagation: Easiest from offsets cut from the base of the plant when formed.

Care: Despite the exotic appearance, this pineapple is easy provided it is not subjected to severe chill for long periods. It grows well in the modern peat-based composts to which a little extra grit has been added. A compost of fairly fibrous texture is best. Feed during active growth. About an 18cm (7in) pot is adequate.

ANANAS COMOSUS
'VARIEGATUS'
(Variegated pineapple)

Description: Variegated form of the commercial pineapple. Similar to *A. bracteatus 'Striatus'*, but much larger. It turns rose-pink when flowering. Height 90cm (3ft).

Position: Moderate warmth and humidity. Good light. Needs moderate space to develop its full height.

Watering: Water generously, but allow to go almost dry between waterings. Water sparingly in winter.

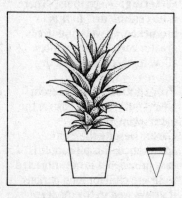

Propagation: Best done by severing offshoots from the base of the plant when formed and potting in warmth in early spring.

Care: The size that the plant can reach, and its demand for congenial warmth and humidity, makes it suitable only where such conditions can be maintained, but with care it can be kept to a 20cm (8in) pot for a useful period. Use a fibrous peat compost. Feed well during summer.

BILLBERGIA NUTANS
(*Angel's tears*)

Description: Bromeliad forming clumps of long grassy leaves. Stems topped with drooping flower clusters combining green, pink and blue. Height 45cm (18in).

Position: Survives temperatures down to almost freezing for short periods. Good light, but shaded in summer with moderate humidity.

Watering: Sparingly in winter, generously in summer.

Propagation: Suckers form freely around the base. Remove and pot, supporting the suckers until well rooted.

Care: One of the easiest bromeliads, surviving considerable neglect regarding both temperature and watering. Survives going dry for short periods. Grows well in most ordinary potting composts, but the peat-based ones are best. Can be kept in 13cm (5in) pots for a long time. Feed with foliar feeds, or the normal types, in summer.

BILLBERGIA PYRAMIDALIS

Description: Bromeliad forming rosette of pale green leaves with a strange reddish flower cluster arising from the centre like a mass of flames. Height about 45cm (18in) at the most.

Position: Similar to *B. nutans*.

Watering: Keep central 'urn'

filled with water. Otherwise similar to *B. nutans*.

Propagation: Cut away suckers or side shoots that form around base of parent. Leave to dry for a few days, and pot in same type of compost.

Care: Much the same as for *B. nutans*, but prefers a compost of peaty open texture. More careful watering is needed during winter if the temperature tends to fall considerably. It is then usually best merely to keep the urn filled, allowing the compost itself to remain on the dry side.

BILLBERGIA × 'WINDII'

Description: Bromeliad: hybrid of *B. nutans* but with much larger pendant pink leaves, and more attractive grey-green foliage. Can reach 45cm (18in) in height, and can be allowed to form a large clump if desired.

Position: Much the same as for *B. nutans*.

Watering: As for *B. nutans*. Keep the base of the leaves well wetted during the growing period, but not in winter.

Propagation: As for *B. nutans*. Can be propagated at frequent intervals if desired.

Care: As for *B. nutans*, but feeding can be more generous. The plant gives a better effect if allowed to develop into a large clump in a hanging basket, provided space is available. This species is also more attractive than *B. nutans* when out of flower, because of its more decorative foliage.

CRYPTANTHUS BEUCKERII (*Marbled spoon*)

Description: Bromeliad forming small rosette of foliage marbled in various shades of green, sometimes pink-tinted. Small head of white flowers.

Position: Moderate warmth, not below about 13°C/55°F, and good light. Does not need much space. Use in bottle gardens.

Watering: Freely during active growth, more sparingly at other times, just sufficient to prevent complete drying out in winter.

Propagation: Offsets cut from around the base when formed in spring.

Care: Grows well in most potting composts mixed with some sphagnum moss to give an open texture. Only small pots needed and very little feeding.

CRYPTANTHUS BROMELIOIDES 'TRICOLOR' (*Earth star*)

Description: Bromeliad:

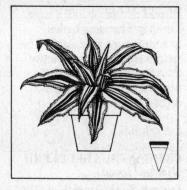

unusual in having leaves on slender stems. They are spreading in habit and striped along their length in cream, yellow, green, rose-pink and white. Can attain about 30cm (12in) in height.

Position: Moderate warmth, and humidity in summer. Drier generally in winter. Best colouring develops in good light – not direct sunshine.

Watering: Needs more careful watering in winter when the compost should be just prevented from drying out completely. Water freely during active growth.

Propagation: From offsets as for other cryptanthus.

Care: Similar to other cryptanthus and the same compost for *C. beuckerii*. This species, owing to its taller upright habit, can be grown well in company with other houseplants.

CRYPTANTHUS FOSTERIANUS (*Pheasant leaf*)

Description: Bromeliad forming a wide spreading rosette of wavy, fleshy, toothed leaves, dark bronze-green branded with silvery grey. Can reach over 45cm (18in) in diameter and needs space to spread, but has little height. (7.5cm (3in)).

Position: Moderate warmth and humidity, slight shade.

Watering: As for *C. beuckerii*.

Propagation: From the little plantlets (offsets) that form freely around the base. These should be potted when they have made a few leaves.

Care: This species is best grown in fairly large half-pots, as used for alpines, using potting compost mixed with sphagnum moss. Old plants lose their attractive colouring, so it is wise to have a young replacement. Feed with foliar feeds.

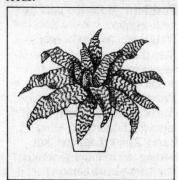

CRYPTANTHUS ZONATUS
(*Earth star*)

Description: Bromeliad very similar to *C. fosterianus* but with greenish-brown leaves (in the form 'Fuscus') which are more narrow and much less spreading. Height 10cm (4in).

Position: Much the same as for *C. fosterianus* but needs less space for spreading.

Watering: As for *C. beuckerii*.

Propagation: As for *C. fosterianus*.

Care: Needs smaller pots than *C. fosterianus*, but use the same potting compost/moss mix. Take extra care to ensure perfect drainage. There is often a better defined small 'urn' at the centre of the rosette in this species. Keep filled with water during the summer. Less important in winter when drier conditions should be maintained. Feed with foliar feeds in summer.

GUZMANIA LINGULATA

Description: Bromeliad forming a rosette of glossy narrow leaves. Showy long-lasting crimson leaves. Leaves up to about 45cm (18in) long. Height about 30cm (12in).

Position: Moderate warmth and humidity, but not stagnant air. Moderate shade.

Watering: Moist at all times, freely in summer with frequent misting. Keep 'urn' filled with water. Use clean rainwater.

Propagation: Allow the little plantlets (offsets) that form around the base to become well rooted before cutting away. Pot in similar compost, see below.

Care: This species will not succeed without adequate warmth and humidity. Pot in a compost made by mixing a peat potting compost with sphagnum moss and bark chips. Feed with foliar feeds in summer. This species does not like alkaline conditions, and is best watered with rainwater if the tap water is limey.

GUZMANIA ZAHNII

Description: Bromeliad with extremely thin yellow-green papery leaves, with thin red stripes, and forming a rosette. Produces stem carrying showy yellow leaves. Leaves reach

about 50cm (20in) in length.
Position: As for *G. lingulata*.
Watering: As for *G. lingulata*.
Clean rainwater is particularly
important if the tap water is
limey. Tap water is also likely to
cause spotting of the delicate
foliage.
Propagation: The same as for
G. lingulata. Handle plantlets
carefully.
Care: Much the same as for *G.*
lingulata. Leaves can easily
become marked. Foliar feeds are
best applied to the root ball. They
should also be diluted or made
up with rainwater if the tap
water is limey. Generally more
exacting than *G. lingulata*.

NEOREGELIA CAROLINAE 'TRICOLOR'
(*Striped blushing bromeliad*)

Description: Bromeliad
forming a rosette of shiny strap-
shaped green saw-edged leaves
striped with cream. Centre turns
rich pink at flowering time.
Height 30cm (12in).
Position: Cool to warm, not
excessive chill. Good light, even
a little dappled sunshine,
develops best colouring. Not
space-demanding.
Watering: Water freely in
summer. Keep just moist rest of
year, and only very slightly
moist in winter if the

temperature falls. Keep the 'urn'
filled, but empty in winter again
if temperature is low.
Propagation: Offshoots should
be taken from around base of
plants whenever possible, see
below. Give them support after
potting until they have rooted.
Care: Grow in a mixture of
John Innes No. 2 compost and
sphagnum moss, or similar
open-textured compost. After
flowering the mother plant dies
– be sure there are some young
plants for replacement.
Propagation should not be
neglected.

NEOREGELIA SPECTABILIS
(*Lady's fingernail*)

Description: Bromeliad
forming a rosette of red-tipped
narrow leathery leaves white-
banded below. Height 30cm
(12in).

Position: Much the same as for *N. carolinae*. The central red coloration remains decorative for a long time.
Watering: As for *N. carolinae*. Keep the urn filled with water.
Propagation: As for *N. carolinae*. Water young plants sparingly until well rooted, or roots may rot.
Care: Likes the same conditions and compost as *N. carolinae*. This plant also dies after flowering, so it is important to propagate often to have replacements.

TILLANDSIA CYANEA
(*Pink quill*)

Description: Bromeliad forming clumpy rosette of narrow green brown-lined leaves, brown at base. Strange spear-shaped clusters of magenta leaves at frequent intervals. Height 22.5cm (9in).
Position: Good warmth and humidity the year round. Moderate shade. A neat plant and not space-demanding.
Watering: Just moist in winter, and very freely the rest of the time. Mist frequently in summer.
Propagation: Detach offshoots that form and root in an ordinary cutting compost.
Care: Success with this species depends on adequate warmth and humidity. For potting use a mixture of John Innes No. 1 compost and sphagnum moss to achieve an open but moisture-retaining texture. Only small pots are needed. Feed with foliar feeds in summer. The winter minimum should not fall below about 13°C/55°F.

TILLANDSIA USNEOIDES
(*Spanish moss*)

Description: Curious pendulous bromeliad: mossy tufts that trail considerable distances. Yellowish-green flowers all summer.
Position: As for *T. cyanea* but best given a considerable height.
Watering: A high humidity at all times. Apply by mist to cover the entire plant frequently in summer.
Propagation: Cut off shoots, tie into clumps, fasten to pieces of a mossy tree branch.
Care: Needs no compost – lives entirely above the soil. Fasten pieces to sections of mossy tree branch and suspend from suitable support. Feed by foliar feed misted over entire plant. Not an easy houseplant unless you have somewhere where water can be sprayed freely. It can be kept small, but will not then look its best.

VRIESIA SPLENDENS
(*Flaming sword*)

Description: Bromeliad forming a rosette of arching strap-shaped leaves, banded across very deep purple. Tall sword-shaped spike of bright red leaves late summer. Grows to about 60cm (2ft) when flowering.

Care: Fairly easy. Pot in 13cm (5in) pots of a peat potting compost with some sphagnum moss added. Also grows well in a ball of moss and compost wired to piece of tree branch. Mature plants lose the leaf banding. Propagate when possible. Feed moderately with foliar feeds in summer.

Position: Moderate warmth, humidity and shade.

Watering: Keep 'urn' filled with water. Water roots sparingly in winter, but freely the rest of the year.

Propagation: Remove offsets that form around the base of the plant when of moderate size and pot into same type of compost.

ORCHIDS

ANGULOA CLOWESII
(*Tulip or cradle orchid*)

Description: Orchid with tulip-shaped yellow flowers on short stalks. It is indigenous to Colombia but despite this tropical origin can be very successfully grown in relatively low temperatures.

Position: Minimum temperature is 10°C/50°F. Slight to moderate shade, where flower scent can be enjoyed.

Watering: With plants growing at low temperature cautious watering is vital if rotting is to be avoided. Begin watering in Spring when new leaves appear and start to feed when leaves are formed. During the Summer months ample feeding and watering are essential. Keep dry when resting in winter.

Propagation: Division when repotting.

Care: Pot in special orchid compost. Plants die back in autumn and should then be left almost dry. Resume watering when leaves appear in spring. This is also the time when repotting or propagation should be carried out.

BRASSIA VERRUCOSA
(*Spider orchid*)

Description: Orchid with pale green, dark-spotted, scented flowers having long, slender petals.

Position: Happy with a minimum temperature of 10°C/50°F. Moderate shade, where scent can be enjoyed. Good window sill plant. Needs little space.

Watering: Never allow to become so dry that the pseudo-bulbs shrivel. Water cautiously in winter and freely during active growth.

Propagation: Division of pseudo-bulbs in spring when they become crowded in pot.

Care: Pot and repot in spring using an orchid compost. Feed plants well established in their pots during active growth. Plants will flower in 13cm (5in) pots. A good orchid for beginners.

CALANTHE VESTITA

Description: Orchid. Deciduous foliage, spikes bearing numerous small white to pink flowers, October to February, when foliage has died. Flower spike rises to 90cm (3ft).

Position: Not lower than 13°C/55°F. Moderate humidity, shady and airy in summer.

Watering: Keep almost dry when resting; water freely during active growth.

Propagation: Each year by division of the pseudo-bulbs.

Care: Put one pseudo-bulb to each 13cm (5in) pot or more in proportion. Use a mixture of John Innes No. 2 compost and sphagnum moss well chopped and mixed. Pot and propagate each year. When foliage yellows in late summer, stop watering until growth resumes in spring. In moderately warm conditions give little occasional water during flowering. Feed plentifully during active growth, but do not overfeed. Likes a rich compost.

CATTLEYA BOWRINGIANA

Description: Orchid. Two-leaved pseudo-bulb with stems bearing 5 to 10 large flowers combining rose-pink, purple and yellow. September to December. Height about 60cm (2ft).

Position: Needs minimum temperature of 10°C/50°F. Good light, but not direct sunlight, and moderate humidity.

Watering: Pseudo-bulbs must not be allowed to shrivel. Water sparingly after flowering until active growth resumes, then increase.

Propagation: Division of pseudo-bulbs when repotting.

Care: Use an orchid compost and clay pots, but slatted orchid baskets allowing plenty of air to reach the roots are better. About 13cm (5in) pots are suitable as average. Repot and take opportunity to propagate when roots form at the base of new shoots, usually a few weeks after flowering.

CYMBIDIUM

Description: Large group of orchids ideal for beginners. Grass-like foliage. Stems with numerous large butterfly flowers of many colours and markings. Height is variable. Very compact miniatures exist.

Position: Minimum is 7°C/45°F in winter. Slight shade when flowering, bright or even full sun at times, see below.

Watering: Water well, allowing compost to become almost dry before re-watering. Water cautiously in winter.

Propagation: Division of the pseudo-bulbs.

Care: Pot firmly with orchid compost. Pot to one side: the pseudo-bulbs with growing roots should face the greatest area of compost to allow room for development. Divide and pot March to May. Expose to full sun

for a time in summer to autumn to help induce flower spike production. Support flower spikes with canes. Many named hybrids.

DENDROBIUM INFUNDIBULUM

Description: Orchid. Tall, hairy stems bearing large, orange-lipped, white roundish flowers. Flower stems rise to about 45cm (18in).
Position: Minimum temperature 10°C/50°F. Moderate humidity. Shade from spring to summer, good light at other times.
Watering: Sparing in winter

but sufficient to prevent pseudo-bulbs shrivelling. Generous rest of year. Ample humidity in summer.
Propagation: Division of root-producing pseudo-bulbs after flowering.
Care: Pot using orchid compost. For the home 13cm (5in) pots are suitable. Moderate humidity is required. In winter the plants must be rested in drier conditions.

DENDROBIUM SUPERBUM

Description: Orchid with tall stems of rose-pink or red-purple spotted, large fragrant flowers. Can rise to 1.2m (4ft).

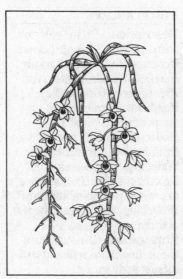

Position: As for *D. infundibulum*, where the lovely scent can be enjoyed.
Watering: As for *D. infundibulum*.
Propagation: Division of pseudo-bulbs as for *D. infundibulum*.
Care: Much the same as for *D. infundibulum*. Old withered flower stems should be removed cleanly. The flowering stems may need support. The species is semi-deciduous and foliage deterioration can be expected, but this should not happen during growth. If it does, pest attack, possibly red spider mite, may be the reason.

LAELIA ANCEPS

Description: Orchid with long stems bearing 2-5 large flowers, December to January. Various coloured hybrids. Flower stem rises to about 60cm (2ft).
Position: Minimum temperature 10°C/50°F. Moderate humidity and good light, but not direct sunlight.
Watering: Little from about December to March, but enough to prevent pseudo-bulbs from shrivelling. Water freely the rest of the year.
Propagation: Division when the pseudo-bulbs send out roots, usually early spring.

Care: Keep pots as small as possible and use an orchid compost. Set pseudo-bulbs one-sided as for *Cymbidium*. Ventilate freely when temperatures permit.

LYCASTE AROMATICA

Description: Orchid with deciduous leaves and short stems of fragrant red-lipped golden-yellow flowers, about early spring.
Position: Moderate warmth, humidity and shade. Minimum temperature is 10°C/50°F but higher level is advisable.
Watering: When the leaves are growing water freely, but very little when they have faded and the plant is resting. Must always be sufficient to prevent pseudo-bulbs from shrivelling.
Propagation: Division of the pseudo-bulbs in spring.
Care: Grow in 13cm (5in) clay pots using orchid compost. Can also be grown on moss in slatted orchid baskets or wired to pieces of mossy tree branch.

MILTONIA SPECTABILIS

Description: Orchid with stems bearing a solitary very large flower, usually purplish, during summer.

Position: Cool and airy, but moderate humidity and shade in summer. Good light rest of year. Minimum temperature 13°C/55°F. Needs little space. Good for window sills.

Watering: Keep moist all the year round.

Propagation: Divide pseudo-bulbs in spring or autumn.

Care: Best grown in slatted orchid baskets or well crocked clay pots. Used orchid compost. Usually needs repotting and propagating every 3 or 4 years. Give maximum light in winter. Ventilate when possible.

ODONTOGLOSSUM BICTONIENSE

Description: Orchid with oval, flattish pseudo-bulbs. Long stems bear numerous butterfly flowers coloured pink, brown and yellow. Flower spike rises to 75cm (2½ft).

Position: Minimum temperature 10°C/50°F. Moderate humidity, but cool and airy. Shade in summer, full light in winter.

Watering: Keep moist all year round, slightly less so in winter.

Propagation: Division in spring or autumn.

Care: Grow in clay pots well crocked, or preferably in slatted orchid baskets. Use orchid compost. This species is more vigorous than most odontoglossums. May need potting and propagation at the same time, fairly frequently. Ventilate when possible.

ODONTOGLOSSUM GRANDE
(*Clown orchid*)

Description: Orchid with spikes of 4-7 large flowers with colours and markings suggesting a clown's face. Flower spike rises to 30cm (12in).

Position: Minimum temperature 10°C/50°F. Happy in average room conditions and a good choice for window sills.

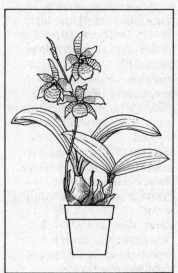

Watering: As for *O. bictoniense*, but keep drier in winter.

Propagation: As for *O. bictoniense* but required less often.

Care: Much as for *O. bictoniense* but this species is less vigorous. Rest it between the end of flowering in autumn and regrowth in spring. During this period provide little water. During summer keep water off the foliage or it may become marked or spotted.

ONCIDIUM ORNITHORHYNCHUM

Description: Orchid with pendulous stems bearing numerous scented rose-lilac flowers, October to December. Flower scapes measure up to 60cm (2ft).

Position: Minimum temperature 10°C/50°F. Moderate humidity and shade in summer, where scent can be enjoyed.

Watering: Just sufficient in winter to maintain the foliage. Water freely in summer.

Propagation: Division during spring.

Care: Grow in well crocked clay pots or slatted orchid baskets using orchid compost. Plant one-sided as for cymbidium. Repotting, with propagation, is usually needed every 2-3 years. Mature plants may need more winter watering than young specimens.

PAPHIOPEDILUM CALLOSUM
(*Slipper orchid*)

Description: Orchid with attractive evergreen mottled foliage. White, green, and purple striped 'slipper' flowers, January to June. Stems rise to 30cm (12in).

Position: Moderate warmth, humidity and shade. A neat window sill plant, but dislikes direct sun, draughts and cold.

Watering: Keep moist all the

year round, but avoid wetting foliage which causes spotting.

Propagation: Division in spring.

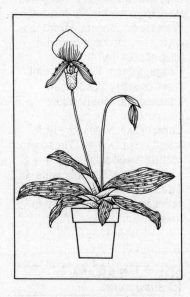

Care: Use 10cm (4cm) pots and orchid compost. Repot about every 2 years, or less if necessary. Moderate humidity is important. Ventilation should be given when temperature permits. Feed moderately in summer.

PAPHIOPEDILUM INSIGNE (*Slipper orchid*)

Description: Orchid with yellowish-green leaves and large yellow-green, brown-spotted and striped slipper flowers. Stems are 25-30cm (10-12in) long.

Position: Temperature can drop to 10°C/50°F. Cool and airy with moderate shade. Can be grown as small plants or allowed to make sizeable clumps, depending on space available. Small specimens make fine window sill plants out of direct sunshine.

Watering: Keep moist all year round. Water more cautiously in cool surroundings.

Propagation: Division of the clumps in spring.

Care: Easy. Use an orchid compost and pot as described for *P. callosum*. If large specimens required, use larger pots or half-pots as used for alpine plants, and allow large clumps to develop without disturbance. Such plants must be fed well during active growth.

CACTI AND SUCCULENTS

AEONIUM ARBOREUM
(*Tree aeonium*)

Description: Succulent best
bought in the cultivated variety
'Atropurpureum', which has
rosettes of shiny purple leaves
on trunk-like stems. Can grow
to about 90cm (3ft).
Position: Bright and airy but
frost-free in winter.
Watering: Moderate from late
spring to autumn, otherwise
keep almost dry.
Propagation: Separate the
leaves from a rosette and insert
them upright in a sandy
compost.
Care: Easy, but minimum
winter temperature should not
fall much below 7°C/45°F. Pot
into gritty or sandy compost.
Little feeding is required but old
plants long established in their
pots may be fed in moderation
during summer.

AEONIUM DOMESTICUM VARIEGATUM
(*Youth and old age*)

Description: Succulent
forming rosettes of green and
cream leaves.

Position: Bright and airy,
exposed to some sunshine.
Popular, bright window sill
plant. Neat and compact, does
not need much space. Keep well
away from frost in winter.
Watering: Moderate from late
spring to autumn, otherwise
keep almost dry.
Propagation: Remove small
rosettes with piece of stem
attached and root in sandy
compost.
Care: Easy. Needs very little
attention or feeding. The rosette
cuttings need shade at first
while rooting. Mature plants will
deteriorate in colour and
variegation if kept too long in
shade.

AGAVE AMERICANA
(*Century plant*)

Description: Succulent
forming large impressive
rosettes of long, narrow saw-
edged leaves with spiny tips.
Best bought in one of the
variegated banded forms. Can
spread and rise to at least 1.2m
(4ft) in a large tub.
Position: Hardy outdoors in
mild areas. Cool, airy, even
draughty, places as long as there
is good light and plenty of space.
Watering: Water and leave to
dry out before re-watering. Keep
dry in winter.

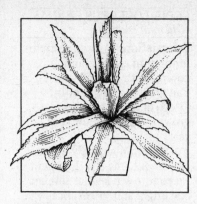

Propagation: Remove offsets with a knife, allow to dry for a day or so, and then pot in sandy compost.
Care: Easy. They grow well in the John Innes potting composts. Large plants, in small tubs or large pots, can be stood outdoors in summer. Mature plants may send up a tall flower spike, but die afterwards. Feed only moderately in summer.
Special points: The hard, sharp spines can inflict serious scratches if handled carelessly.

ALOE VARIEGATA
(Partridge breast)

Description: Succulent with compact clumps of erect, stiff pointed leaves, dark-green edged and cross-banded with greenish-silver. Height 12in.
Position: Excellent neat plant for a bright window sill, but

do not allow temperature to drop to freezing in winter.
Watering: Thorough, but allow to become almost dry before re-watering. Keep almost dry in winter.
Propagation: Remove small offsets that form around the parent plant and pot in sandy compost. Can also be grown from seed.
Care: Very easy. Grows well in most of the usual potting composts but add extra grit for drainage. Potting on is not often required. Well grown plants produce tall spikes of orange-red tubular flowers.

APOROCACTUS
FLAGELLIFORMIS
(Rat-tail cactus)

Description: Forest cactus forming long pendulous tail-like stems covered with reddish spines and bearing rich pink tubular flowers in summer.
Position: Containers need to be raised to give room for the 'tails' to hang. Bright with moderate humidity in summer. Can be grown in hanging pots or baskets or on walls or shelves. Does not require space. Temperature must not fall below 7°C/45°F in winter.
Watering: Moderate in summer, frequently during

flowering. Keep almost dry in winter.

Propagation: Break off pieces of stem, allow to dry, and insert in a sandy compost.

Care: Fairly easy, but must be rested practically dry throughout the winter. Grows well in most potting composts but add some extra grit for perfect drainage. Can be kept in 13cm (5in) pots for some time.

ASTROPHYTUM MYRIOSTIGMA
(*Bishop's cap cactus*)

Desription: Globular cactus, shaped like a bishop's mitre, with a whitish floury surface. Showy yellow flowers at the top during summer. Can grow to about 20cm (8in).

Position: Very bright airy window sill or similar. Do not allow temperature to drop to freezing in winter.

Watering: Moderate in summer, allow to rest dry in winter.

Propagation: Easy to grow from seed.

Care: Generally easy, but must have a winter rest almost dry if it is to flower well in the summer. Grows well in John Innes potting composts with extra grit added for drainage. Can be fed sparingly during summer.

CEPHALOCEREUS SENILIS
(*Old man cactus*)

Description: A striking cactus forming an erect column covered with long silky hairs. Can grow to a height of 1m (3½ft) or more, but slow-growing – 20mm (¾in) per year.

Position: Moderately warm, very bright, and airy. Excellent for picture windows or similar and bright sun rooms. Keep well above zero in winter.

Watering: Moderate, without waterlogging, in summer and during active growth. Keep dry in winter. See below.

Propagation: Usually easy from seed.

Care: Fairly easy, but take special care to see that potting compost is free-draining. John Innes No. 1 with added grit is usually suitable. Make sure the pots are well crocked. Feed moderately in summer when plants are established in final pots.

CEREUS PERUVIANUS
(*Column cactus*)

Description: Cactus forming a tall ribbed column, the ribs being edged with long brownish spines. Can reach a height of 2m (6½ft) or more.

Position: Bright, airy, above

freezing in winter. A good plant for a sunny picture window or sun room. The white flowers (rare indoors) open at night.

Watering: Keep moist in summer, dry in winter.

Propagation: Tops of columns can be cut off, allowed to dry for a couple of days, and then rooted in a sandy compost. See below. Can also be propagated from seed.

Care: To encourage branching and to keep down height the columns can be pruned. Removed pieces are useful for propagation. For feeding, a high potassium tomato feed gives the best results. Grit should be added to the potting compost for perfect drainage.

CEROPEGIA WOODII
(Hearts entangled)

Description: Trailing succulent with long thread-like stems bearing small marbled heart-shaped leaves and small pitcher-shaped dark reddish flowers.

Position: Moderate warmth, not below 10°C/50°F in winter. Airy, with slight shade in summer. Can trail as much as 2m (6½ft), so the hanging containers need plenty of height.

Watering: Moderate in summer, keep dry in winter.

Propagation: From cuttings or from little nodule-like tubers that form along the stems. Remove and pot in sandy compost.

Care: It forms a large tuber which is prone to rot if kept too damp. Compost must be very well drained and the pots well crocked. Remove the growing tips of young plants to encourage branching. Feed sparingly.

CHAMAECEREUS SILVESTRII
(Peanut cactus)

Description: Cactus of creeping habit forming many long prickly stems of about finger thickness. Profusion of starry scarlet flowers in early summer.

Position: Survives almost freezing temperatures and considerable neglect. Excellent for sunny and airy window sills. Low-growing, and best given wide shallow pans so that it has room to spread.

Watering: Moderate in summer, but keep dry in winter especially when conditions are cold. Will survive without water for long periods. It may shrivel, but will soon recover when watering resumes.

Propagation: Very easy. Small

pieces can be broken off and rooted in sandy compost.

Care: Extremely easy. Grows well in most composts provided they are reasonably drained. Although it survives neglect, it will look better and flower more freely if given care. Feed moderately in summer.

CRASSULA ARGENTEA
(*Jade plant*)

Description: Succulent of shrubby habit forming thick branching stems, bearing oval, thick, glossy green leaves. Exceeds 75cm (2½ft) in height and spread, but rarely flowers.

Position: Cool to warm, but can survive almost to freezing temperatures. Bright to slight shade, airy conditions. Not a fussy plant. Can reach a considerable size if well cultivated and well established.

Watering: Water freely, then allow to go dry before repeating. Keep almost dry in winter. Can survive without water for long periods.

Propagation: Cuttings root readily. Plants sometimes form aerial roots.

Care: Extremely easy. Grows in almost any compost that is well drained. To keep plants small, delay repotting for as long as possible, and feed sparingly.

CRASSULA FALCATA
(syn. *Rochea falcata*)
(*Scarlet paintbrush*)

Description: Succulent with erect stems of thick sickle-shaped green leaves with greyish velvety surface. Terminal clusters of small scarlet bell-shaped flowers. Grows to about 60cm (2ft).

Position: Bright and airy position, cool but above freezing temperatures in winter. A good window sill plant. Demands little space.

Watering: Keep moist from spring to autumn and almost dry in winter.

Propagation: Leaves can be removed after flowering and rooted in sandy compost, or cuttings treated the same way.

Care: Fairly easy, but watering needs are a little greater than many other succulents. Ensure that the compost is well drained by the addition of extra grit. A high-potassium tomato feed is recommended.

ECHEVERIA SETOSA

Description: Succulent forming clumps of spoon-shaped green leaves with fine white hair and red-tipped around the edges. Height 3 inches.

Position: Moderate warmth, bright and airy. Good window

sill plant, very neat and compact. Well grown plants produce red flowers on short stems in summer.

Watering: Moderate most of the year, except in winter when it should be kept almost dry.

Propagation: Carefully remove leaves and root in sandy compost.

Care: Free-draining compost is required. John Innes No. 2 with a generous addition of grit is suitable. Too much moisture around the base of the plant leads to rotting. Winter temperaure should not fall below 5°C/41°F.

ECHINOCACTUS GRUSONII
(*Golden barrel cactus*)

Description: Cactus of globular shape with ribs bearing golden-yellow spines. Can eventually reach 90cm (3ft) in diameter, but extremely slowly.

Position: Bright, airy, cool but above freezing in winter. Young plants are small and neat and ideal for sunny window sills.

Watering: Moderate watering in summer but keep dry from October to about March when the plants rest.

Propagation: From seed sown in spring.

Care: Fairly easy, needing little attention, and can be kept in small pots for many years. Grow in John Innes potting compost No. 2 to which about one-third volume of grit has been added. Feed established plants moderately in summer. Mature specimens may produce yellow flowers around the top.

EPIPHYLLUM HYBRIDS
(*Orchid cactus*)

Description: Forest cactus, forming flattened fleshy stems with notched edges. Notable for enormous showy flowers, May to June, in white and shades of yellow and red. There are a number of named hybrids. Can grow to about 90cm (3ft).

Position: Warm, moderately humid and slightly shaded. Not below 7°C/45°F in winter, preferably a few degrees higher. Useful plants for shaded window sills, not south-facing, when in flower. Not very attractive when out of flower.

Watering: Keep moist throughout the year, but only slightly so in winter.

Propagation: Pieces of stem or removed side shoots root readily in spring.

Care: Plants can become leggy, tall and untidy with age, and may then flower poorly. Propagate frequently. Tall plants may need a cane for support.

A–Z

Flowers well in 13cm (5in) pots using modern peat composts.

EUPHORBIA MILII
(syn. *E. splendens*)
(*Crown of thorns*)

Description: Shrubby plants with spear-shaped succulent leaves and long spines from the stems. Clusters of red or yellow flowers the year round, but mostly in winter. Height 24ins.

Position: Does not require much space. Needs reasonable warmth and good light but not direct sunshine. Enjoys a drier atmosphere than most houseplants prefer.

Watering: From spring to summer water freely, but very sparingly at other times when the plant must be rested. Overwatering causes leaves to turn yellow and fall.

Propagation: From seed sown on window sill in spring; or from cuttings in summer, inserted in coarse sand.

Care: A long-lived plant in the right conditions. If deterioration occurs through overwatering (this is common), allow plant to go dry for two months. New shoots should then begin to show and watering can gradually be resumed.

Special points: The sap that exudes when stems are cut is poisonous.

KALANCHOE BLOSSFELDIANA HYBRIDS
(*Blushing Katy*)

Description: Succulent with dwarf shrubby habit, fleshy green leaves and flower clusters in shades of red and yellow. Height 12 inches.

Position: Cool and airy, a winter minimum of 7°C/45°F, slight shade in summer. Hybrids are dwarf and compact and are often specially treated by nurseries for selling with out-of-season winter flowers. Spring and summer is the normal flowering time.

Watering: Never allow to go completely dry.
Propagation: Hybrid seed is available. Also from cuttings.
Care: Repot cuttings to 13cm (5in) pots using any modern potting compost. Growing from seed is best not undertaken in the home. Will survive

temperatures below 7°C/45°F but above freezing if kept on dry side. Excessive humidity may cause mould. Excessive watering causes basal stem rotting. Feed moderately during bud formation.

LOBIVIA FAMATIMENSIS
(*Sunset cactus*)

Description: Cactus forming short columns with ribs edged with sharp spines and producing large yellow flowers. Height 6 inches.

Position: Bright and airy. Excellent for a sunny window sill where space is limited.
Watering: In summer water freely, keep dry in winter, and water slightly the rest of the time.
Propagation: Sections, when formed, can be removed and rooted in sandy compost. Also from seed.
Care: Fairly easy. Temperature can fall to just above freezing in winter during the resting period. Pot in John Innes No. 1 or 2 compost with extra grit added for drainage.
Special Points: Handle carefully. Spines can cause skin irritation if they penetrate.

MAMMILLARIA BOCASANA
(*Pincushion cactus*)

Description: A small globular cactus which, as it grows, multiplies to form a small mound. The surface is covered with short spines covered with silky hair. Height 6 inches.
Position: Cool, airy, bright. Ideal for a sunny window sill, where space is limited. Winter minimum temperature about 5°C/41°F.
Watering: During summer water freely, but do not allow water to run between the globes. Keep dry in winter.

Propagation: The little globes can be removed and rooted in a sandy compost.

Care: Fairly easy. Grows well in John Innes potting composts with extra grit added. Plants can be propagated when they become too large for 13cm (5in) pots. Feed moderately during summer.

Special points: Handle carefully. The spines, concealed by hair, can irritate the skin if they penetrate.

OPUNTIA MICRODASYS
(*Bunny ears*)

Description: Cactus forming branching stems of flattish oval segments uniformly surfaced with tufts of yellowish fine bristle. Can reach about 90cm (3ft) in height with time, but is slow-growing. Rarely flowers.

Position: Cool airy and bright. Minimum winter temperature of 7°C/45°F.

Watering: In summer water generously and sufficiently to prevent complete drying out in winter.

Propagation: Remove segments in early summer and root in sandy compost.

Care: Likes a fairly rich compost. Use John Innes No. 3 with added grit for drainage. Should not be allowed to dry out completely in winter. Can be grown in 13cm (5in) pots for a long time.

Special Points: The bristles can cause skin irritation if they penetrate.

OPUNTIA ROBUSTA
(*Prickly pear*)

Description: Vigorous growing cactus similar in habit to *O. microdasys*, but with rounder segments bluish-green and with more widely spaced tufts, sometimes with yellowish spines. Size can vary a lot and dwarf forms are available.

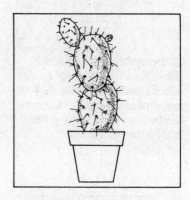

Position: Same as for *O. microdasys*, but considerably more space may be needed.

Watering: As for *O. microdasys*.

Propagation: As for *O. microdasys*.

Care: As for *O. microdasys*. *O. robusta* seems to have a number of variants. There is a form that is hardy in mild areas in the south and west, as well as types which appear far less vigorous and grow more compactly. These are worth propagating, although the species generally is not an ideal houseplant.

PACHYPHYTUM OVIFERUM
(*Sugared almond plant or pearly moonstones*)

Description: Small shrubby succulent, the stems clustered with leaves shaped like sugared almonds, having delicate purplish tints and covered with a whitish bloom. White bell-shaped flowers attached to arching stems in spring.
Position: Similar to echeveria. Good light is essential for best colouring.
Watering: As for echeveria, but special care is needed in winter to get conditions just right – not wet, not dry.
Propagation: Leaves should be carefully detached and inserted in sandy compost. Also from seed.
Care: Much the same as for echeveria. During handling, potting and the like, care should be taken not to rub off the attractive bloom.

REBUTIA SENILIS
(*Fire crown*)

Description: Small spherical cactus forming clumps and covered with numerous whitish spines. Brilliant red flowers from late spring to summer.
Position: Bright and airy. Excellent for a sunny window sill where space is limited. Temperature should not be allowed to drop below 5°C/41°F in winter.
Watering: Water thoroughly then allow to go almost dry before re-watering. In winter give just sufficient water to prevent shrivelling.
Propagation: Very easy from seed, which is produced freely by the plants – seedlings may appear around the parent. Also from offsets removed and potted in sandy compost.
Care: Easy. Grows well in most potting composts if grit is added to ensure perfect drainage. Feed moderately in summer.

RHIPSALIDOPSIS ROSEA
(*Easter cactus*)

Description: Forest cactus. Neat, shrubby at first becoming trailing. Freely branching succulent stems, flattish and sometimes angled. Pretty flowers in shades of carmine or white, May to June.

Position: Moderate warmth and humidity, shade in summer. A dainty trailer for shelf or wall pots, but young plants may have a more erect habit.

Watering: Never allow to dry out completely. Mist in summer. Keep drier if conditions are cool in winter.

Propagation: Very easy from pieces of stem rooted in a cutting compost during summer.

Care: Fairly easy. Will survive quite cold winter temperatures, almost down to freezing, if kept dryish. Will shrivel, but recover with return of warmth and watering. Grows well in peat-based potting composts, and in small pots. Feed when buds begin to form.

SCHLUMBERGERA ×
BUCKLEYI
(*Christmas cactus*)

Description: Forest cactus with trailing stems composed of flattish succulent segments. Profusion of showy rose-pink to magenta flowers, December to February.

Position: Moderate warmth and humidity. Good light but not direct sunlight in summer. Useful for small hanging baskets, shelf or wall pots.

Watering: Keep moist at all times, drier in winter if temperature drops.

Propagation: Pieces of stem root easily during summer in a cutting compost.

Care: Erratic watering during flowering causes bud drop. Stand plants outdoors during summer, out of sun, and keep watered. Reduce watering in autumn to rest the plants. Resume watering, and also feed, when buds begin to form. Grows well in most potting composts.

BULBS

ACHIMENES HYBRIDS
(*Hot water plant*)

Description: The named hybrids are grown from small underground stems. They grow upright or as trailers; some varieties grow both ways. The plants become smothered with richly coloured flowers, mainly blue, purple or pink, from summer to late autumn. They can successfully be used in hanging baskets especially the 'Michelssen Hybrids'.
Position: Moderate warmth and humidity needed, with some slight shade.
Watering: Keep compost moist.
Propagation: Easiest from the underground stems, which usually multiply freely.
Care: Plant the underground stems about 5 to each 13cm (5in) pot, just below compost surface February to April on warm window sill. Water cautiously at first until growth is strong. Use twiggy sticks for support unless trailing is desired in appropriate varieties. After flowering, gradually allow pots to dry. Store frost-free over winter. Next planting time turn out pots, separate the tubers and repot.

AMARYLLIS
see HIPPEASTRUM

CANNA HYBRIDS
(*Indian shot*)

Description: Handsome erect banana-like foliage. Gladiolus-like flowers. The form 'Lucifer' is less tall than some cultivars, growing to about 60cm (2ft).
Position: Warm, bright and airy. Good for a bright large window.
Watering: Keep moist.
Propagation: Division of the roots of the underground stem when potting, and when shoots can be seen.
Care: Pot in early spring using 18cm (7in) posts and commercial potting compost. Keep warm but do not water freely until growth is strong. Most garden cannas are unsuitable as houseplants. Store the pots dry and frost-free over winter. Repot and propagate, if desired, following spring. Feed well in summer.

CRINUM × POWELLII
(*Cape lily*)

Description: Large bulb with strap-shaped foliage and handsome lily-like trumpet flowers, pink to white, July to September. Grows to 45cm (18in) or more in height.

Position: Hardy outdoors in mild areas. Cool, airy, slightly shaded.

Watering: Keep moist, but only slightly so in winter.

Propagation: From offsets that form around parent bulb.

Care: Pot in spring in any potting compost. Leave long neck tip of bulbs well protruding from compost surface. About 18cm (7in) pots, or 3 bulbs in larger pots if desired. Water sparingly until growth is well away. Feed generously during active growth. Keep frost-free over winter. Repot or pot on every third year or so.

CROCUS

Description: Small corm producing well known flowers in a wide range of colours. Height 6-10cm (2½-4in).

Position: Cool and airy, slightly shaded to make flowers last as long as possible. Unsuited to warm stuffy rooms.

Watering: Keep moist.

Propagation: Self-propagating from little cormlets when planted outdoors. These can be taken up and potted when mature.

Care: Choose choice cultivars or species for pots. Pot in autumn using a proper potting compost and planting closely,

tops just covered with soil. Plunge pots in moist clean sand or peat outside, but *not* where it can become waterlogged. Do not bring into a cool room until they have formed plenty of roots and are beginning to grow. After flowering, plant outdoors. Feed during leaf development.

CYCLAMEN PERSICUM

Description: Corm. A most popular gift around Christmas time. Height 15-22.5cm (6-9in).

Position: Slight shade. Ideal temperature is about 10°C/50°F. Wilts in widely fluctuating temperatures, cold and draughts as well as warm stuffy conditions and in bright sunlight.

Watering: Avoid extremes. Water best kept off the top of the corm.

Propagation: From seed. Not advised in the home.

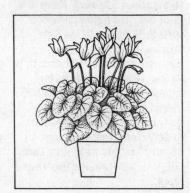

Care: Can be grown from corms potted July/August, convex (root covered) side downwards, one to each 13cm (5in) pot. Corm top just above compost surface. Water cautiously until growth is active. To save plants, rest them in a cold frame outdoors, keeping them dry during the summer. The new 'minicyclamens' are dainty miniatures. They need similar treatment but greater care in watering because of their small pots.

GLORIOSA ROTHSCHILDIANA (*Glory lily*)

Description: Elongated tuber. Climber with lance-shaped tendril-tipped leaves and showy red and yellow flowers like reflexed lilies. Can reach a height of 1.8m (6ft).

Position: Cool to warm, moderate humidity, slight shade. Give canes for support.

Watering: Keep moist during growth.

Propagation: Self-propagating, see below.

Care: Start tubers into growth early spring, as for begonia. Growth begins at tuber tips. Place centrally in 18cm (7in) pot with potting compost just covering. As the plant grows the

old tuber shrivels. At least two new ones form. At end of year let pots go dry. Store frost-free over winter. Next starting time, tip out pots and separate the new tubers.

HIPPEASTRUM HYBRIDS (*Amaryllis*)

Description: Huge bulb. Strap-shaped evergreen leaves. Enormous trumpet flowers on thick stems. Flower stem can exceed 90cm (3ft).

Position: Cool, slight shade.

Watering: Generous when leaves are growing. See overleaf for details.

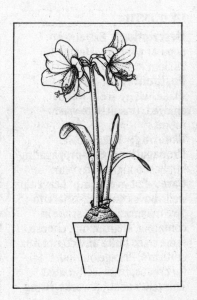

Propagation: From offsets formed around mature bulbs.
Care: Pot by the end of January in 18cm (7in) pots with top well protruding above potting compost. Keep moderately warm. Flower may form before leaves. Do not water until these appear. Best kept slightly moist over winter to preserve foliage, but some people let pots go dry and store frost-free until next starting time. 'Prepared' bulbs for early flowering should be grown as instructed on the pack. Feed when foliage is growing, rather than pot on. Grows well in most potting composts.

HYACINTH

Description: Extremely popular pot bulb. Height 15-22.5cm (6-9in).
Position: Cool, airy, slight shade, where scent can be enjoyed. Unsuited to warm rooms.
Watering: Keep moist.
Propagation: Self-propagating but best bought each year.
Care: Pot in autumn. Leave tip well above compost surface to give maximum root space in container. If grouping, choose same sized bulbs and do not mix cultivars. Plunge outdoors, as for crocus, until well rooted. This takes about 8 weeks. Bring

into the cool and expose to full light gradually over a few days. After flowering, plant outdoors. In time bulbs multiply by offsets. When mature these can be taken up and potted. Bulbs for Christmas flowering are

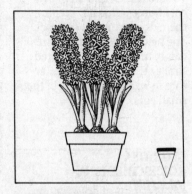

specially prepared and must be purchased annually. In all cases feed when the foliage is growing. High temperatures in the early stages can inhibit flowering.

HYMENOCALLIS (ISMENE)
(*Peruvian daffodil*)

Description: Hybrids of two species usually sold. Large bulbs with highly scented daffodil-like white to cream flowers, March to April.
Position: Cool but not cold, moderate humidity and slight shade. Where powerful scent can be enjoyed.

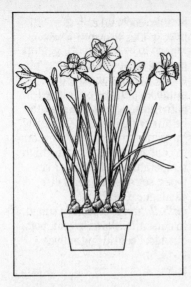

Watering: Keep moist when growing. Almost dry in winter.
Propagation: Remove any offsets when repotting and put them singly in pots of growing compost. Pot on as necessary, they will reach flowering size in two years.
Care: Grow as for Hippeastrum but keep dry over winter or bulbs may rot. Buy large bulbs, as small ones may not have reached flowering size. 'Zwanenburg' is hardy in mild areas outdoors. 'Advance' is popular and has very large flowers but is rather more tender. The pale yellow form is 'Sulphur Queen'. Winter temperature must not fall to freezing point.

IRIS (BULBOUS)
(*English, Spanish, Dutch, irises*)

Description: Neat-growing flowers. Many colours, May to June. *I. reticulata* is popular for pots because of its low growth and late-winter purple flowers. Some types can exceed 60cm (2ft).
Position: Similar to crocus. Good for a bright window sill.
Watering: Keep moist.
Propagation: Self-propagating, similar to crocus.
Care: Grow named cultivars if possible. Place about 5 bulbs in each 13cm (5in) pot (or in proportion) in autumn. Use John Innes No. 2 compost. Place outdoors. A cold frame or similar protection is ideal, but keep moist. Do not bring into the home until buds begin to show colour. Feed during active leaf growth.

LACHENALIA
(*Cape cowslip*)

Description: Bulb with tubular red, yellow, and purple flowers, December onwards.
Position: Cool, airy, slight shade. Above 13°C/55°F may inhibit flowering. Pots and hanging baskets.
Watering: Keep moist during active growth.

Propagation: From offsets when repotting.

Care: Plant early to mid-autumn. Grow *L. bulbifera* in hanging wire baskets, lined with moss. Set bulbs on the moss with tips pointing down through the moss, level with the wire mesh, 5-8cm (2-3in) apart. Fill with potting compost. Set a few more bulbs around top edge. Plants grow through the moss and a 'ball' of bloom results. After planting put basket in cool place, ideally 7°C/45°F. Water sparingly until foliage is well away. Grow *L. aloides* similarly, in ordinary pots not hung. Allow both to dry when foliage has died and expose to full sun. At re-potting time tip out and separate offsets.

LILY

Description: Scaly bulb. Flowers trumpet or reflexed, often scented. Height 90cm-1.2m (3-4ft).

Position: Cool, slightly shaded. Unsuited to warm rooms. Most houseplant lilies are short, but taller types are ideal for porches, etc.

Watering: Keep moist, never wet.

Propagation: Offsets or scales removed when repotting.

Care: Pot autumn to early spring. Leave tip just protruding, but cover those known to be stem rooting. Most potting composts suitable. Pots must be well drained. Put outdoors plunged or covered with moist peat. When growth begins bring indoors. Gradually introduce to full light. Grow on in cool airy place, avoiding high temperatures. There are many types, so consult a specialist catalogue. Compact *L. umbellatum* is especially suited to pots. After flowering put pots outside. Feed during active growth.

NARCISSUS

Description: Well known, but has various forms including daffodil. There are multifloras, giant flowered, double, miniatures which are especially good for pots, and highly scented types like 'Jonquilla'.

Position: As for crocus and hyacinth. Where fragrance can be enjoyed.

Watering: Keep moist.

Propagation: Self-propagating as crocus and hyacinth, but best bought each year.

Care: Much the same as for crocus and hyacinth. Do not crowd bulbs in containers or pot too deeply as roots may push up the bulbs. Prepared bulbs are

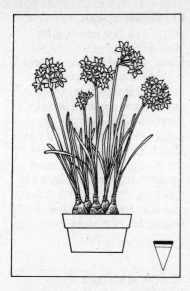

Propagation: Offsets when formed.

Care: Always buy named hybrids, *not* garden forms, for potting. Pot in August, one bulb to each 13cm (5in) pot. Leave tip well above compost level. Put outdoors in sunny frame if possible. Give no water until growth begins, then water freely. Bring indoors for flowering. Afterwards cut off faded flowers and water until foliage yellows. Allow to go dry and store pots where they can get sunshine until next starting time. Repot only after several years. Feed well when foliage is forming. Always keep frost-free.

now sold and should be grown as suppliers instruct. Bulb catalogues indicate varieties suitable for gentle forcing. In all cases excessive warmth inhibits flowering.

NERINE
(*Guernsey lily*)

Description: Named types each with large bulb giving umbels of flowers. Many colours, often with glistening sheen. Height 60cm (2ft).
Position: Cool but not cold. Slight shade. Impressive window sill plants for autumn display.
Watering: Moist when growing. Dry in winter.

ORNITHOGALUM THYRSOIDES
(*Chincherinchee*)

Description: Bulb producing cream to white spikes, famous for their ability to remain fresh for weeks in water as cut flowers. Height 45cm (18in).
Position: Bright, airy window sill during late spring and summer.
Watering: Keep moist during active growth. See below.
Propagation: From buds that form around the parent bulb.
Care: Put several bulbs in each pot. Use any potting compost. After flowering, put the

containers outdoors in sunny position and keep watered. When foliage dies down, allow to go dry and repot the bulbs in autumn. Tends to be an untidy pot plant. Thin canes may be needed for support. Remove faded flower heads promptly. Feed while the foliage is growing. Can be gently forced for earlier flowers.

RECHSTEINERIA CARDINALIS
(*Cardinal flower*)

Description: Tuber. Velvety leaves with purplish sheen. Clusters of long brilliant scarlet tubular flowers throughout summer. Grows to 30cm (12in).
Position: Moderate warmth and humidity. Moderate shade. Does not require much space.
Watering: Moderate while growing. Keep dry in winter.

Propagation: Easy from seed, or by division of tubers as for begonia.
Care: Start as for begonia and pot similarly. Repot seedlings in 10cm (4in) pots. May flower same year as sowing if done in February. Thin cane may be needed to support flower stems. After foliage has died at end of the year, let pots go dry. Store free from frost over winter until repotting time. Old large tubers may not flower well and are best propagated or discarded.

SINNINGIA HYBRIDS
(*Gloxinia*)

Description: Tubers. Velvety leaves and clumps of huge exotic trumpet flowers in autumn. Height 9 inches.
Position: Cool to warm, moderate humidity and shade. Excellent window sill plants, but keep out of full sun.
Watering: Moist when growing.
Propagation: As for begonia, also from F1 hybrid seed.
Care: As for begonia. One tuber to each 13cm (5in) pot. F1 hybrid seed sown February may give plants flowering in autumn. Old tubers that are 'corky' may not flower well and can be discarded. Winter storage as for begonia. Numerous named

cultivars. Best flowering is obtained from 2 year old tubers. Keep water off foliage, otherwise spotting will occur. Avoid direct sunshine.

TULIP

Description: Bulb. Well known flowers, single or double, in many colours.

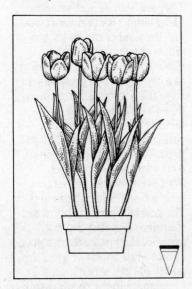

Position: As for narcissus.
Watering: Keep moist.
Propagation: Self-propagating, as narcissus, but for pots it is best to buy them annually.
Care: Not all tulips do well in pots. Consult specialist catalogue when choosing. The

dwarf doubles are especially easy and desirable. There are numerous named cultivars. They make lovely groups in bowls, but do not mix types; they may not all flower at the same time. A favourite single for gentle forcing is 'Brilliant Star', neat with dazzling crimson colour.

BONSAI

Every year at the Chelsea Flower Show the Japan Society of London stage a meticulous display of Bonsai plants, many of them older than the show itself. Perhaps in the entire show there are no plants more beautiful than these delicate trees. They display to perfection the charm of maturity in miniature, the windswept branches and gnarled trunk of a mountain tree less than ten inches high. Growing in dishes that hardly seem to hold sufficient soil to maintain the plant for months, let alone years, these superb plants are ample proof that with proper care in potting, pruning and feeding it is possible to develop and sustain plants over literally hundreds of years. It is, doubtless, more of a challenge to care for trees as Bonsai, as it demands patience and artistic sense to achieve the proportions and stylistic beauty of a good tree; but the results are very rewarding.

There is a wide range of different types of tree to choose from. One of the most attractive, ideally suited to the beginner, is the Japanese maple (*Acer palmatum*) with its beautiful scarlet or bronze foliage. The firethorn (*Pyracantha coccinea*) and cotoneaster are also colourful, both bearing flowers followed by scarlet berries and, though the firethorn needs rigorous pruning, repay care with spectacular display. The white pine (*Pinus parviflora*) and juniper have a pleasing oriental appearance to western eyes that make them effective Bonsai. They are both perfect subjects, being almost natural dwarf trees, and the juniper can be chosen either as an upright (which should be as erect as possible) or as a cascade which grows down from the pot like a tree growing down a cliff. Hawthorn (*Crataegus oxyacartha*) is particularly suitable to plant in groups as it is rather thin on its own. Plant in odd numbers (three or five) with the largest tree in front, for the best effect. The gnarled trunks of hornbeam (*Carpinus betulus*) and crab apple (*Malus*) make them a good choice while the latter gives the additional pleasure of blossoming in the spring. Many traditional British trees can be used to good effect; the beech (*Fagus sylvatica*) and ash (*Fraxinus excelsior*) can be trained into interesting shapes, particularly their weeping varieties.

Position: It is important to

remember that Bonsai are not naturally houseplants and deprived of outside air circulation and light will shed their leaves and may die. Although American miniaturization of tropical trees has produced Bonsai that can live permanently indoors, for all other plants (including the ones mentioned here) it is essential that they be kept out of doors for the majority of the time, as they are still trees, however small. A sheltered balcony or patio makes an ideal location, or they can be

Juniper

protected above and to the side by a shelter of wooden laths or plastic sheeting. When brought indoors they should be given as much natural light as possible and kept free from draughts and excessive heat. Their stay indoors should not exceed five or six days and care should be taken not to remove a Bonsai from a warm room directly to a winter atmosphere. Acclimatize by placing it in a cold room first and, if very cold, protect the roots with peat or straw when first returned outside. Bonsai trees can be alternated so that one is always inside.

Watering: In winter and wet springs the tree will survive on the rainfall it receives during its time outdoors. When inside and during warm spells it is essential to water it regularly and keep the soil moist. In hot weather this can mean watering up to twice a day and must not be neglected as even short deprivation can kill a tree. Rainwater is best, if available, or tap water left to stand overnight. Feed with a weak liquid fertilizer every ten days to two weeks. Trees benefit from regular spraying.

Propagation: Established Bonsai can be bought from a good plant retailer, but if you want to start one yourself suitable subjects can often be found in garden centres. Look for deciduous plants or shrubs with small leaves. Hawthorn or hornbeam plants being sold for hedging are best as these will be smaller than ones sold as feature plants for the garden. Crab apples must be grown from seed as they are generally sold as mature trees. Sow seed in autumn or strike cuttings about 20 cm (8 inches) long in October. Plant out initially in sandy soil. Cotoneaster may be grown from cuttings inserted into a sandy mixture or young plants can be bought.

An inexpensive way to acquire plants is to take young seedlings of two or three years from under parent trees in early spring. Choose a well-proportioned seedling and prune out any crowded or spindly branches. If it has a small mass of fibrous roots near the trunk it can safely be planted in a container. If the roots are long, prune back to within six inches of the trunk and plant out in the garden for a year.

When potting, choose your pot carefully to complement the plant. Check it has good drainage holes. Place perforated zinc covers over the holes and pot the tree in a mixture of loam, leaf mould (or peat) and sharp sand. Water after potting. **Care:** It is essential to prune a Bonsai tree to maintain its health and make it look beautiful. Firethorn and white pine are especially in need of it as they tend to be rather congested, but all plants benefit from it. During winter and early spring cut away dead or unnecessary branches near to the trunk. Pinch out growth on junipers and other evergreens with needle-like leaves. Fruiting trees should not be pruned until the middle of July, except for their tips. To achieve a tree with a strong trunk, firm branches and a good twiggy outline, shorten all growth to the first or second leaf or set of leaves. Careful pruning to a suitably positioned bud can usually achieve branches following a desired direction. With all Bonsai subjects the shape of the

Acer Trifidum

tree is one of the most important requirements, so that a small plant, even when defoliated, will remain attractive. To give an interesting twist or curve to a too-straight trunk or branch wiring can be employed. This should be done in the early years of a tree's development in June or July, when the plant is at its most supple. Choose a wire slightly less pliable than the branch (copper wire no. 8 for the trunk, no. 16 for soft branches) and anchor it in the soil or round the trunk. Wind it loosely around the branch or trunk then gently bend it to the desired position. Wires will have to remain in place for six months to a year before removal.

Repotting should take place in the early spring every one or two years for young plants (under ten years), two to ten years for older trees. On the whole evergreens need repotting less frequently than deciduous trees. Gently free roots from the soil. Tease the outer roots away till they hang freely and prune back to one third. Any strong tap roots should also be reduced in size. Wash out the container and repot in fresh compost, in the same pot. If the tree is in danger of becoming top-heavy (Japanese pine is particularly susceptible) thread wire through the drainage holes and secure around the lower part of the tree for stability. Do not prune and cut back roots at the same time, to minimize shock.

Contributor
David Squire

HOW TO DISPLAY YOUR PLANTS

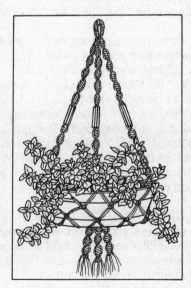

DISPLAY

POTS AND CONTAINERS

Traditional clay pots Until the late 1950s houseplants had always been grown in earthenware clay pots – containers that had a natural colour and texture that blended with all plants. Then plastic pots were introduced and the whole plant pot scene changed.

Clay versus plastic Each of these materials has its devotees, but invariably the majority of plants are now sold in plastic pots – the type most preferred by nurserymen. Plastic pots are light to handle, cheaper to transport, easily stored and less likely to break. They are available in a wide range of colours and can be selected to complement most plants and room decor. In them plants require less water than those in clay pots, and although they do not deteriorate or break easily those made from thin plastic are brittle.

Saucers and square pots As well as plastic pots, saucers are also available and these greatly help to keep polished surfaces free from moisture. These saucers are light to handle and can be easily cleaned. Recent years have seen the introduction of large, square, box-like plastic containers in a wide range of vivid colours. Although plants can be set directly in small ones, the larger ones are best reserved as ornamental decorative outer containers. Their square shape and vivid colours make them ideal for use with 'architectural' foliage plants in modern, perhaps clinical, settings. Because they can so often be startling to the eye do not use them excessively as they will create too many focal points.

Ornate plant holders The Victorians and Edwardians with their love of plants created many specialized and distinctive containers for displaying plants or to hide the utilitarian nature of the actual pot. Ornate palm stands and pot surrounds were widely seen. Today we are not so rigid in our ideas about what makes an attractive surround for a pot. The soft brown shades of large earthenware pots, highly ornate and glazed pots, wicker-work surrounds, enamel

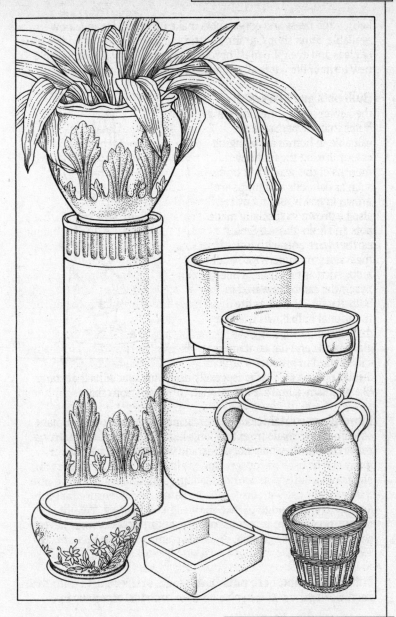

kettles and brass and copper pots make up the wide range now available. Junk shops, granny's attic and jumble sales provide a feast of ideas and even the most obscure container can often be given a new term of life – it is all a matter of using your imagination.

Bulb pots and glasses It is the winter and spring-flowering bulbs that are particularly valuable in homes for bringing colour during the first few months of the year. Most bulbs such as daffodils and tulips are grown in bowls, but many can also be grown in specially made pots and bulb glasses. Small earthenware pots with holes in their sides are superb for small bulbs such as crocuses, while hyacinths can be flowered in bulb glasses. As well as the traditional bulb bowls used for daffodils and tulips, highly-glazed wide and flat containers can be used to produce a large display of flowers. This is especially useful for hyacinths that stand like guardsmen and are low enough to be seen from above.

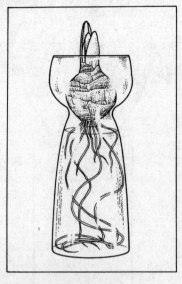

Fibre-glass containers An increasing number of outdoor plant containers are made from this long-lasting and immensely strong material. But they may not withstand violent knocks. However, many can be used in conservatories either as direct containers for plants or as outer pots for houseplants, and can be introduced into the home for use with large foliage plants. Always ensure that the floor is strong enough to take the weight of compost. Weight is usually no problem in a conservatory, but in a room it may have to be spread over a large area. For large plants in offices these make ideal containers.

Milk coolers and herb pots Earthenware milk coolers, with their narrow, elegant shape, can be used for daffodils, especially in conservatories where they might benefit from being raised off the floor and set amid other plants. In such places, herb pots with notch-like holes in their sides can be used for small bulbs. Like milk coolers, many other artefacts of yesterday can also be used to display and grow plants like bulbs that have a limited life and carry their own food reserves.

WALL-MOUNTED PLANT HOLDERS

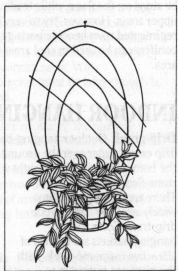

Wire frames These wall-mounted plant holders are usually formed of wire – sometimes plastic-covered – but unlike the wire half-baskets have space for a small plastic saucer to be placed under the pot. These containers are not always pleasing to the eye and in such cases are best used for foliage plants that trail around them. A few types do not have bases and drip saucers, just a circular wire frame holding the pot in place. These are suitable only for use outdoors in stone-floored conservatories.

Plants for wall-mounted plant holders Plants that exhibit a 'face-side' or those that just trail can be used here, such as the small-leaved and variegated ivies, devil's ivy (*Scindapsus aureus*), tradescantias and *Zebrina pendula*. The asparagus fern (*Asparagus densiflorus*) produces a cascade of wiry stems covered with small mid-green leaves, while the creeping fig (*Ficus pumila*) displays heart-shaped, pointed, dark green leaves, prominently veined. The mother of thousands (*Saxifraga stolonifera*) seldom fails to gain attention, its red thread-like runners often reaching several feet in length. The best form is 'Tricolor', with variegated leaves.

A few trailing flowering plants are also suitable, such as

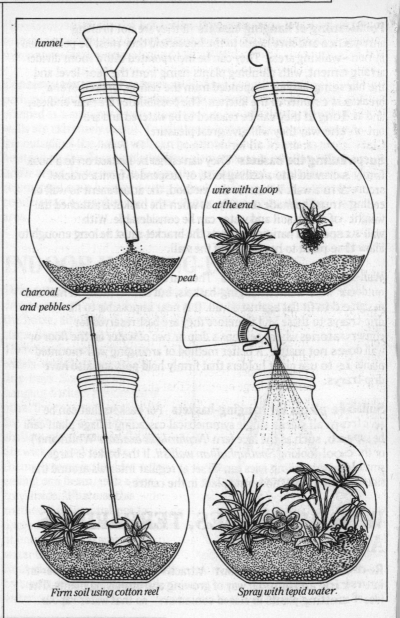

funnel

wire with a loop at the end

charcoal and pebbles

peat

Firm soil using cotton reel

Spray with tepid water.

Plant Display

given off by leaves condenses on the glass and returns to the compost – was popularized by the keen entomologist Dr Nathaniel Ward. In the early 1840s while trying to pupate a hawk moth in a closed glass jar he noticed that a small fern also in the container continued to grow with no ill-effect. He subsequently constructed miniature closed greenhouses and experimented with a range of ferns and other small plants.

Glass containers of all kinds Since then, Dr Ward's idea has spread to include the use of every sort of glass container, including large industrial chemical flasks, bottles, glass sweet jars, giant brandy snifters and flagon cider bottles. Terrariums and fish tanks are also used with sheets of glass for covers, preferably sloping so that the water vapour after condensing does not drop on to the plants but runs to the sides and subsequently into the compost. Plastic materials are frequently used as containers, but the moisture tends to remain in clouds on the inside, obscuring your view of the plants.

Choosing the plants Selecting suitable plants for these containers must always be done with care, as they need to form a balanced community. Invasive plants soon smother their neighbours, causing leaves to remain moist and encouraging decay. Larger-leaved and fast-growing plants are best reserved for terrariums or for those glass containers with large openings that allow the plants to be trimmed back regularly. Those containers with narrow openings are best planted with slow-growing and relatively hard-surfaced plants. These will enable the container to be left alone for a long period before it becomes overcrowded.

Ferns for containers Many small ferns can be safely used, but beware of large ones. Some of these are native and found in the wild, while others have to be bought from specialist nurseries. The following ferns are suitable for large carboys and bottles: maidenhair fern (*Adiantum cuneatum*), small lady fern (*Athyrium filix-femina*), bladder fern (*Cystopteris bulbifera*), common polypody (*Polypodium vulgare*), hart's tongue fern (*Phyllitis scolopendrium*), maidenhair spleenwort (*Asplenium trichomanes*) and *Blechnum penna-marina*. These last two also do well in small containers.

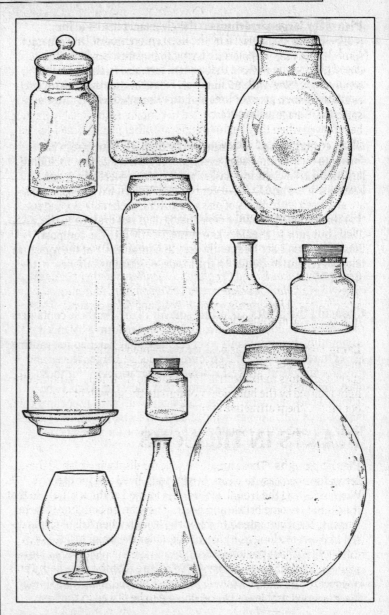

PLANT DISPLAY

Plants for large terrariums In their infancy spider plants (*Chlorophytum capense*) can be used, but as they spread are best removed. The same applies to many other plants. Small bromeliads, cordylines, *Stromanthe amabilis*, *Fittonia verschaffeltii*, *Dracaena sanderiana*, *Pilea cadierei* and small palms in their early years, such as *Chamaedorea elegans* (often sold as *Neanthe bella*). Plants with spreading foliage are best restricted to containers that enable them to be removed when they begin to suffocate other plants. Small-leaved ivies can also be used. Selaginellas, plants that have the structure of ferns and delicacy of mosses, can be used as a cover for the compost, forming a foil for the other plants. All of the plants suitable for containers with small openings can also be used in terrariums.

Plants for carboys and small flasks For long-term success these plants must be slow-growing and have leaves tough enough to resist decay through too much water vapour falling on them. Suitable plants include the bromeliads *Neoregelia carolinae* 'Tricolor', *Cryptanthus acaulis* and *Cryptanthus bivittatus*. Other plants are *Sansevieria hahnii*, *Codiaem variegatum pictum*, *Marantas*, the smooth-leaved *Peperomia magnoliifolia* and *Pilea cadierei*, which may require trimming back occasionally.

Lamp bottles As well as positioning planted bottles and flasks under small spot lamps, many upright flasks can be fitted with special adaptors to fix electric light bulbs to their tops. Although the light emitted by the bulb does not initiate the growth of plants, it does make them attractive at night.

PLANTS IN TROUGHS

Plastic troughs These are invaluable for displaying plants; they are waterproof, easy to clean, bright, long-lived and inexpensive. When selecting the trough ensure it is formed of thick plastic so that it does not become brittle and break. They can be bought in several lengths, but if you intend to move the trough when full of plants do not buy one too long as it may break under the weight. One 60cm (2ft) long is about the longest to buy and it will hold three or four plants in 10-12.5cm (4-5in) pots. To ensure that the rims of the pots are covered troughs 15cm (6in) deep are needed. This will allow a layer of small pebbles or coarse shingle to be placed in the base.

Filling the troughs Because there is no drainage of excess water from the trough a layer of small pebbles or shingle must be placed in the bottom. On top of this the plants in their pots can be stood. If you intend to change the plants in the trough fairly frequently just place them on the drainage material, but if they are long-term foliage plants the compost in the pots can be kept cool and moist by packing moist peat around them. This is especially useful during summer and particularly if the trough is in good light near to a window where transpiration is high.

Planting directly into the troughs Although this is often the simplest way to fill the trough it is not the best, as there is then no place for excess water to escape to and in time the compost will become sour and lack air. But if this method does appeal to you it is best to set all of the plants in a trough with drainage holes drilled in its base and to place it in an outer, waterproof plastic trough. All of the plants must be relatively slow-growing and not invasive if the collection is to remain together for a long time. For this 'all-in-one' planting do not mix long-term foliage plants with short-lived flowering plants.

Attractive trough surrounds If the appearance of plastic troughs is not pleasing enough, attractive wooded and wicker-work outer containers are available. Wooden ones are easy enough to make and sand-papered and varnished wood has a richness and beauty seldom equalled by other materials.

Troughs on stands Ornate wooden troughs with 30cm (1ft) or so long legs screwed into them form ideal homes for plastic troughs full of plants. And although these stands are vulnerable to the activities of small children they can be placed out of playing areas, perhaps near to the protection afforded by an armchair. These stands can also be used in conjunction with hanging indoor-baskets so that they form an attractive room divider.

Plants for troughs As long as the plants are not planted directly into a single mass of compost in the trough there is no problem about mixing flowering and foliage plants, rapid growers and those that develop more slowly. In fact, by changing them every few weeks and moving them around the house interest can be created from just a few plants. Small trailing plants such as ivies, *Setcreasea purpurea*, tradescantia, *Zebrina* and *Fittonia* can be positioned to cascade over the front, with upright foliage plants set in the centre. Select only the more robust flowering plants for the troughs. cinerarias (*Senecio*), chrysanthemums and *Campanula isophylla* are excellent.

Homes for daffodils Daffodils bought in bud ready to flower can be placed in troughs. The pots can be stood in the trough, with pebbles or shingle under their bases and damp peat packed around and over them, just covering the surface.

LARGE FLOOR-LEVEL CONTAINERS

Mixture of plants Groups of plants standing at floor-level need to be a mixture of sizes to create interest at all levels. Large tree-like foliage plants can be combined with small upright foliage types and trailing ones that will soften the edges of the container.

Dominant plant Usually one plant becomes dominant, creating the main interest and lasting for many years. The other plants are secondary and used as temporary space fillers to give interest during early years. Once the main plant becomes tree-like and shades the soil in the container it is doubtful whether any plant would last there for more than a few weeks without being given a respite in a healthier place.

Very heavy Strong containers are essential for these large plants and the copious amounts of compost they require. These large containers do not usually have drainage holes, plants being set directly in the compost. A few inches of coarse drainage material is needed in the base, overlaid with moist peat and then the compost. Because of the heavy weight of the filled container it is best positioned and then filled with compost, at the same time setting the plants in position. If the floor is formed of a concrete slab there is no problem about the weight, but if – as in most homes – the floor-boards rest on joists a steel plate may be required under the carpet. This will spread the load over four or more joists.

Suitable plants There are many combinations of plants for large containers, but those chosen must be compatible in their needs for light, warmth and water if they are to flourish over a long period. The A-Z Sections give details of a wide range of plants and their cultural requirements and below are suggested combinations of plants for large containers.

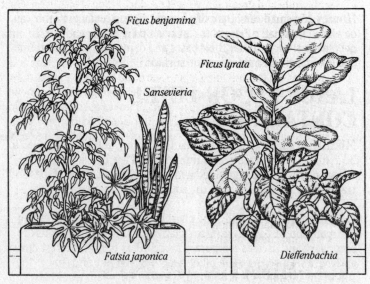

1. A tall weeping fig (*Ficus benjamina*) brings height to the collection, with *Fatsia japonica* displaying its mid-green shining palm-like leaves at the front. Mother-in-law's tongue (*Sansevieria trifasciata*) with its long, rigid, spiky leaves can be set at one side. A white container shows off the foliage of the fatsia and sansevieria to perfection. The *Fatsia japonica* is commonly known as the Japanese aralia or false castor oil plant. The weeping fig can be pruned to fit a corner of a room. Its leaves have a 'face' side and so the plant does not need to be turned frequently.
2. The mother-in-law's tongue can again be used to give interest centrally at the base, with the spiky theme being carried upwards with *Dracaena marginata* displaying a tuft of sharply-pointed leaves at its top. To soften the base set young dumb canes (*Dieffenbachia maculata*) around the edges.

3. A two-plant combination could be the distinctive *Philodendron bipinnatifidum* which grows to about 1.2m (4ft) and displays large, three-lobed deeply-incised deep green leaves up to 45cm (18in) long and 30cm (1ft) wide. It is both a compact and spreading plant and the space under its lower leaves can be used for the spider plant (*Chlorophytum*). This has long, narrow leaves with white and green stripes and produces long stems from which develop small versions of the parent. This is a plant, by the way, that has small tuberous roots and in time often pushes itself out of the pot.

4. A clinical and modern creation could be *Dracaena fragrans* and small-leaved trailing foliage plants around the base so that they trail over the side of the container. Older specimens of dracaena eventually have bare stems and tufts of leaves at the top, allowing the eye to travel beyond the plants. If the combination becomes bare at compost level do not be afraid of using small white pebbles to give extra interest.

5. Another two-plant combination is the fiddle-back fig (*Ficus lyrata*) and dumb cane (*Dieffenbachia maculata*).

6. The false castor oil plant (*Fatsia japonica*) and the spider plant (*Chlorophytum*) also form a good combination, with the stems of the spider plant trailing over the container. Combinations of leaf shape and colour always create interest.

ILLUMINATING PLANTS

Quality of light Any artificial light falling on a plant will highlight its foliage and make it more interesting, but only light within a certain wave band will activate the green pigments within leaves and initiate growth.

The normal tungsten-filament bulbs used to illuminate most homes do not help plants grow. Some fluorescent tubes initiate growth and specially designed ones for use with plants are available from garden centres. These involve installing electrical fittings and it is wise to have these checked by a competent electrician or your local electricity board.

Influence on flowering Plants vary in their reaction to light; some are termed short-day plants and only begin to initiate flower buds when the length of the dark period in every twenty-four hours is longer than the light part. Conversely, some plants flower when the light period is longer than the dark part, while others do not have their flowering influenced at all by the relative dark and light periods, and these are called day-neutral plants. A further complication is that temperatures have to be right for light to influence flowering.

Nurserymen are well aware of the factors that influence the flowering of plants and by manipulation of light and dark periods, and by keeping temperatures right for bud initiation, they are able to flower such plants as chrysanthemums and *Kalanchoe blossfeldiana* all year round. And by doing this nurserymen have discovered that all-year-round chrysanthemums – whether grown for sale in pots or as cut flowers – last much longer than those grown and flowered normally.

Strip lights Because these lights are frequently installed under shelves so they cannot be seen – yet the light falls on the plants – there is the possibility that hot air may build up in layers and damage plants. Therefore it is best to use either one of the strip lights that activates growth in plants, or one that produces a cool light.

Spot lights Wall-mounted spot lights can be attractive in themselves and produce an eye-catching effect on plants. Large foliage plants especially benefit from this. Plants in alcoves can be easily illuminated. Standard lights usually illuminate quite large areas beneath them with subdued light and are best reserved for small flowering plants.

Lights and mirrors These tend to go together like sausages-and-mash and can in combination create an impressive display. The greatest benefit, besides making the plants attractive for a longer period, is to fool the eye into thinking a room is much larger than it is. An alcove in a bedroom or living-room with a floor to ceiling mirror positioned at the back and a trough of plants in front – with a concealed strip light above – is a captivating sight.

Dimmed lights and spot-lights in combination Many living rooms have dimmer switches that enable the intensity of light to be reduced. If this is done while leaving a spot light on a large and distinctive plant such as a palm the result is stunning. Spot-lights can also be used to bounce light off a light-coloured wall with a plant silhouetted against it.

African Violets These small plants with violet-like flowers in a wide range of colours are highly suited for growth under lights. They are compact, floriferous and can be flowered the year through.

Lights, mirrors and bookcases If you have a large bookcase and wish to give it added interest fit small mirrors cut to fit between two shelves. The mirror does not have to extend across the full width of the bookcase. Then if a 'cool' concealed light is fitted to shine on to the mirror and a few small plants set in front of it a hole-in-the-wall effect is created.

PLANTS IN GROUPS

Shapes and colours Plants benefit from being grouped together, forming a micro-climate more humid than if on their own. And setting plants in groups so that the foliage is either complementary or in contrast creates further interest. For instance, a group of all-green foliage plants could become dull, but if a distinctively variegated-leaved one were placed among them each would highlight the other. The same can be done with leaf shapes.

Creating further interest

Many of the long-lived green-leaved foliage plants can be given added interest by placing either flowering or variegated foliage houseplants around their bases. If these temporary plants have a scrambling habit they are best raised from the floor to prevent damage to them. However, be careful in winter that the plants are not exposed to floor-level draughts and ensure they will survive the low-light conditions frequently found at floor-level. If the area is draughty in winter it is best to use the hardiest of variegated foliage plants. In summer there is no reason to think that flowering types will not grow satisfactorily in such positions – as long as they are not constantly being knocked.

Keeping plants in their own pots

Rather than planting individual plants in one large container it is better to leave them in their own pots and just to group them. Each plant – especially during winter – needs to be watered individually to satisfy its own distinctive need for water. If all the plants are in the same soil this becomes impossible. If, however, you have a large, ornate container that you wish to use as a decorative feature in its own right – as well as to hold plants – the individual pots can be placed in it and moist peat packed around them. Remember though that ornamental plant pots may be damaged by the acids in the peat and constant moisture, and should be replaced with clay pots. By doing this the pots can still be watered individually.

Corner groups

Several plants in the corner of a room – giving interest at different heights – can be very attractive. If the area is cool and light a half-standard fuchsia placed in the corner with flowering plants around is ideal.

Window sill groups These are ideal places for many plants, but take care that the window sill is protected from water draining from the pots. Long plastic trays are excellent for this and moist peat can be packed around them to reduce moisture loss. As well as providing a home for mature plants, large plants still in their infancy can be placed on window sills. For instance, a weeping fig set to one side of the window will give a good display before it grows so large that it has to be placed on the floor.

ARCHITECTURAL PLANTS

Eye catchers There are a few foliage plants – and they need not be exceptionally large – with such distinctive outlines and leaf shapes that they can be strategically placed to attract the eye or perhaps complement a feature in the room.

Stately palms Few other plants can match the grace of palms, and they have been used in the home for decoration certainly since the Victorians made them popular. Many of the large ones, such as *Howeia forsteriana* (also sold as *Kentia forsteriana*) with a height up to 3m (10ft), 1.8m (6ft) spread and feathery, graceful drooping fronds, and the date palm (*Phoenix canariensis*) which frequently rises to 1.8m (6ft) and spreads at its top, are worth growing. These tall palms are best stood on the floor, but some of the lower-growing ones are better seen when positioned on stands. These include the parlour palm (*Chamaedorea elegans*, often sold as *Neanthe bella*) and the butterfly palm (*Chrysalidocarpus lutescens*) often sold as *Areca lutescens*). The butterfly palm is very attractive, the leaves initially joined at their tips giving a skeletonized appearance before expanding.

The palm-like dracaenas These are often called ribbon plants because their leaves are frequently striped. Although most of them are ultimately tree-like they are slow growing enough to make excellent houseplants. *Dracaena deremensis* easily rises to 1.2m (4ft) or more, with a tuft of sword-like glossy dark green leaves with silver strips down them. The dragon tree (*Dracaena draco*) and *Dracaena fragrans* are also worth growing. In its native habitat in tropical Guinea *Dracaena fragrans* will grow to 6m (20ft). 'Massangeana', the one usually sold as a houseplant, has cream-striped foliage.

The sword-like yuccas Several hardy yuccas grow well outside in gardens, but some tender ones such as *Yucca elephantipes* (sometimes sold as *Yucca guatemalensis*) are suited to the home, bearing long, sword-shaped and sharply-pointed glossy green leaves. As it ages it tends to bush out from its base. If you have young children beware of its pointed leaves which are extremely sharp.

Swiss Cheese Plant This has become one of the most popular houseplants, able with its large, glossy-green and deeply incised leaves to become a talking point wherever it is placed, but it does need a temperature of 13°C (55°F) to maintain healthy growth.

The ficus family The India rubber plant (*Ficus elastica*) is so well known that it hardly needs description, only to say that eventually it makes tree-like proportions with a bushy habit at its base. For this reason it is a useful 'architectural' plant for filling a large area. The fiddle-back fig (*Ficus lyrata*) similarly attains tree-like stature with large, fiddle-shaped leaves, and the weeping fig (*Ficus benjamina*) is also vigorous, frequently attaining 1.8m (6ft) with drooping, spear-shaped dark green leaves.

FLAMBOYANT PLANTS

BOUGAINVILLEA

One of the easiest is bougainvillea. The flowers remain brilliant for several months from summer to autumn and are borne in great profusion, creating a most striking sight. The plants literally glow with colour – rich red, purple and orange shades predominating.

There are about 16 species of bougainvillea, most of them scrambling climbers of shrubby character and originating from South America. There are a number of delightful and attractive hybrids. A common name sometimes given to these plants is paper flower.

The best bougainvillea for room cultivation is *B. glabra*. They have the great advantage that they will give lots of colour as small and young plants. By suitable training, they can be kept compact and bushy and dissuaded from rambling.

Young plants can be grown in 15-20cm (6-8in) pots, John Innes potting compost No. 2 suiting them very well. If you wish to restrict development, snip off the tips of the stems when they reach 15cm (6in) long in their early stages. This encourages the free production of more shoots to give a bushy habit. These shoots can then be allowed to grow as much as space permits. If a plant with a taller habit is wanted, provide a cane for support to the desired height (usually about 1.2-1.5m (4-5ft) high is advisable). Allow one or more stems to grow up the support, securing where necessary. Side shoots on the main stem, or stems, should then be cut back to about 15cm (6in) from the main shoots.

A position in good light is absolutely vital. Keep the plants well watered in summer, spraying them regularly. In autumn, when flowering is over, reduce watering and rest the plants. In winter, give only sufficient water to prevent the compost drying out completely. When growth begins again, watering can gradually be resumed.

Cutting back bougainvilleas do not like being continuously cut back. In conservatories they are best allowed as much freedom as possible. Train them on wires or on a wall trellis.

Propogation can be effected from cuttings taken in summer, but they need about 21°C (70°F) for rooting. The seed is easy to germinate, although it is a gamble whether a plant will be produced up to the standard of the named hybrids.

STEPHANOTIS

Another flamboyant climber is *Stephanotis floribunda*, popularly called the wax flower because of the texture of the flowers. It is also called the Madagascar jasmine because of the exquisite and powerful scent of the flowers. This species frequently appears in florists' shops as a houseplant, and is then usually in flower and trained around and over a wire loop. The leaves are evergreen, bluntly spear-shaped, thick, green and shiny, making the plant usefully decorative the year round. The flowers are tubular, with flared petals at the tip, giving a starry effect. They are born in clusters, and are waxy white. These flowers are born very freely from May to October on well grown specimens. One small plant fills the home with scent.

Size Although when bought this plant is relatively small, it is able to reach at least 3m (10ft) in height, climbing by means of its twining stems. If height and space allow, it is a good idea carefully to disentangle the stems from the wire loop and pot into a larger pot equipped with stout bamboo canes.

Conservatories This species also make a superb conservatory plant, but its temperature requirement is a minimum of about 10°C (50°F) in winter, and preferably a few degrees higher.

Composts The plant grows extremely well in the modern peat-based potting composts, and in summer should be given moderate humidity and slight shade. It needs to be freely watered.

Pots By keeping the plants in relatively small pots, their growth and development will be slowed down, which is helpful when limited for space. However, if this is done the plants must be fed properly during their growing period, using a balanced houseplant fertilizer. Restriction of the pot's size also tends to increase the freedom of flowering.

In winter, reduce watering to maintain only moist conditions for the roots. If kept on the dry side the plants may survive temperatures much lower than the minimum recommended. They will probably lose leaves and become tatty-looking, but resume growth with the return of warmer conditions in spring. However, too much chill for too long is very risky and the plants may die.

OLEANDER

Oleander, sometimes called rose bay, and it is a shrub that will reach a considerable size, although it can be flowered easily in small pots. Seedlings, for example, will flower in the third year from sowing, in 18cm (7in) pots. N.B. The stems and leaves of this plant are highly toxic.

The plant is extremely easy to grow and has pleasing, slightly shiny, spear-shaped evergreen foliage, as well as a wonderful show of flowers from summer to autumn.

Types There are a number of types bearing large clusters of flowers in rich red to purplish shades, pink and white. The blossom may be single or double. There is also a cultivar with smaller but very tight double flowers and a form with cream-variegated foliage and pink flowers. Anyone with a spacious conservatory, little more than frost-free in winter, could form a most attractive collection of these plants. Neriums are also extremely useful for cool porches, entrance halls or foyers, provided the light is good.

The plant grows well in any of the usual potting composts. It often grows naturally in very moist soils and should be watered well from spring to autumn. In winter very little water is needed, usually just enough to prevent drying out. If the temperature is very low, watering should be even more sparing.

Where space is limited the development of neriums must be checked by drastic cutting back after flowering. New shoots will arise from the base. It is important to remove the shoots that grow from the bases of the flower trusses promptly. If this is not done the plants soon become large, straggly and ungainly. Even with constant cutting back and pruning, moving on to a 25cm (10in) pot or small tub is usually necessary. Cuttings taken in summer usually root easily if stood in a jar of water.

STRELITZIA

The bird of paradise flower, once seen, is never forgotten. It is a native of South Africa and belongs to the banana family. In spite of its spectacular appearance it is one of the easiest houseplants to grow. Moreover, it will delight you with its amazing flowers at Christmas time, as well as in summer.

The plant is clump-forming, growing as rather fan-shaped groups of foliage. The leaves are large, stout, bluntly spear-shaped, evergreen and borne on long stout stems spear-fashion. The entire flower is shaped like a bird's head, hence its common name.

Well grown plants produce two or more flowers twice a year at the times already stated, and this assumes they are growing in 25cm (10in) pots. The flowers are long-lasting and can be cut for floral decoration.
Young strelitzia plants are now sold by a number of nurseries.

When received, they should be given pots just large enough to take the roots comfortably. Any of the potting composts can be used.

Flowering Plants will not flower until they have reached maturity. From seed this may take from about three to five years. Before flowering, the plants will have to be large enough to demand 25cm (10in) pots. Flowering may be encouraged by keeping the plants slightly pot-bound, but feeding must not be neglected during summer. If plants tend to be reluctant to flower, a little superphosphate incorporated with the upper layers of compost in spring may help. Once flowering begins, it will usually be repeated every year afterwards. The plants will eventually need dividing. This is best done in early spring. It may be quite a mammoth operation and the plant is best cut through with a very sharp knife, since this does less damage to the very fleshy roots than attempts to pull them apart, which may cause bruising and lead to rotting.

TIBOUCHINA

Because of its exquisite flowers, like giant purple-blue pansies with satin-like petals, borne from summer to autumn, *Tibouchina semidecandra* has long been a highly prized conservatory plant, and has now been introduced as a houseplant. In a modern home, with large picture-windows, it will grow quite well. Although native to Brazil, it is easy to grow with a minimum temperature of about 7-10°C (45-50°F). As well as a profusion of glorious flowers, about 10cm (4in) across, the velvety dark-green leaves may give reddish tints in autumn where conditions are cool. The plant is then only semi-evergreen.

As a houseplant, tibouchina can be conveniently accommodated in 18cm (7in) pots, using any of the modern potting composts, preferably a rich one such as John Innes potting compost No. 3. Give one or more bamboo canes as necessary for support and secure the stems as they grow. If the plant is a young one bought in spring, it may need stopping to encourage several shoots which subsequently should be trained up canes. If possible, give young plants a minimum temperature of 10°C (50°F). Plants grown in conservatories or garden rooms are best trained up a wall trellis and given either large pots or small tubs, or planted in a border.

COLOUR SCHEMES WITH HOUSEPLANTS

Colour schemes Adherence to strict rules about colour schemes inhibits experimentation, and positioning a plant against a colour-clashing background creates no real problem as it can soon be moved. It is better to have tried a plant in a certain position and to know it does not suit than to keep wondering if it would.

The colour contrast of plants against light-coloured backgrounds creates a feeling of spaciousness. Rooms with plants set in an all-white background appear clinical, whereas light-coloured plants against dark backgrounds create a sense of closeness and constriction. Soft pastel-coloured flowering plants against a warm, delicately patterned wallpaper immediately bring an overall feeling of comfort and ease. Therefore, high contrasts are best retained for dining areas and halls and gentle patterns and soft colours for living rooms and bedrooms. But that is not to say that a teenager might not be more appreciative of the bizarre rather than the orthodox. Very young children's bedrooms, of course, must not be garish, but give a feeling of security.

Orange and yellow flowers Black-eyed Susan (*Thunbergia alata*) is always a summer delight with its chocolate-brown centred orange-yellow flowers. Chrysanthemums, in variety, crocus, daffodils and primulas all have varieties that parade these colours. And the slipper flower (*Calceolaria* × *herbeohybrida*) has yellow flowers, often speckled and dabbled a range of other colours.

Orange and yellow foliage *Dieffenbachia picta* 'Exotica' (often sold as *Dieffenbachia maculata* 'Exotica') has leaves suffused with pale yellow. By the way, this plant is known as the dumb cane, the sap being poisonous. Keep the plant out of reach of animals and children. The ever-reliable coleus often shows orange and yellow foliage, as do many varieties of *Codiaeum variegatum pictum*.

Red and pink flowers Cyclamen and busy Lizzie (*Impatiens*) both have forms with these attractive colours, as does *Cineraria cruenta* (often sold as *Senecio*), gloxinia (*Sinningia speciosa*) hybrids also produce red and pink flowers.

Red and pink foliage Coleus are like the Jacob's Coat of the colour world for foliage, some inevitably displaying these colours. If you already have plants displaying these colours you may wish to perpetuate them from cuttings. The cabbage palms *Cordyline fruticosa* 'Firebrand' and 'Guilfoylei' both have leaves with pink or red. Many forms of caladium also display these colours.

Blue flowers *Campanula isophylla*, varieties of hyacinths and *Ipomoea rubro-caerulea* are all known for their blue flowers. Some hydrangeas have blue flower heads.

Blue foliage *Eucalyptus gunnii*, *Aechmea fasciata* (also sold as *Aechmea rhodocyanea* or *Billbergia rhodocyanea*) and many species of sedum have bluish-green leaves.

Purple flowers The Cape primrose (Streptocarpus) is a real summer delight with its foxglove-like flowers. The variety 'Constant Nymph' displays blue-purple flowers with darker veins in its throat. *Saintpaulias*, with their wide colour range, also display this colour. Other plants include crocus, cineraria (*Senecio*), *Brunfelsia calycina* and *Browallia speciosa*.

Purple foliage Perhaps the most distinctive of these is *Setcreasea purpurea*, with long, purple leaves and a sprawling but neat habit. The climbing and trailing *Gynura aurantiaca* has eye-catching leaves smothered with bright purple hairs. Its only failing is its grounsel-like yellow flowers that have an unpleasant aroma. But these February flowers can always be cut off. *Iresine herbstii* develops shiny, heart-shaped purple leaves. It does best in good light.

White flowers As well as the blue-flowered *Campanula isophylla* there is a white-flowered form. Cyclamen, hyacinths, daffodils, and chrysanthemums also have white-flowered varieties. Two heavily-scented climbing plants for the home are the Madagascar jasmine (*Stephanotis floribunda*) and *Jasminum polyanthum*. Both need their own supporting framework so that they can be grown in a conservatory or greenhouse when not in flower. Gardenias, with their heavily-scented white flowers, can be grown in the home but they do require high temperatures and a heated greenhouse or conservatory in which they can be grown the rest of the year.

PLANT DISPLAY

CAMOUFLAGING UNSIGHTLY FEATURES

Nature's way All houses have some feature best hidden or blended into its surrounds. Modernized Victorian or Edwardian houses may have walls festooned with gas or water piping, or even electricity conduit. Modern homes that have had home extensions added to them may have similar problems. Such unsightly features, could, of course, be boarded over, but this might create problems should maintenance be needed and will also be expensive. Far better to use plants with foliage that can be trained over them. But take care the foliage does not touch hot-water pipes, although these can be lagged.

Some useful trailing and climbing foliage plants Many of these are excellent for training as a screen, such as the Canary Island ivy (*Hedera canariensis* 'Variegata'), *Hedera helix* 'Chicago', grape ivy (*Rhoicissus rhomboidea*), sweetheart vine (*Philodendron scandens*)

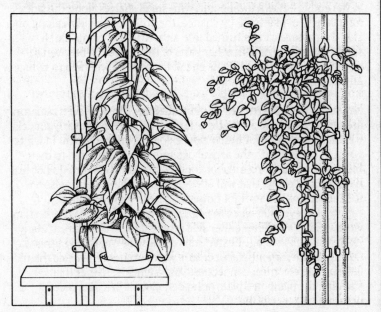

and kangaroo vine (*Cissus antarctica*). Some good trailers include the devil's ivy (*Scindapsus aureus*) and its variegated dapple-white relative *Scindapsus aureus* 'Marble Queen'. The ever-reliable tradescantias and *Zebrina pendula* can also be used.

Improving outside views Few gardens are brilliant in colour the whole year and a window opening on to a dreary view may benefit from a few plants. Plants can be stood on window sills, but for extra display a shelf or two placed across the window will enable more plants to be housed. Position trailing foliage plants at either side on the top shelf. The shelves often prevent casement windows being opened and the whole display may have to be adjusted during summer, when in any case there is colour in the garden to look out upon.

Giving purpose to small places Flats formed from old Victorian houses often have odd-shaped rooms or narrow passages that have no practical purpose. Narrow passages that have been blocked off can be turned into pleasant retreats by placing a large foliage plant at the end to act as a focal point, with small shelves along the sides for a variety of plants. If, by chance, the area has a window along one side the passage can be turned into an area where plants barely surviving dull corners in other parts of the house can be given a sojourn. Mirrors placed at the end of the passage will help to reduce any feeling of claustrophobia.

Seasonal improvements to old radiators Most modern radiators are unobtrusive and aesthetic as far as they can be, but early models were less pleasing. Not much can be done to improve them in winter when in use but with the arrival of summer a board fitted to their tops can be a standing area for trailing foliage plants. But do not just have trailing plants that will obviously cover the radiator, also include one or two upright flowering plants that will initially capture the eye. A *Jasminum polyanthum* in the centre with Persian violets (*Exacum affine*) either side is bound to create interest. Many electrical night-storage heater units can also be improved in this way during summer months, but ensure water cannot drip inside them and damage electrical connections and elements. Rather than standing the plant on a plate or holder, place it in a deep-sided ornamental pot or dish.

Fooling the eye Not all rooms are perfectly shaped; some are too high, others excessively long and narrow. For long and narrow rooms large foliage plants and hanging-baskets assist in dividing up the area, or at least in arresting the eye. Victorian rooms are frequently imposingly high and unless the eye is captured by a focal point relatively low in the room the eye will wander too much. However, it must be said that although high-ceilinged rooms are difficult to heat adequately in winter, during summer they present a cool, light, airy atmosphere so desired by many plants. And they do give the opportunity to grow large palms and foliage plants.

Creating focal points All rooms need an area that creates interest and initially attracts the eye. Unfortunately, many modern centrally-heated homes that formerly relied upon fireplaces to do this job are now box-like. The same applies to many converted flats that initially boasted attractive fireplaces. Collections of plants, some large and permanent, others ephemeral, present only during a relatively brief flowering period, can assume this role. They can even be integrated with an attractive piece of furniture. And because they are movable they need not be positioned in the centre of one wall, but in a corner or perhaps at the opposite end of the room to the window. In such a position a carefully placed mirror will directly reflect light entering the room.

HIGHLIGHTING GOOD FEATURES

Capturing attention Arches, window surrounds and unused fireplaces are just a few of the features in a home that can be enhanced and highlighted by plants. And in many instances this can be accomplished quite cheaply. For instance, a small window perhaps high up in a wall would benefit from the trailing mid-green, toothed, heart-shaped leaves and star-shaped August and September blue flowers of *Campanula isophylla*. Should this colour not suit the decor then a white form is available, and both are inexpensive and easily grown, demanding little attention but water and the removal of dead flowers.

Highlighting windows Small windows, as we have seen, can be enhanced, but so can large picture windows and French windows. To take the eye directly to large windows the wooden and often not very aesthetic surrounds can be camouflaged with climbing foliage plants such as the grape ivy (*Rhoicissus rhomboidea*). In a normal-sized pot it easily grows to 1.2m (4ft) but if given a large one will continue well up to the ceiling, even in high Victorian rooms. A few twining and scrambling shoots can be taken over the top of the window. It clings to a framework by means of tendrils, displaying dark green shiny leaves formed of three-stalked diamond-shaped leaflets.

Several other climbing foliage plants will create a frame for the window, including the kangaroo vine (*Cissus antarctica*) and *Philodendron scandens* with dark green heart-shaped leaves. If the decor demands variegated foliage then the lax appearance of *Cissus discolor* with triangular, vivid-green leaves with purple undersides and white-and-purple mottled uppersides is well worth considering, but it does require a high temperature and may drop a few leaves during winter. The ever-reliable Canary Island ivy (*Hedera canariensis* 'Variegata') with its large, variegated leaves is always a delight and superb for cool areas.

Plants for alcoves If you have one attractive alcove you are blessed; if you have two you are twice blessed. Small, recessed areas – perhaps illuminated – can be effectively used to display plants. If the recess has a rounded top with a concealed light the plants look even better. Don't clutter these areas with plants packed cheek by jowl. Rather, use just one plant in each. Ferns take kindly to these areas and if large enough the robust and foliage-packed Boston fern (*Nephrolepis exaltata* 'Bostoniensis') or spreading *Adiantum raddianum* are excellent. Because these have a spreading and somewhat trailing sweep to their fronds they are ideal for placing on strong glass shelves fixed two-thirds up the alcove. If, however, as in some Victorian houses there is a small cupboard at the base of the alcove this can be used to house ferns best admired from above, such as the bird's nest fern (*Asplenum nidus*) or button fern (*Pellaea rotundifolia*).

Alternatively, large but vulnerable specialist plants such as palms can be safely placed there, out of the direct routes of children. Such a palm – and one that seldom fails to attract the attention of visitors – is the butterfly palm (*Chrysalidocarpus lutescens*, but also widely known as *Areca lutescens*). This produces small clumps with bamboo-like stems and glossy yellowish leaves.

Highlighting arches Often integral sitting and dining areas are separated only by an arch or beam across the room. Arches, with their attractively curved sides, can be enhanced by setting plants in wall plant holders around them, although if the room has a natural clinical appearance it would be a mistake to use too many and clutter the surface. Instead, a wall-mounted small-leaved variegated ivy on either side helps to take away the sense of bareness but at the same time does not intrude on the lines of the arch. On the dining area side of the arch the theme could be changed with perhaps a climbing foliage plant trailing around the arch.

Enhancing furniture Sometimes pieces of furniture with large, polished surfaces can be enhanced with an attractive container and plant that harmonizes with them. Copper and brass are metals that have a pleasingly warm appearance with low tray-like containers with mound-forming foliage plants such as *Begonia boweri*, with small, emerald-green leaves blotched chocolate-brown, are a delight. In such places do not use plants that dominate the setting as they detract attention from the piece of furniture.

PLANT DISPLAY

Houseplant Care and Selection Chart

NAME	TEMP	TYPE	INTEREST/TIME	LIGHT NEEDED	SPACE/POT SIZE	CULTURE
ABUTILON HYBRIDS	5°C/41°F	shrub	flowers/years	slight shade	small/18cm/7in	easy
ACACIA ARMATA	5°C/41°F	shrub	flower/fol/years	good light	small/18cm/7in	easy
ACACIA DEALBATA	5°C/41°F	shrub	flower/fol/years	good light	mod/23cm/9in	easy
ACACIA PODALYRIIFOLIA	5°C/41°F	shrub	flower/fol/years	good light	mod/23cm/9in	easy
ACACIA VERTICILLATA	5°C/41°F	shrub	flower/fol/years	good light	small/18cm/7in	easy
ACALYPHA HISPIDA	16°C/61°F	shrub	flowers/years	good light	small/18cm/7in	difficult*
ACHIMENES HYBRIDS	13°C/55°F	rhizomes	flowers/years	slight shade	small/13cm/5in	easy
ACORUS GRAMINEUS	hardy	aquatic	foliage/years	bright	small/18cm/7in	easy*
ADIANTUM CAPILLUS-VENERIS	5°C/41°F	fern	foliage/years	slight shade	small/13cm/5in	easy
ADIANTUM RADDIANUM	10°C/50°F	fern	foliage/years	mod. shade	small/18cm/7in	moderate
AECHMEA CHANTINII	10°C/50°F	bromeliad	flower/fol/years	slight shade	small/13cm/5in	easy*
AECHMEA FASCIATA	10°C/50°F	bromeliad	flower/fol/years	slight shade	small/13cm/5in	easy*
AECHMEA FULGENS	10°C/50°F	bromeliad	flower/fol/years	slight shade	small/13cm/5in	easy*
AEONIUM ARBOREUM	10°C/50°F	succulent	form/years	good light	small/13cm/5in	easy
AEONIUM DOMESTICUM VARIEGATUM	10°C/50°F	succulent	form/years	good light	small/13cm/5in	easy
AGAVE AMERICANA	5°C/41°F	succulent	form/flower/years	good light	mod/23cm/9in	easy
AGLAONEMA COMMUTATUM	13°C/55°F	evergreen	foliage/years	good light	mod/18cm/7in	moderate
AGLAONEMA MODESTUM	13°C/55°F	evergreen	foliage/years	shade	small/13cm/5in	easy

NOTE: The temperature given is the minimum temperature required.
The pot size given is the size in which the plant will be happiest for a considerable time.

Species	Temperature	Type	Category	Light	Size	Ease
ALOE SPECIES	7°C/45°F	succulent	form/flower/years	good light	small/13cm/5in	easy
ANANAS BRACTEATUS STRIATUS	13°C/55°F	bromeliad	fol/flower/years	good light	small/18cm/7in	moderate*
ANANAS COMOSUS	13°C/55°F	bromeliad	fol/flower/years	good light	small/18cm/7in	moderate*
ANGULOA CLOWESII	10°C/50°F	orchid	flower/scent/years	slight-mod.	small/13cm/5in	moderate*
ANTHURIUM ANDREANUM	13°C/55°F	evergreen	flower/fol/years	slight shade	small/13cm/5in	moderate
ANTHURIUM CRYSTALLINUM	13°C/55°F	evergreen	foliage/years	mod. shade	mod/18cm/7in	difficult
ANTHURIUM SCHERZERIANUM	16°C/61°F	evergreen	flower/fol/years	slight shade	small/18cm/7in	easy
APHELANDRA SQUARROSA	10°C/50°F	evergreen	fol/flower/years	slight shade	small/18cm/7in	easy
APOROCACTUS FLAGELLIFORMIS	13°C/55°F	cactus	form/flower/years	slight shade	small/13cm/5in	easy
ARAUCARIA HETEROPHYLLA	7°C/45°F	shrub	foliage/years	slight shade	mod/23cm/9in	mod-easy
ARECA LUTESCENS	18°C/64°F	palm	foliage/years	slight shade	large/25cm/10in	difficult*
ASPARAGUS DENSIFLORUS	5°C/41°F	evergreen	foliage/years	slight shade	small/18cm/7in	very easy
ASPARAGUS SETACEUS	5°C/41°F	evergreen	foliage/years	slight shade	small/13cm/5in	very easy
ASPIDISTRA ELATIOR	5°C/41°F	evergreen	foliage/years	slight shade	small/18cm/7in	very easy
ASPLENIUM NIDUS	13°C/55°F	fern	foliage/years	mod. shade	small/18cm/7in	easy
ASTROPHYTUM MYRIOSTIGMA	7°C/45°F	cactus	form/flower/years	good light	small/13cm/5in	easy
AUCUBA JAPONICA	hardy	shrub	foliage/years	not critical	mod/23cm/9in	easy
AZALEA	see entry	shrub	flowers/see entry	slight shade	small/18cm/7in	see entry*
BEGONIA BOWERI	10°C/50°F	evergreen	fol/flower/years	slight shade	small/13cm/5in	easy
BEGONIA CATHAYANA	10°C/50°F	evergreen	foliage/years	mod. shade	mod/18cm/7in	moderate

(*=special requirement: see entry)

NAME	TEMP	TYPE	INTEREST/TIME	LIGHT NEEDED	SPACE/POT SIZE	CULTURE
BEGONIA COCCINEA	10°C/50°F	evergreen	fol/flower/years	slight shade	mod/18cm/7in	easy
BEGONIA CORALLINA	10°C/50°F	evergreen	fol/flower/years	slight shade	mod/18cm/7in	easy
BEGONIA FUCHSIOIDES	10°C/50°F	evergreen	fol/flower/years	slight shade	mod/18cm/7in	easy
BEGONIA HAAGEANA	10°C/50°F	evergreen	fol/flower/years	good light	mod/18cm/7in	easy
BEGONIA MANICATA	10°C/50°F	evergreen	fol/flower/years	slight shade	small/13cm/5in	easy
BEGONIA MASONIANA	10°C/50°F	evergreen	foliage/years	slight shade	small/13cm/5in	easy
BEGONIA METALLICA	10°C/50°F	evergreen	fol/flowers/years	slight shade	mod/18cm/7in	easy
BEGONIA REX	10°C/50°F	evergreen	foliage/years	slight shade	small/13cm/5in	easy
BEGONIA SEMPERFLORENS	10°C/50°F	evergreen	flowers/few years	good light	small/13cm/5in	easy
BEGONIA TUBERHYBRIDA	10°C/50°F	tuberous	flowers/years	slight shade	small/18cm/7in	easy
BELOPERONE GUTTATA	7°C/45°F	shrub	flowers/years	good light	small/18cm/7in	easy
BILLBERGIA NUTANS	7°C/45°F	bromeliad	flower/years	good light	small/13cm/5in	easy*
BILLBERGIA PYRAMIDALIS	7°C/45°F	bromeliad	flower/years	good light	small/13cm/5in	easy*
BILLBERGIA × WINDII	7°C/45°F	bromeliad	flower/years	good light	small/13cm/5in	easy*
BLECHNUM GIBBUM	13°C/55°F	fern	foliage/years	slight shade	small/18cm/7in	moderate
BOUGAINVILLEA GLABRA	7°C/45°F	shrub/cl.	flowers/years	good light	large/23cm/9in	easy
BRASSIA VERRUCOSA	13°C/55°F	orchid	flowers/years	mod. shade	small/18cm/7in	moderate*
BROWALLIA SPECIOSA	13°C/55°F	biennial	flowers/months	slight shade	small/13cm/5in	easy

Name	Temp	Type	Feature	Light	Size	Difficulty
BRUNFELSIA CALYCINA	13°C/55°F	evergreen	flower/years	good light	small/13cm/5in	moderate
CALADIUM BICOLOR	15°C/59°F	tuberous	foliage/years	slight shade	small/13cm/5in	easy
CALANTHE VESTITA	15°C/59°F	orchid	flower/years	slight shade	small/18cm/7in	moderate*
CALATHEA LANCIFOLIA	13°C/55°F	evergreen	foliage/years	mod. shade	small/13cm/5in	mod/easy
CALATHEA MAKOYANA	13°C/55°F	evergreen	foliage/years	mod. shade	small/13cm/5in	mod/easy
CALATHEA ORNATA	13°C/55°F	evergreen	foliage/years	mod. shade	small/13cm/5in	mod/easy
CALATHEA ZEBRINA	15°C/59°F	evergreen	foliage/years	mod. shade	small/18cm/7in	difficult
CALCEOLARIA	5°C/41°F	biennial	flowers/weeks	mod. shade	small/13cm/5in	easy
CALLISIA ELEGANS	10°C/50°F	trailer	foliage/years	good light	small/13cm/5in	easy
CAMPANULA ISOPHYLLA	4°C/40°F	trailer	flowers/years	slight shade	small/13cm/5in	easy
CANNA HYBRIDS	10°C/50°F	rhizomes	flower/fol/years	good light	mod/23cm/11in	easy
CAPSICUM ANNUUM	16°C/61°F	annual	berries/weeks	good light	small/13cm/5in	very easy
CATHARANTHUS ROSEUS	13°C/55°F	shrub	flowers/fol/years	slight shade	small/18cm/9in	easy
CATTLEYA BOWRINGIANA	10°C/50°F	orchid	flowers/years	good light	small/18cm/9in	moderate*
CELOSIA ARGENTEA	7°C/45°F	annual	'flowers'/months	good light	small/13cm/5in	easy
CEPHALOCEREUS SENILIS	10°C/50°F	cactus	form/years	good light	small/13cm/5in	easy
CEREUS PERUVIANUS	10°C/50°F	cactus	form/years	good light	small/13cm/5in	easy
CEROPEGIA WOODII	10°C/50°F	suc/trail	'leaves'/fl/years	good light	small/13cm/5in	easy
CHAMAECEREUS SILVESTRII	5°C/41°F	cactus	form/flower/years	good light	small/13cm/5in	very easy
CHAMAEDOREA ELEGANS BELLA	10°C/50°F	palm	foliage/years	slight shade	mod/23cm/9in	moderate

NAME	TEMP	TYPE	INTEREST/TIME	LIGHT NEEDED	SPACE/POT SIZE	CULTURE
CHAMAEROPS HUMILIS	7°C/45°F	palm	foliage/years	slight shade	large/23cm/9in	easy
CHLOROPHYTUM COMOSUM	7°C/45°F	trailer	foliage/years	slight shade	small/18cm/7in	easy
CHRYSANTHEMUM	4°C/40°F	perennial	flowers/months	slight shade	small/18cm/7in	easy
CISSUS ANTARCTICA	7°C/45°F	climber	foliage/years	good light	large/23cm/9in	easy
CISSUS DISCOLOR	16°C/61°F	trailer	foliage/years	good light	small/18cm/7in	difficult
CITRUS MICROCARPA	7°C/45°F	shrub	fruit/flower/years	good light	small/18cm/7in	easy*
CLIVIA MINIATA	10°C/50°F	evergreen	flowers/years	slight shade	small/18cm/7in	easy
CODIAEUM VARIEGATUM	15°C/59°F	evergreen	foliage/years	good light	small/18cm/7in	moderate
COFFEA ARABICA	13°C/55°F	evergreen	foliage/years	good light	small/18cm/7in	moderate
COLEUS	13°C/55°F	annual	foliage/months	good light	small/13cm/5in	easy
COLUMNEA × BANKSII	13°C/55°F	trailer	flower/fol/years	slight shade	small/13cm/5in	moderate*
COLUMNEA GLORIOSA	13°C/55°F	trailer	flower/fol/years	slight shade	small/13cm/5in	moderate*
CORDYLINE AUSTRALIS	7°C/45°F	shrub	foliage/years	good light	mod/18cm/7in	easy
CORDYLINE TERMINALIS	13°C/55°F	shrub	foliage/years	slight shade	small/18cm/7in	moderate
CRASSULA ARGENTEA	7°C/45°F	succulent	foliage/years	good light	small/18cm/7in	very easy
CRASSULA FALCATA	7°C/45°F	succulent	fol/flower/years	good light	small/13cm/5in	easy
CRINUM × POWELLII	2°C/36°F	bulb	flower/years	good light	mod/23cm/9in	easy
CROCUS	hardy	corm	flowers/years	good light	groups	easy

Name	Temp	Type	Grown for	Light	Size	Difficulty
CROSSANDRA INFUNDIBULIFORMIS	13°C/55°F	shrub	flower/fol/years	slight shade	small/13cm/5in	moderate
CRYPTANTHUS BEUCKERII	10°C/50°F	bromeliad	foliage/years	good light	small/13cm/5in	easy*
CRYPTANTHUS BROMELIODIES	10°C/50°F	bromeliad	foliage/years	good light	small/13cm/5in	easy*
CRYPTANTHUS FOSTERIANUS	10°C/50°F	bromeliad	foliage/years	good light	small/13cm/5in	easy*
CRYPTANTHUS ZONATUS	10°C/50°F	bromeliad	foliage/years	good light	small/13cm/5in	easy*
CTENANTHE OPPENHEIMIANA						
CUPHEA IGNEA	7°C/45°F	annual	flowers/weeks	not fussy	small/13cm/5in	easy
CYANOTIS KEWENSIS	10°C/50°F	trail/cl	fol/flower/years	slight shade	small/13cm/5in	easy
CYCLAMEN PERSICUM	10°C/50°F	corm	fol/fl/some years	mod. shade	small/13cm/5in	easy
CYMBIDIUM	7°C/45°F	orchids	flowers/years	good light	small/18cm/7in	easy
CYPERUS ALTERNIFOLIUS	10°C/50°F	aquatic	foliage/years	good light	small/13cm/5in	easy*
CYPERUS PAPYRUS	10°C/50°F	aquatic	foliage/years	good light	mod/18cm/7in	easy*
CYRTOMIUM FALCATUM	7°C/45°F	fern	foliage/years	mod. shade	small/18cm/7in	easy
CYTISUS	7°C/45°F	shrub	flowers/years	slight shade	mod/18cm/7in	easy
DAVALLIA CANARIENSIS	5°C/41°F	fern	foliage/years	slight shade	small/13cm/5in	easy
DENDROBIUM INFUNDIBULUM	13°C/55°F	orchid	flowers/years	good light	small/18cm/7in	moderate*
DENDROBIUM SUPERBUM	13°C/55°F	orchid	flowers/years	good light	mod/18cm/7in	moderate*
DIDYMOCHLAENA TRUNCATULA	10°C/50°F	fern	foliage/years	shade	mod/18cm/7in	mod/easy
DIEFFENBACHIA MACULATA	15°C/59°F	evergreen	foliage/years	good light	mod/18cm/7in	difficult
DIONAEA MUSCIPULA	13°C/55°F	aquatic	traps/fl/years	good light	small/13cm/5in	mod/diff*

NAME	TEMP	TYPE	INTEREST/TIME	LIGHT NEEDED	SPACE/POT SIZE	CULTURE
DIPLADENIA SPLENDENS	13°C/55°F	climber	flower/fol/years	good light	mod/18cm/7in	moderate
DIZYGOTHECA ELEGANTISSIMA	16°C/60°F	shrub	foliage/years	good light	mod/18cm/7in	moderate
DRACAENA DEREMENSIS	13°C/55°F	shrub	foliage/years	slight shade	mod/18cm/7in	mod/diff
DRACAENA DRACO	7°C/45°F	shrub	foliage/years	good light	large/23cm/9in	easy
DRACAENA FRAGRANS	13°C/55°F	shrub	foliage/years	slight shade	mod/18cm/7in	moderate
DRACAENA MARGINATA	16°C/60°F	shrub	foliage/years	slight shade	mod/18cm/7in	mod/easy
DRACAENA SANDERIANA	13°C/55°F	shrub	foliage/years	slight shade	mod/18cm/7in	moderate
ECHEVERIA SETOSA	5°C/41°F	succulent	fol/fl/years	good light	small/13cm/5in	easy
ECHINOCACTUS GRUSONII	5°C/41°F	cactus	form/fl/years	good light	small/13cm/5in	easy
EPIPHYLLUM HYBRIDS	10°C/50°F	cactus	flowers/years	slight shade	small/18cm/7in	easy
EPIPREMNUM AUREUM	10°C/50°F	climber	foliage/years	slight shade	large/23cm/9in	moderate
ERICA HIEMALIS	5°C/41°F	shrub	flowers/years	good light	small/18cm/7in	moderate*
EUCALYPTUS CITRIODORA	7°C/45°F	shrub	fol/scent/years	slight shade	small/18cm/7in	mod/easy
EUCALYPTUS GLOBULUS	2°C/36°F	shrub	fol/scent/years	good light	large/23cm/9in	easy
EUCALYPTUS GUNNII	hardy	shrub	foliage/years	good light	large/23cm/9in	easy
EUONYMUS JAPONICUS	hardy	shrub	foliage/years	slight	small/18cm/7in	easy
EUPHORBIA MILII	13°C/55°F	succulent	bracts/years	good light	small/13cm/5in	easy
EUPHORBIA PULCHERRIMA	13°C/55°F	shrub	bracts/weeks	slight shade	small/13cm/5in	easy

EXACUM AFFINE	10°C/50°F	annual	fl/scent/weeks	slight shade	small/13cm/5in	easy
× FATSHEDERA	5°C/40°F	shrub/cl	foliage/years	slight shade	mod/23cm/9in	easy
FATSIA JAPONICA	hardy	shrub	foliage/years	not fussy	large/23cm/9in	very easy
FICUS BENGHALENSIS	15°C/59°F	shrub	foliage/years	good light	mod/18cm/7in	moderate
FICUS BENJAMINA	15°C/59°F	shrub	foliage/years	slight shade	mod/18cm/7in	moderate
FICUS DELTOIDEA	7°C/45°F	shrub	berry/fol/years	mod. shade	small/18cm/7in	easy
FICUS ELASTICA	15°C/59°F	shrub	foliage/years	good light	mod/18cm/7in	mod/easy
FICUS LYRATA	15°C/59°F	shrub	foliage/years	good light	mod/18cm/7in	mod/easy
FICUS PUMILA	7°C/45°F	climb/tr	foliage/years	mod. shade	small/13cm/5in	easy
FICUS RADICANS	16°C/61°F	trailer	foliage/years	slight shade	small/13cm/5in	easy
FITTONIA VERSCHAFFELTII	16°C/61°F	trailer	foliage/years	mod. shade	small/13cm/5in	mod/diff
FUCHSIA	5°C/41°F	shrub	flowers/years	slight shade	small/18cm/7in	easy
GARDENIA JASMINOIDES	15°C/59°F	shrub	fl/scent/years	slight shade	small/18cm/7in	mod/diff
GERBERA	10°C/50°F	perennial	flowers/years	slight shade	small/18cm/7in	easy
GLORIOSA ROTHSCHILDIANA	10°C/50°F	tuber/cl	flowers/years	slight shade	small/18cm/7in	easy
GREVILLEA ROBUSTA	7°C/45°F	shrub	foliage/years	not fussy	mod/18cm/7in	easy*
GUZMANIA LINGULATA	13°C/55°F	bromeliad	fol/flower/years	slight shade	small/13cm/5in	moderate*
GUZMANIA ZAHNII	13°C/55°F	bromeliad	fol/flower/years	slight shade	small/13cm/5in	moderate*
GYNURA AURANTIACA	13°C/55°F	trail/cl	foliage/fl/years	good light	small/13cm/5in	easy
GYNURA PROCUMBENS	13°C/55°F	climber	foliage/years	good light	small/13cm/5in	easy

NAME	TEMP	TYPE	INTEREST/TIME	LIGHT NEEDED	SPACE/POT SIZE	CULTURE
HEDERA CANARIENSIS	7°C/45°F	climber	foliage/years	not fussy	mod/23cm/9in	easy
HEDERA HELIX	7°C/45°F	climb/tr	foliage/years	not fussy	variable	easy
HELIOTROPIUM	7°C/45°F	perennial	fl/scent/some years	slight shade	small/13cm/5in	easy
HIBISCUS ROSA-SINENSIS	15°C/51°F	shrub	flowers/years	slight shade	mod/18cm/7in	easy
HIPPEASTRUM HYBRIDS	13°C/55°F	bulb	flowers/years	slight shade	small/18cm/7in	easy
HOWEIA BELMOREANA (KENTIA)	10°C/50°F	palm	foliage/years	slight shade	large/23cm/9in	moderate
HOWEIA FORSTERIANA (KENTIA)	10°C/50°F	palm	foliage/years	slight shade	large/23cm/9in	moderate
HOYA BELLA	10°C/50°F	shrub/tr	flowers/years	mod. shade	small/13cm/5in	easy
HOYA CARNOSA	5°C/41°F	climber	fol/fl/scent/years	not fussy	mod/18cm/7in	easy
HYACINTH	10°/50°F	bulb	flower/scent/years	not fussy	small/13cm/5in	easy
HYDRANGEA	7°C/45°F	shrub	flower/see entry	slight shade	small/18cm/7in	easy*
HYMENOCALLIS	7°C/45°F	bulb	flower/scent/years	slight shade	small/18cm/7in	easy
HYPOCYRTA GLABRA	15°C/59°F	shrub	flowers/years	mod. shade	small/13cm/5in	easy
HYPOESTES PHYLLOSTACHYA	10°C/50°F	evergreen	foliage/years	slight shade	small/13cm/5in	easy
IMPATIENS	13°C/55°F	annual	flowers/see entry	not fussy	small/13cm/5in	easy
IPOMOEA TRICOLOR	13°C/55°F	annual/cl	flowers/months	good light	small/18cm/7in	easy
IRESINE HERBSTII	13°C/55°F	evergreen	foliage/years	good light	small/13cm/5in	easy
IRIS (BULBOUS)	hardy	bulb	flowers/years	good light	groups	easy

Name	Temperature	Type	Features	Light	Size	Difficulty
JASMINUM POLYANTHUM	7°C/45°F	climber	flower/scent/years	good light	large/23cm/9in	easy
KALANCHOE BLOSSFELDIANA	7°C/45°F	succulent	flower/years	good light	small/13cm/5in	easy
LACHENALIA	10°C/50°F	bulb	flowers/years	slight shade	small/13cm/5in	easy
LAELIA ANCEPS	10°C/50°F	orchid	flowers/years	good light	small/18cm/7in	moderate*
LANTANA CAMARA	7°C/45°F	shrub	flowers/years	good light	small/18cm/7in	easy
LILY	13°C/55°F	bulb	flowers/scent/years	slight shade	small/18cm/7in	easy
LOBIVIA FAMATIMENSIS	2°C/36°F	cactus	form/flowers/years	good light	small/13cm/5in	easy
LYCASTE AROMATICA	10°C/50°F	orchid	flower/scent/years	slight shade	small/18cm/7in	moderate*
MAMMILLARIA BOCASANA	5°C/41°F	cactus	form/fl/berry/years	good light	small/13cm/5in	very easy
MARANTA LEUCONEURA	13°C/55°F	evergreen	foliage/years	mod. shade	small/13cm/5in	easy
MILTONIA SPECTABILIS	13°C/55°F	orchid	flowers/years	mod. shade	small/18cm/7in	moderate*
MIMULUS HYBRIDS	7°C/45°F	annual	flowers/some weeks	good light	small/13cm/5in	very easy
MONSTERA DELICIOSA	13°C/55°F	evergreen	foliage/years	slight shade	large 23cm/9in	easy
MUSA ENSETE	13°C/55°F	evergreen	foliage/years	slight shade	large/23cm/9in	easy
NARCISSUS	hardy	bulb	flower/scent/years	good light	small/18cm/7in	easy
NEOREGELIA CAROLINAE	13°C/55°F	bromeliad	fol/flower/years	good light	small/13cm/5in	easy*
NEOREGELIA SPECTABILIS	10°C/50°F	bromeliad	fol/flower/years	slight shade	small/13cm/5in	easy*
NEPHROLEPSIS EXALTATA BOSTONIENSIS	10°C/50°F	fern	foliage/years	slight shade	small/13cm/5in	easy

NAME	TEMP	TYPE	INTEREST/TIME	LIGHT NEEDED	SPACE/POT SIZE	CULTURE
NEPHROLEPSIS EXALTATA						
WHITMANII	10°C/50°F	fern	foliage/years	slight shade	small/13cm/5in	moderate
NERINE	10°C/50°F	bulb	flowers/years	slight shade	small/13cm/5in	easy
NERIUM OLEANDER	7°C/45°F	shrub	flowers/years	slight shade	mod/22cm/9in	easy
NERTERA GRANADENSIS	1°C/34°F	perennial	berry/years	good light	small/13cm/5in	moderate
NICANDRA PHYSALODES	hardy	annual	see entry/months	good light	small/13cm/5in	very easy
NOLINA RECURVATA	15°C/51°F	shrub	foliage/years	good light	mod/23cm/9in	easy
ODONTOGLOSSUM BICTONIENSE	10°C/50°F	orchid	flowers/years	slight shade	small/18cm/7in	moderate*
ODONTOGLOSSUM GRANDE	10°C/50°F	orchid	flowers/years	slight shade	small/18cm/7in	moderate*
ONCIDIUM ORNITHORHYNCHUM	10°C/50°F	orchid	flowers/years	mod. shade	small/13cm/5in	moderate*
OPUNTIA MICRODASYS	7°C/45°F	cactus	form/years	good light	small/13cm/5in	easy
OPUNTIA ROBUSTA	7°C/45°F	cactus	form/fl/years	good light	mod/18cm/7in	very easy
ORNITHOGALUM THYRSOIDES	7°C/45°F	bulb	flower/years	good light	small/18cm/7in	easy
PACHYPHYTUM OVIFERUM	10°C/50°F	succulent	form/years	good light	small/13cm/5in	easy
PACHYSTACHYS LUTEA	10°C/50°F	evergreen	fol/flower/years	good light	small/18cm/7in	easy
PAPHIOPEDILUM CALLOSUM	13°C/55°F	orchid	flower/years	mod. shade	small/18cm/7in	moderate*
PAPHIOPEDILUM INSIGNE	10°C/50°F	orchid	flower/years	mod. shade	small/18cm/7in	moderate*

Name	Temperature	Type	Flower/Foliage	Light	Size	Difficulty
PASSIFLORA CAERULEA	5°C/41°F	climber	flower/years	good light	large/23cm/9in	easy
PELARGONIUM (ALL TYPES)	10°C/50°F	perennial	flower/scent/years	good light	small/18cm/7in	easy
PELLAEA ROTUNDIFOLIA	5°C/41°F	fern	foliage	slight shade	small/18cm/7in	easy
PELLIONIA REPENS	13°C/55°F	evergreen	foliage/years	slight shade	small/13cm/5in	moderate
PEPEROMIA ARGYREIA	13°C/55°F	evergreen	foliage/years	slight shade	small/13cm/5in	difficult
PEPEROMIA CAPERATA	10°C/50°F	evergreen	fol/fl/years	slight shade	small/13cm/5in	moderate
PEPEROMIA GLABELLA	10°C/50°F	trailing	foliage/years	slight shade	small/13cm/5in	difficult
PEPEROMIA GRISEOARGENTE	10°C/50°F	evergreen	foliage/years	slight shade	small/13cm/5in	moderate
PEPEROMIA MAGNOLIFOLIA	10°C/50°F	evergreen	foliage/years	slight shade	small/13cm/5in	easy
PEPEROMIA MARMORATA	10°C/50°F	evergreen	foliage/years	slight shade	small/13cm/5in	easy
PEPEROMIA OBTUSIFOLIA	7°C/45°F	evergreen	fol/fl/years	slight shade	small/13cm/5in	very easy
PEPEROMIA SCANDENS	16°C/61°F	evergreen	foliage/years	slight shade	small/13cm/5in	difficult
PERSEA	5°C/41°F	shrub	foliage/years	good light	mod/18cm/7in	very easy
PHILODENDRON BIPENNIFOLIUM	13°C/55°F	climber	foliage/years	good light	large/23cm/9in	moderate*
PHILODENDRON BIPINNATIFIDUM	13°C/55°F	evergreen	foliage/years	good light	large/23cm/9in	moderate
PHILODENDRON DOMESTICUM	13°C/55°F	climber	foliage/years	good light	large/23cm/9in	moderate*
PHILODENDRON ERUBESCENS	13°C/55°F	climber	foliage/years	good light	large/23cm/9in	mod/easy*
PHILODENDRON MELANOCHRYSUM	13°C/55°F	climber	foliage/years	good light	large/23cm/9in	difficult*
PHILODENDRON SCANDENS	13°C/55°F	trail/cl	foliage/years	not fussy	small/13cm/5in	easy

NAME	TEMP	TYPE	INTEREST/TIME	LIGHT NEEDED	SPACE/POT SIZE	CULTURE
PHILODENDRON SELLOUM	13°C/55°F	evergreen	foliage/years	good light	large/23cm/9in	moderate
PHOENIX CANARIENSIS	10°C/50°F	palm	foliage/years	good light	large/23cm/9in	very easy
PHOENIX ROEBELENII	10°C/50°F	palm	foliage/years	slight shade	small/18cm/7in	moderate
PILEA CADIEREI	10°C/50°F	shrub	foliage/years	slight shade	small/13cm/5in	easy*
PILEA INVOLUCRATA	13°C/55°F	shrub	foliage/years	good light	small/13cm/5in	easy
PILEA MICROPHYLLA	10°C/50°F	shrub	foliage/see entry	slight shade	small/13cm/5in	easy
PILEA MOLLIS	10°C/50°F	evergreen	foliage/years	good light	small/13cm/5in	easy
PILEA NUMMULARIFOLIA	10°C/50°F	trailer	foliage/years	mod. shade	small/13cm/5in	easy
PIPER ORNATUM	16°C/61°F	climber	foliage/years	good light	small/18cm/7in	difficult*
PLATYCERIUM ALCICORNE	10°C/50°F	fern	foliage/years	slight shade	see entry	moderate*
PLECTANTHUS COLEOIDES	10°C/50°F	semi-tr	fol/fl/years	slight shade	small/13cm/5in	easy
PLECTANTHUS OERTENDAHLII	10°C/50°F	trailer	fol/fl/years	slight shade	small/13cm/5in	easy
PLUMBAGO AURICULATA	7°C/45°F	shrub/cl	flowers/years	good light	large 23cm/9in	easy
PRIMULA × KEWENSIS	5°C/41°F	perennial	flower/some years	slight shade	small/13cm/5in	easy
PRIMULA × POLYANTHA	hardy	perennial	flower/some years	slight shade	small/13cm/5in	easy
PRIMULA MALACOIDES	5°C/41°F	biennial	flower/weeks	slight shade	small/13cm/5in	easy
PRIMULA PRAENITENS	5°C/41°F	perennial	flower/some weeks	slight shade	small/13cm/5in	easy*
PRIMULA VULGARIS	hardy	perennial	flower/some years	slight shade	small/13cm/5in	easy

Name	Temperature	Type	Interest	Light	Size	Difficulty
PTERIS CRETICA ALBOLINEATA	7°C/45°F	fern	foliage/years	slight shade	small/13cm/5in	easy
PUNICA GRANATUM NANA	7°C/45°F	shrub	fl/berry/years	good light	small/13cm/5in	easy
REBUTIA SENILIS	7°C/45°F	cactus	form/flower/years	good light	small/13cm/5in	easy
RECHSTEINERIA CARDINALIS	10°C/50°F	tuber	fl/fol/years	good light	small/13cm/5in	easy
REINWARDTIA TRIGYNA	13°C/55°F	shrub	flowers/some years	good light	small/18cm/7in	moderate*
RHIPSALIDOPSIS ROSEA	7°C/45°F	succulent	flowers/years	slight shade	small/13cm/5in	easy
RHOEO SPATHACEA	13°C/55°F	evergreen	fl/fol/some years	good light	small/13cm/5in	moderate
RHOICISSUS CAPENSIS	10°C/50°F	climber	foliage/years	good light	mod/18cm/7in	moderate
RHOICISSUS RHOMBOIDEA	10°C/50°F	climber	foliage/years	mod. shade	large/23cm/9in	mod/easy
ROSA CHINENSIS	hardy	shrub	flower/years	good light	small/13cm/5in	easy
RUELLIA MACRANTHA	16°C/61°F	shrub	fl/fol/years	mod. shade	mod/18cm/7in	moderate
RUELLIA MAKOYANA	10°C/50°F	evergreen	fl/fol/years	slight shade	small/13cm/5in	moderate
SAINTPAULIA IONANTHA	13°C/55°F	perennial	flower/years	good light	small/13cm/5in	mod/easy
SALPIGLOSSIS SINUATA	5°C/41°F	annual	flower/months	good light	small/13cm/5in	easy
SANCHEZIA NOBILIS	13°C/55°F	shrub	fl/fol/years	good light	mod/18cm/7in	difficult
SANSEVIERIA TRIFASCIATA	10°C/50°F	evergreen	foliage/years	not fussy	small/18cm/7in	easy*
SAXIFRAGA COTYLEDON	hardy	perennial	fl/fol/years	good light	small/13cm/5in	easy*
SAXIFRAGA STOLONIFERA	5°C/41°F	trailer	fl/fol/years	mod. shade	small/13cm/5in	easy
SCHEFFLERA ACTINOPHYLLA	10°C/50°F	shrub	foliage/years	mod. shade	mod/23cm/9in	easy
SCHEFFLERA ARBORICOLA	10°C/50°F	shrub	foliage/years	mod. shade	small/18cm/7in	easy

NAME	TEMP	TYPE	INTEREST/TIME	LIGHT NEEDED	SPACE/POT SIZE	CULTURE
SCHEFFLERA DIGITATA	2°C/36°F	shrub	foliage/years	mod. shade	large/23cm/9in	easy
SCHIZANTHUS PINNATUS	5°C/41°F	annual	flower/fol/months	slight shade	small/13cm/5in	easy
SCHLUMBERGERA × BUCKLEYI	13°C/55°F	succulent	flower/years	good light	small/13cm/5in	easy
SENECIO BICOLOR	hardy	perennial	foliage/some years	good light	small/18cm/7in	easy
SENECIO × HYBRIDUS	5°C/41°F	biennial	flower/months	slight shade	small/13cm/5in	easy
SENECIO MACROGLOSSUS	10°C/50°F	climber	fl/fol/years	slight shade	large 23cm/9in	moderate
SENECIO MIKANIODES	10°C/50°F	climber	fol/fl/years	good light	large 23cm/9in	mod/easy
SENECIO ROWLEYANUS	10°C/50°F	trailer	fol/fl/scent/years	good light	small/13cm/5in	easy
SETCREASEA PALLIDA	5°C/41°F	trailer	foliage/years	good light	small/13cm/5in	very easy
SINNINGIA HYBRIDS	10°C/50°F	tubers	flowers/some years	slight shade	small/13cm/5in	easy
SOLANUM PSEUDOCAPSICUM	2°C/36°F	shrub	berry/months	slight shade	small/13cm/5in	easy*
SOLEIROLIA SOLEIROLII	5°C/41°F	trailer	foliage/years	not fussy	small/13cm/5in	easy
SPARMANNIA AFRICANA	5°C/41°F	shrub	flowers/some years	good light	mod/18cm/7in	easy
SPATHIPHYLLUM 'MAUNA LOA'	13°C/55°F	perennial	fol/fl/years	slight shade	mod/18cm/7in	moderate
SPATHIPHYLLUM WALLISII	10°C/50°F	perennial	fol/fl/years	slight shade	small/18cm/7in	moderate*
STENOCARPUS SINUATUS	1°C/34°F	shrub	foliage/years	good light	mod/18cm/7in	easy
STEPHANOTIS FLORIBUNDA	10°C/50°F	climber	flower/scent/years	slight shade	mod/18cm/7in	mod/easy
STRELITZIA REGINAE	5°C/41°F	perennial	flower/fol/years	good light	large/23cm/9in	easy

STREPTOCARPUS	10°C/50°F	perennial	flowers/years	slight shade	small/13cm/5in	mod/easy
STROMANTHE AMABILIS	13°C/55°F	evergreen	foliage/years	mod. shade	small/13cm/5in	moderate
SYNGONIUM PODOPHYLLUM	13°C/55°F	climber/tr	foliage/years	slight shade	mod/18cm/7in	mod/diff
TETRANEMA ROSEUM	10°C/50°F	as annual	flower/months	mod. shade	small/13cm/5in	easy
THUNBERGIA ALATA	10°C/50°F	an/cl/tr	flower/months	not fussy	small/13cm/5in	easy
THUNBERGIA GRANDIFLORA	10°C/50°F	climber	flower/years	slight shade	large/23cm/9in	moderate
THUNBERGIA GREGORII	10°C/50°F	climber	flower/entry	slight shade	large/23cm/9in	moderate
THUNBERGIA LAURIFOLIA	15°C/59°F	climber	flower/fol/years	slight shade	large/23cm/9in	mod/diff
TIBOUCHINA URVILLEANA	7°C/45°F	shrub	flower/years	slight shade	large/23cm/9in	mod/easy
TILLANDSIA CYANEA	13°C/55°F	bromeliad	fol/fl/years	slight shade	small/13cm/5in	moderate*
TILLANDSIA USNEOIDES	13°C/55°F	brom/tr	fol/fl/years	mod. shade	see entry	mod/diff*
TOLMIEA MENZIESII	7°C/45°F	trailer	fol/fl/years	mod. shade	small/13cm/5in	easy
TORENIA FOURNIERI	10°C/50°F	annual	flowers/months	slight shade	small/13cm/5in	easy
TRADESCANTIA BLOSSFELDIANA	10°C/50°F	trailer	fol/fl/years	good light	small/18cm/7in	easy
TRADESCANTIA FLUMINENSIS	7°C/45°F	trailer	foliage/years	good light	small/13cm/5in	very easy
TULIP	hardy	bulb	flowers/years	good light	group	easy
VRIESIA SPLENDENS	15°C/59°F	bromeliad	fol/fl/years	slight shade	small/13cm/5in	moderate*
YUCCA ELEPHANTIPES	7°C/45°F	shrub	foliage/years	good light	large/23cm/9in	easy
YUCCA FILAMENTOSA	hardy	shrub	fol/fl/years	good light	large/23cm/9in	easy
ZANTEDESCHIA AETHIOPICA	2°C/36°F	aquatic	flower/fol/years	slight shade	small/18cm/7in	easy*
ZEBRINA PENDULA	10°C/50°F	trailer	foliage/years	slight shade	small/13cm/5in	very easy

AT A GLANCE GUIDE TO PLANT TYPES AND CONDITIONS

FLOWERING PLANTS

Abutilon
Acacia
Acalyphya
Aechmea
Anthurium
Azalea
Begonia
Beloperone
Billbergia
Bougainvillea
Browallia
Brunfelsia
Calceolaria
Campanula
Catharanthus
Chrysanthemum
Citrus
Clivia
Cobaea
Columnea
Crocus
Crossandra
Cuphea
Cyanotis
Cyclamen
Cytisus
Dipladenia

Epiphyllum
Erica
Euphorbia
Exacum
Fuchsia
Gardenia
Gerbera
Gloriosa
Heliotropium
Hibiscus
Hippeastrum
Hoya
Hyacinth
Hydrangea
Hypocyrta
Impatiens
Ipomoea
Iris
Jasminum
Kalanchoe
Lantana
Mammillaria
Mimulus
Narcissus
Nerium
Nicandra
Pachystachys
Passiflora
Pelargonium
Plectranthus

Plumbago
Primula
Punica
Rebutia
Reinwardtia
Rosa
Ruellia
Saintpaulia
Salpiglossis
Sanchezia
Schizanthus
Schlumberga
Spathiphyllum
Stephanotis
Streptocarpus
Strelitzia
Tetranema
Thunbergia
Tibouchina
Vriesia

FOLIAGE PLANTS

Acorus
Adiantum
Aechmea
Aglaonema
Ananas
Aphelandra

Araucaria
Asparagus
Aspidistra
Asplenium
Aucuba
Begonia
Billbergia
Caladium
Calathea
Callisia
Capsicum
Celosia
Chlorophytum
Cissus
Citrus
Codiaeum
Coffea
Coleus
Cordyline
Cryptanthus
Ctenanthe
Cyperus
Dieffenbachia
Doinaea
Dizygotheca
Dracaena
Epipremnum
Eucalyptus
Euonymus
Fatshedera
Fatsia
Ficus
Fittonia
Grevillea
Gynura
Hedera
Howeia
Hypoestes
Iresine
Maranta

Monstera
Musa
Nephrolepsis
Nertera
Nolina
Opuntia
Pellionia
Peperomia
Persea
Philodendron
Pilea
Piper
Pteris
Rhoeo
Rhoicissus
Sansevieria
Saxifraga
Schefflera
Senecio
Setcreasea
Solanum
Soleirolia
Sparmannia
Spathiphyllum
Stenocarpus
Stromanthe
Syngonium
Tolmiea
Torenia
Tradescantia
Yucca
Zantedeschia
Zebrina

FERNS

Adiantum
Asparagus
Asplenium
Blechnum

Cyrtomium
Davallia
Didymochlaena
Nephrolepsis
Pellaea
Platycerium
Pteris

PALMS

Areca
Chamaedorea
Chamaerops
Howeia
Phoenix

BROMELIADS

Aechmea
Ananas
Billbergia
Cryptanthus
Guzmania
Neoregelia
Tillandsia
Vriesia

CACTI

Aporocactus
Astrophytum
Cephalocereus
Cereus
Chamaecereus
Echinocactus
Epiphyllum
Mammillaria
Opuntia
Rebutia
Rhipsalidopsis

Schlumbergera

SUCCULENTS

Aeonium
Agave
Aloe
Ceropegia
Echeveria
Euphorbia
Kalanchoë
Lobivia
Pachyphytum

BULBS

Achimenes
Canna
Crinum
Crocus
Cyclamen
Gloriosa
Hippeastrum
Hyacinthus
Hymenocallis
Iris
Lachenalia
Lilium
Narcissus
Nerine
Ornithogalum
Rechsteineria
Sinningia
Tulip

ORCHIDS

Anguloa
Brassia
Calanthe

Cattleya
Cymbidium
Dendrobium
Laelia
Lycaste
Miltonia
Odontoglossum
Oncidium
Paphiopedilem
Pleione

CLIMBING PLANTS

Cissus
Cyanotis
Dipladenia
Epipremnum
Hedera
Hoya
Ipomoea
Jasminum
Passiflora
Philodendron
Rhoicissus
Senecio
Stephanotis
Thunbergia

TRAILING OR HANGING PLANTS

Achimenes
Asparagus
Begonia
Callisia
Campanula

Chlorophytum
Columnea
Cyanotis
Ficus
Hedera
Saxifraga
Senecio
Setcreasia
Thunbergia
Tradescantia
Zebrina

PLANTS FOR SHADE

Araucaria
Aspidistra
Aucuba
Cyperus
Dizygotheca
Euonymus
Fatshedera
Fatsia
Ferns
Hedera
Maranta
Pellaea
Philodendron
    scandens
Rhoicussus
Ruellia
Saxifraga
Tolmiea

PLANTS FOR DRY ATMOSPHERES

Aechmea

Ananas
Billbergia
Clivia
Cryptanthus
Cacti
Grevillea
Pelargonium
Sansevieria
Succulents
Yucca

PLANTS FOR SUN

Beleperone
Campanula

Cacti
Capsicum
Citrus
Coleus
Hippeastrum
Impatiens
Pelargonium
Rosa
Solanum
Succulents

LOTS OF WARMTH IN WINTER

Anthurium

Aphelandra
Caladium
Codiaeum
Columnea
Crossandra
Dieffenbachia
Dizygotheca
Dipladenia
Fittonia
Maranta
Pelliona
Piper
Reinwardtia
Saintpaulia
Spathiphyllum
Stephanotis

INDEX

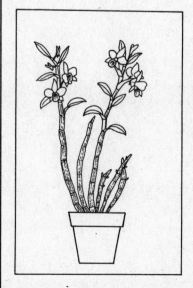

INDEX